HITLER'S LAST CHRISTMAS

*The Day the Entire Mighty 8th Air Force
Entered the Battle of the Bulge*

Y0-BCV-989

DONALD F. KILBURG, JR.

outskirts
press

"More than 70 years later, I can see General Castle's plane on our right wing falling from formation and feel my own adrenaline-driven fight for my life in the worst mission of my 32 bombing missions over Europe. This is a great documentation of that extraordinary day."

— W. Henry Hughey, *Ball Turret Gunner on Richmond C. Young's crew, Christmas Eve 1944*

"Kilburg's book brought me back to my 18-year-old self and my last flying mission with the 487th Bomb Group, a day that I thought I was about to meet my Maker. Thanks, Don, for a great book. It brings to my mind others who paid a terrible price, the families who lost brothers, sons, husbands and sweethearts, fathers who never saw their children. Your book captures the experience of tens of thousands of ordinary American young people, thousands of miles from home, in a strange environment—and then facing death, injuries, or capture by the enemy. It also reminds me how they persevered and succeeded in victory. Finally, we have a comprehensive look at the largest bombing mission of all time, one that helped lead to the demise of the mastermind of the evil Nazi regime!"

— Robert G. Yowan, *Ball Turret Gunner and one of only four survivors on Kenneth W. Lang's crew, Christmas Eve 1944*

This account of the largest aerial bombing mission ever is dedicated to the memory of those brave young men who participated in it, the ground crews who supported them, and the families at home who hoped and prayed for them. Certainly, the highest ranking among these brave souls was General Frederick Castle, who has long been the icon of this mission. As Harry E. Slater, historian of the 94th Bomb Group, has written, "Those who knew Castle have stated that if it were possible for him to debrief his final mission, he would simply have said: 'The job of dying for a general leading the 8th Air Force over Germany is no more or less demanding than for a gunner in the Tail End Charlie.'"

Special thanks for assisting in telling the story of this event are given to Walter Wright and Susanna Glidden for sharing their personal recollections of Frederick Castle, to Donald L. Miller and Danny Parker for their excellent documentation of the history of 8th Air Force in Europe and the Battle of the Bulge, to Ivo de Jong for his comprehensive documentation of the 487th Bomb Group history and the events of Christmas Eve 1944, to Cindy Neal for her collection of the individual stories of the men of the 487th BG, the Quinten Jeffers family and to Joost de Raft for his excellent digital detail of Mission 760 (http://24december1944.com/). Thanks also to Jerry Ogle, Lee Hauenstein, Paul Webber, Deb Denbeck, and the past officers of the 487th Bomb Group Association who have done so much to keep this proud history together and accessible. And thanks to Patricia Kilburg for her help and support in pulling the story of the Christmas Eve mission together.

TABLE OF CONTENTS

Prologue I

Chapter 1: Mission 760 Remembered.................................... 1

Chapter 2: Hitler's Adlerhorst (Situation) 6

Chapter 3: Eisenhower's Versailles (Situation)................... 20

Chapter 4: High Wycombe The Plan (Situation) 36

Chapter 5: Frederick Walker Castle 52

Chapter 6: Seventeen Minutes of Hell and Heroes of the
      Rest of the Initial Attack 61

Chapter 7: The Missed Target of Opportunity 93

Chapter 8: The Targets of the First Attack Force............... 98

Chapter 9: The Targets of the Second Attack Force 137

Chapter 10: The Targets of the Third Attack Force......... 165

Chapter 11: Fighters "Little Friends" 205

Chapter 12: Results of Mission 760.................................... 234

Chapter 13: The Aftermath 240

Glossary 252

Appendix A: Aircraft of Mission 760 257

Appendix B: Maps 267

Appendix C: 8th Air Force in England December 1944 273

Appendix D: Targets 24Dec1944.. 278

Bibliography 281

Index 291

PROLOGUE

Mission 760, Christmas Eve 1944,
the Greatest Day in the History of Aerial Warfare.

The global scale of the Second World War has left a legacy of recorded and recounted events that document the unprecedented involvement of humanity in mortal conflict to a level never before experienced. There is no doubt that the outcome of the Second World War changed the course of civilization around the globe and what might have been. The events of the war have been documented in official records, books, movies, and song. For the most part the great events are well-known and have been frequently studied and analyzed. Yet, one of the greatest feats of aerial warfare, never again duplicated, has received scant attention in the record of the war.

It took place on Sunday, December 24, 1944, when the US Army Air Corps launched every plane at its disposal in Great Britain and in occupied Europe flying in formation to thirty-four distinct tactical targets throughout Germany. There were more than 21,000 airmen in flight in a combat environment that had no concept of foxholes and no taking of cover. The objective was the immobilization of German aircraft, supply lines, and communication centers that were the life support for the Fuhrer's Ardennes Offensive.

Whereas the heavy bombers of the 8th Army Air Corps had been spending months in aggressive attacks on strategic targets providing essential supplies of fuel, ammunitions, food, equipment, and parts, the bombers of the 8th suddenly switched their attention to the support of Allied ground troops engaged in brutal conflict with the advancing German soldiers. It was also a desperate effort by the Allies to support the troops hopelessly hunkered down in the frigid weather of the Battle of the Bulge. The eventual success of those beleaguered troops was to some great measure due to the success of that Christmas Eve air mission.

Dramatic events on the ground have, perhaps rightfully, eclipsed the events in the air in the documentation of those bitter days and weeks that began with the surprise of Hitler's last major offensive. The early hours of Mission 760 included the death of one of only five general officers to die in the northern European campaign, Brigadier General Frederick Castle. As mission commander, Castle was in the lead plane of this most massive formation in the history of air combat. The death of such a high-ranking officer who also happened to be one of the founding member of the 8th Army Air Corps in England, a West Point graduate, and the godson of the chief of the Army Air Corps, Henry "Hap" Arnold served to focus attention at the time on the downed general officer and a major portion of his lead formation. The notoriety of these events has inadvertently served to diminish awareness of the successful completion of this air battle of all air battles. The mis-filing of the details of that 8th Air Force mission #760 shortly after the war was completed and the eagerness of the returning airmen to get on with life have served to conceal the glory of that day in December 1944 until recently.

The basic facts and statistics of the mission have been known and documented, particularly in the annals of the 8th Air Force. But it is only as the participants have aged and begun to share their stories that the true picture of what occurred that day has begun to be revealed. Hearing many of those stories firsthand caused the author to launch a search for the rest of the story. Queries to the National Archives and the historical library of the 8th Air Force yielded nothing of the official record, though the National Archives contains the original documents of most air missions before and after the one in question. In July of 2010 a search was made at the archives of the Air Force Historical Research Agency at Fort Maxwell in Montgomery, Alabama. There, the musty documents of this great event saw daylight for the first time in more than fifty years.

On Christmas Eve 1944, the 8th Air Force launched the largest air armada in the history of warfare. On that December 24, the traditional prayers for peace on earth, goodwill toward men seemed all the more urgent and yet unattainable. America had been consumed by the war effort for four successive Christmases. American forces pressed on in the Pacific, in the Philippines, Burma, and Iwo Jima. Europe was devastated after six Christmas seasons of wanton aggression and destruction. Most of the estimated 78 million people who died in the war were already dead. And on December 24, 1944, it seemed to many that the carnage was never going to end.

Most certainly it seemed to the Allied ground troops mired in the mud, snow, and record cold of the Ardennes region of Luxembourg, Belgium, and Germany that their war experience would only end as a frozen corpse lying in the snow. The Supreme Allied Commander, General Dwight Eisenhower, was in hiding in response to an assassination threat from German agents disguised as American soldiers. General "Tooey" Spaatz, commander of the Allied Air Forces, had predicted the end of the war for 1944 and now had reconsidered and concluded it might go on for another year.

When asked why the account of the greatest air mission of all times seemed lost in histories of the war, one aged veteran simply responded, "It was a very big war." Nonetheless, while actual re-cords of the complete mission have been lost, or rather, misplaced for much of the past sixty-five years, the accounts of the event have lived on in the memories of those brave flyers of the 8th Air Force who participated in it. The purpose of this book is to give voice to their memories and praise to their accomplishments.

Chapter 1

MISSION 760 REMEMBERED

OWEN FLINT STOOD before a ballroom full of octogenarians, their families, and their friends just south of Phoenix, Arizona, in October 2009 and brought the house to a hushed silence. With a few simple words, he transported them back to vivid memories of an event that took place nearly sixty-five years prior. He held them spellbound with a simple expression of gratitude. Owen had traveled to Phoenix from his native England because of the most senior men in the room. And before he was done, they and their families found tears welling up in their eyes.

Owen had been a young boy in war-torn England. He had vivid memories of the horror of enemy attack on his homeland. He had memories of the excitement of watching American B-24s and B-17s lumbering, heavily laden down the runway and off to bombing missions on the Continent. He had memories of counting the planes back in, some ragged and in obvious distress, as they made their way back to the airfield and others never returning. But one of his fondest memories brought his audience back to December 1944, when Owen was a lad of six, full of anticipation of Christmas and knowing that in the darkest days of war Father Christmas was going to have a difficult time making his rounds.

In his mind's eye, the bent, gray-haired men before him were the vibrant young Yanks he knew as a wee lad. They looked up at him—stooped over, leaning on a cane, or from their wheelchair or walker—with admiration in their eyes, as he had once—as Owen the boy—looked

Christmas Party for village children

up at them so many years ago, with glowing admiration. Owen the man recalled that wondrous Christmas of 1944 when he and all the children of his town were invited to celebrate at the American air base. The excitement of it all was overwhelming. The prospect of seeing Father Christmas and receiving a gift was fantastic. The promise of sweets after so many years of rationing because of the war was incredible. Thoughts of that wonderful Hershey's chocolate that the playful Yank airmen occasionally shared as they teased the young lads on the street or tossed a ball with them were more than young Owen could stand. To this day, it was one of the most wonderful things he had ever tasted.

Then, when he awoke that Christmas Eve morning, concern filled Owen's mind. The village literally rumbled with the activity at the air base. The weather had been like frosted pea soup for the prior week, bad even for England. But this morning — for the first time in a week — the skies were clear and blue. As he dressed, he could see that beautiful blue sky dotted with countless formations of heavy bombers, more than he had ever seen in his young but war-filled life. This couldn't be just his American friends; this had to be the whole American Air Force, he thought. He hurriedly gave his mum a buss on the cheek and ran to consult with his mates in the lane. What was going on? Would it interfere with the Christmas celebration? Would they beat Hitler once and for all?

Sixty-five years later the aging Owen told his old friends that he had no understanding on that Christmas Eve of what they were going through. He noted that his later knowledge of the magnitude of the mission and the horror experienced by "his Yanks" — the men of the 487th Bomb Group who led the largest mission in the history of air warfare — made that day forever memorable to him. He wonders now how they could have continued on with that evening's festivities for the youth of Lavenham after losing nearly a quarter of their aircraft and almost as many fliers that day. On that day in October 2009, Owen Flint emotionally thanked the remnant of that 487th Bomb Group from the bottom of his heart.

As Owen spoke, memories of that Christmas Eve so long ago flashed through the gray heads of many of the veterans in attendance. Bob Yowan was nineteen again, pumping with adrenaline as he fired at the oncoming attack of Focke-Wulf 190s lined up for a company front attack. He was writhing with pain as a 20mm shell fractured his Plexiglas turret and pierced his hip. He was blind with thoughts of survival as he struggled out of the ball turret of a B-17 and found dead comrades. And he relived the joy of knowing that he was alive as he parachuted peacefully under the beautiful blue sky with its few puffy clouds, thinking to himself, *what a wonderful day to be alive*.

Bob Densmore flashed back to "the worst mission I ever had."

Again, he was a pilot in the low/low formation flying on the lead of Lloyd Reed and squadron air leader Lloyd Nash. He was following their turn when he saw smoke from their wing and their tail gunner bail out. He knew it was over for them. It was then that he looked around and realized there was no more squadron. His own plane was in distress, having taken a 20mm hit in the supercharger for the number one engine. Bob relived the relief of setting down successfully on a backup field in France.

The visions of being a nose gunner that day flashed through Mike Quiring. He again saw those planes coming in and several of the German fighters breaking off for attack. His memory once again made the images real, Focke-Wulf 190s zooming up so close you could almost touch their Iron Crosses.

For Don Kilburg Sr., Owen's comments brought visions of the Christmas Eve when they were all first surprised by ground fire flak over what was supposed to be friendly territory. Then he relived the shock of enemy fighter attack and visions of planes falling from formation. There were resurging memories of his friend and pilot John "Pappy" Edwards and Deputy Air Commander Major Mayfield, flying as co-pilot, assuming command of the entire mission as General Frederick Castle's lead plane fell from formation, exploded, and burned. Kilburg recalled the moments that seemed like hours as Edwards and Shilling regrouped the scattered and broken formation, putting it back on point. He relived the realization that he was now the lead bombardier on the lead target of the largest single mission of the war and he knew that his training had prepared him for this moment.

The 487th was the lead group in Mission #760 of the 8th Air Force by chance. Lead assignments came on a rotational basis, and it was their turn. Eisenhower's command for maximum effort and chance put a composite of the 836th and 838th squadrons of the 487th Bombardment Group in the low/low position of the lead formation.

A delay in fighter support left them exposed and vulnerable resulting in six downed aircraft, twenty-one deaths, and numerous other casualties. Ironically, General Castle's lead plane, though flying with the 839th Squadron in the middle formation, was also normally assigned to the 836th and accounted for five additional deaths. The magnitude of the initial contact with the enemy south of Liege, Belgium, was most apparent in the barracks of the 836th Squadron on Christmas morning, where eighty bunks remained undisturbed.

Owen Flint went on to explain why he felt compelled to fly to the US from England in 2009 to share time with this dwindling group of his own heroes. As he grew to adulthood in the postwar years, he began to learn the history of World War II and for the first time heard the story of December 24, 1944 — the day the entire 8th Air Force took flight in support of the struggling Allied ground troops who were being pounded by the Nazis' Ardennes Offensive. It was the day that the men before him in Phoenix had led the largest air armada in the history of warfare on a single mission. It was a day that they had suffered tremendous losses of comrades and equipment. It was a day when they had done lethal damage to the support, supply, and defense of the enemy in the Battle of the Bulge. Owen told them he wanted to thank them personally. He told them that understanding now that they held a Christmas party for the children of Lavenham, England, just after returning from that horrendous battle, made the memory of that bite of luscious Hershey's chocolate all the sweeter.

"Soldiers of the Western Front! Your great hour has arrived! Today strong attacking armies have attacked the Anglo-Americans. I need not say more. You all feel that this is it! Consider the sacred commitment to give everything and to perform beyond human possibilities for the Fatherland and our Fuhrer!"

-Generalfeldmarschall Gerd von Rundstedt

Chapter 2

HITLER'S ADLERHORST (SITUATION)

DECEMBER 1944 FOUND the fliers of the 8th Air Force growing frustrated and impatient. Common wisdom was that the end of the war was near. The Russians and the western Allies on the ground were in a race to reach and take Berlin. The airmen in England were in combat mode, but all they saw was fog. Several strategic bombing missions had been successfully completed in early December 1944. German rail yards had been hit on the 2nd and the 4th. Munitions and tank works were hit on the 5th. On the 6th, oil refineries and more rail yards were targeted. A small contingent of the 1st Division hit airfields and rail targets near Stuttgart on the 9th. On the 10th, a larger formation from the 2nd and 3rd Bomb Division attacked rail targets along the Rhine River at Bingen and Koblenz. On the 11th the largest force of bombers to date — 1,586 — were dispatched to marshalling yards at Frankfurt am Main and the surrounding area, dropping 3,648 tons of explosives. On the 12th a smaller contingent hit additional marshalling yards in the same area. Bad weather kept them down for the next three days. On the 16th extremely poor weather conditions kept all but 124 bombers on the ground. Those few that got up hit marshalling yards in Stuttgart. Weather grounded them all on the 17th. A mission was attempted on the 18th targeting communications and tactical targets along the Rhine, but extensive cloud cover forced the recall of more than half of the force. That impossible weather kept nearly every air base in Britain under wraps from that point until Christmas Eve.

The lousy weather was something that Adolf Hitler had been counting on. His "Thousand-Year Reich" had been on the run since the landing of the Allies on the beaches at Normandy on the previous June 6. His bold and aggressive advances of the prior five years had been reversed. Despite his tight defenses, the Americans and British were advancing on the "Fatherland" from the west, and the Russians were moving with the same determination and speed from the east. Hitler's own officers attempted to assassinate him in July. The persistent British night bombing had left most major German cities in ruins. The persistent day bombing by the Americans had left him dangerously short of armaments and, most critically, fuel. From January 1944 to December 1944, German monthly production of finished oil products had fallen from 900,000 to 303,000 pounds. His fighting forces had been decimated in the retreat as the Allies advanced. Many of his "men" in uniform were teens newly acquired from the Hitler Youth or old men previously thought too old to fight. Many of his generals believed the end was near. After his brush with death on July 20, Hitler didn't trust most of them.

Toward the end of September 1944, Hitler convened a secret meeting of his select circle at *Wolfsschanze* or "Wolf's Lair," his bunker in East Prussia. Those present were General Wilhelm Keitel, General Alfred Jodl, Generaloberst Heinz Guderian, General Major Eckhard Christian, General Wilhelm Burgdorf, Sturmbannführer Otto Gunsche, SS-Obergruppenführer Hermann Fegelein, and General Lieutenant August Winter. Both Keitel and Jodl had been injured during the July attempt on Hitler's life. At the start of the meeting all were sworn to secrecy and made to sign an oath. They were put on notice that if word of their mission leaked, they and their families would be shot. Jodl had been commissioned by Hitler on September 25th to develop a plan for a surprise attack on the Anglo-American forces in Belgium, Alsace, and France. Later, on the 12th of October, Jodl had presented his initial thoughts to the Fuhrer. The objective was to be Antwerp, the major resupply port of the Allies. Securing Antwerp would also drive a wedge between the Americans in France and the British in Holland. Success of the plan hung on surprise and quick action. Hitler was convinced that, more than anything else, the mission required either air superiority of the Luftwaffe or bad weather that would allow him to move his forces into striking position without being detected.

As the plans jelled among the small group surrounding Hitler, he summoned the legendary commando Otto Skorzeny to Wolfsschanze to receive special orders directly from the Fuhrer. Skorzeny had been the hero of at least ten daredevil commando missions including the rescue of Mussolini from prison. This new operation was to be part of the Ardennes Offensive and involved the establishment of a special brigade — Panzer Brigade 150 — under Skorzeny's command that would infiltrate through enemy lines, using US uniforms and equipment to capture one or more of the bridges over the Meuse river before they could be destroyed. Hitler also remarked that such a unit could cause great confusion among the enemy by giving false orders, upsetting communications, and misdirecting troops. Hitler said, "I want you to create special units wearing American and British uniforms. They will travel in captured Allied tanks. Think of the confusion you could cause? I envisage a whole string of false orders which will upset communications and attack morale." This Special Forces plan was code named Operation Greif.

The overarching Ardennes offense plan was given the code name *Wacht am Rhein* or "the Watch on the Rhine" as a part of the ruse to trick the Allies into believing the Germans were amassing forces west of the Rhine in the region between Cologne and Bonn for a defensive battle against the rapidly approaching Allies intent on crossing the Rhine in their march to Berlin. Hitler believed rightly that western intelligence had cracked his sophisticated Enigma encoding system. He ordered there would be no mention or even acknowledgment of any of the operations associated with the actual attack by radio or telephone. Messages were only to be transmitted personally or by highly guarded courier. Their messages supporting the hoax were broadcast and, for the most part, the Allies fell for it. General Omar Bradley said after the war that he and Eisenhower received a number of reports from the top-secret ULTRA intelligence system that a German offensive was in the works. But they believed only a fool would attempt such a move through the difficult terrain of the Ardennes, particularly with the compounding factors of snow, fog, and mud. The Allied commanders had tremendous respect for the cold, calculating Generalfeldmarschall Gerd von Rundstedt, commander of German forces in the west, and doubted he would attempt such a foolish maneuver. They were unaware that Hitler himself had taken command of the operation. It was the determined Hitler who commanded that his army move with speed, surprise, and overwhelming force.

The German attack was tentatively scheduled for late November when the gloom of winter could be expected to block the view from the sky and handicap the forces of their enemy. It was also understood by the planners that, despite shortages caused by the Allies' strategic bombing of synthetic fuel plants, the required reserve of fuel could be established by that time. In the end, Hitler trusted the weather more than he did the more frequently hollow promises of air support from Hermann Goering. The resilient German production machine had produced over 40,000 aircraft during 1944, of which 25,285 were fighters (including 12,800 Me109s and 7,488 Fw190s), but battle attrition was high, causing a shortage of serviceable aircraft. More importantly the Luftwaffe decline during the year had left a definite shortage of skilled, trained pilots by December. Goering had promised Hitler 3,000 aircraft for the offensive, but Hitler quickly discounted that number to 2,000 in light of Goering's tendency to exaggerate. On December 16 Goering successfully launched only 800 to 900 aircraft for the offensive, including battle, reconnaissance, and transport planes.

To provide the needed cover, the operation was not to begin until Hitler's chief meteorologist, Professor Werner Schwerdtfeger, issued a forecast of at least five days of poor flying weather. Schwerdtfeger had established his reputation as the wizard of weather in the early 1930s as a graduate student at the Leipzig Institute, spending hours manning successful weather balloon flights detecting and documenting the fine structure of fluctuating vertical winds. In 1943, he was assigned as chief of the ZWG, the main weather analysis and forecast center of the German Air Force during the second World War. Recognized for professional knowledge and predictive accuracy, ZWG, located at Wildpark west of Potsdam, had regular contact both with the supreme command of the Air Force and Hitler's Wolfsschanze headquarters.

In November Schwerdtfeger received a directive: "Two days before occurrence in the coming month of December, you must

Adolf Hitler and General Gerd von Rundsted.

forecast the date of a period of five days or more in which fog and/
or low clouds will cover continuously a wide area west of the River
Rhine north of the 50°N parallel approximately, including the region of the Ardennes." He was not informed of the purpose of the
request, though he surmised it was related to a last desperate counterattack. Questioning the assignment, he was told the "absolute
minimum" would be a forecast given at least one day ahead, for
three days or more of no-flight weather conditions. In retrospect,
years after the event, he mused: "I was never told what the consequences were if no forecast of the required weather conditions
could be given, not even for one day. It was a disturbing thought."

During the third week of November, Hitler returned to Berlin briefly, catching up on matters of state and the progress of the war. One of his many meetings during his two weeks there was with the SS-Obersturmbannführer Otto Skorzeny to review the status of organization and training for his special false flag operation. The two discussed how Skorzeny's men would join the advance crews and then blend with the retreating Americans.

December 10th, after a two-week stop in Berlin, Hitler traveled on his special train from Berlin to Giessen and then continued to Bad Nauheim, a small village located halfway between Frankfurt am Main and Giessen. The reconditioned twelfth-century Kransberg castle near the village of Ziegenberg, a formidable structure that General Field Marshall Gerd von Rundstedt used as his home and headquarters, was located a short distance from the town. Just beyond it, a half mile back in the woods, was a complex of concrete bunkers craftily disguised as a traditional rustic country village. Constructed in 1939 as Hitler's headquarters during the invasion of France, Belgium, and Holland, it was called *Adlerhorst*, which translates as "Eagles Nest." Though it possessed a spartan interior, it was highly secure and protected, and Hitler preferred it to the palatial, though exposed, accommodations of Ziegenberg Castle. Today the site of the destroyed Adlerhorst bunker is occupied by the modern village of Wiesental.

On December 12, the commanding generals of the 5th and 6th Panzer armies, Hasso von Manteuffel and Josef "Sepp" Dietrich, were summoned to Bad Nauheim without explanation. They were each ordered to come in a single vehicle without any other officers. Upon arrival they realized they were joining various army, corps and division commanders. It was clear that none of them knew why they were there. Without explanation, they were ordered to leave their pistols and briefcases at the Ziegenberg castle and they were herded out to an awaiting bus. Moments later they found themselves at Hitler's *Adlerhorst*. They exited the bus between two grim

General Josef "Sepp" Dietrich   *General Hasso von Manteuffel*

lines of SS men and were ushered into the bunker. At a reception table, each was then forced to sign a declaration of their willingness to maintain the secrecy of what they were to hear. They acknowledged that they understood that they would be shot if word of their mission were leaked.

The now very curious and attentive generals were seated in a room where SS men were lining the walls when suddenly Adolf Hitler entered accompanied by Generals Jodl and Keitel. After the war ended, several of those summoned to this meeting observed that the Fuhrer appeared old and broken, his hands visibly shaking as he held the notes of his speech. His all-too-familiar harangue went on for two hours. The first hour was a history lesson about German generals who had triumphed over adversity. Then he moved into the shocking details of the planned offensive. He urged them on, saying: "The German people can no longer endure the

Ziegenberg Castle, von Rundstedt's headquarters

heavy bombing attacks. The German people are entitled to action from me." He informed them that he had come up with a masterful plan that would turn the course of the war. He said the Allies believed the Ardennes was the least likely place for the Germans to advance. Accordingly, they had the weaker defenses there than anywhere else along the Siegfried line. He told them they would reach Antwerp in six days, cut off the vital source of supply from the harbor, and cut off the British from the Americans flanking both sides. He told them they would repeat the historic rout of Dunkirk. He told them the Reich would be victorious. Later some noted that they were impressed not only by the enormity of the plan, but also by Hitler's dramatic presentation of it and the energy and determination he seemed to gain as he presented it. No one else spoke.

At the end of Hitler's tirade, the generals were individually introduced to the Fuhrer and each given a few minutes to talk to him. Soon all were reminded of the consequences of violating their individual oaths of secrecy and hustled back to Ziegenberg to celebrate von Rundsted's seventieth birthday.

Returning to their units, Hitler's generals anxiously made final preparations and awaited the command to begin what was to be the last major German offensive of World War II. Many of them felt woefully unprepared for such a major assault. Weather conditions were the cover that was key to Hitler's plans, but they were also the bane of the heavy equipment that was intended to be moved rapidly into the salient. The region of Hitler's Ardennes Offensive was scenic land with few direct roads capable of transporting the armies that were about to occupy them. Numerous rivers, streams, and wetlands made crossing challenging. Bridges presented a difficult conundrum. They were needed for efficient crossing in the advance. Destroying them would delay Anglo-American advances into Germany, but it would also hamper resupply and retreat, should that be necessary.

In the weeks leading up to the third week of December, German High Command had amassed an impressive force in the Eifel mountain region and surrounding area. It included more than 250,000 troops, 970 tanks, 1,900 pieces of artillery, and a mammoth logistical supply system. Most of this force, equipment, ammunition, and rations had been transported at night and under heavy camouflage. In some cases, loaded railcars were stored in tunnels and forests during daylight hours to avoid detection. Because of limited rail in the region of the planned assault, military equipment and supply loaded on horse-drawn carts were common. Two common problems vexed many of the generals who had pledged their loyalty and secrecy to the Fuhrer, however. The first was the lack of fuel. Prolonged and successful Allied bombing of refineries and synthetic fuel production facilities was showing its impact. The official plan for the offensive called for a speedy advance fueling from supplies captured along the way from the Allies.

The German commanders in the field were keenly aware of the risky nature of such a plan. They were also aware that the long war, with its early successes and advances followed by humiliating defeats and retreat, had more than decimated their fighting force. In five years of warfare the Wehrmacht had lost 3,360,000 men killed, wounded, or missing; 466,000 of those casualties had come in August 1944 alone. Many of the fighters under their command were "green" youngsters newly advanced from the Hitler Youth or old men in their sixties or more, originally thought too old for combat. Morale of those who were experienced was low for the most part. Hitler had confidently promised them strong air support for their advance from more than 2,000 planes from the Luftwaffe. Yet they well knew that the same weather that was being counted on to keep the Allies' bombers and fighters on the ground would also ground their own planes. Additionally, it was widely rumored that, while aircraft production had continued successfully despite repeated bombing of factories by the Allies, Luftwaffe pilot mortality in battle was high, and replacement pilots were poorly trained and inexperienced in general.

Herman Goering, who had come to the gathering in his lavish personal train, was still reeling from Hitler's lack of confidence in his ability to get desired results from the Luftwaffe. He was also feeling the sting of the lack of confidence in his leadership that was being expressed by many in his command. In the months just prior to this final assault, the Luftwaffe had generally moved from offense on both Eastern and Western fronts to a primarily defensive mode protecting what was left of the Reich from the incessant aerial attacks by the Allies. Those attacks had become more lethal early in 1944 with the introduction of the P-51B Mustang fighter by the Americans. It flew thirty miles an hour faster than Goering's Me109s and some twenty miles an hour faster than the Fw190s. The revised Mustang fighters also had a combat radius of more than 800 miles, enabling them to escort American bombers into the heart of the Reich. Additionally, the Americans had extended the range of the P-47 Thunderbolt to 500 miles and the P-38F Lightning to

700 miles with the addition of drop tanks. Combat losses of many of the seasoned aces of the Luftwaffe and shortages of fuel also left Goering with the weakest force since the beginnings of the war. After the war Albert Speer, Reich minister of armaments and war production, revealed that prior to September of 1944, the German monthly requirements for liquid fuel were 160,000 to 180,000 tons. Because of the Allied bombing, only 30,000 tons per month were available.

Despite the misgivings of his commanders (Jodl and von Rundstedt were clearly opposed to the risky offensive), the Fuhrer had spoken. As they took their leave, several them were troubled by his paranoid wishfulness and detachment from the reality of the situation. Intent on restoring his status with his Fuhrer, Goering quickly diverted two-thirds of his day-fighter force and a third of his night-fighter force from their defensive duties in order to support the advance of the Wehrmacht on the ground in the Ardennes. In his eagerness to please, Goering promised Hitler some 1,000 aircraft in support of the offensive, roughly a quarter of Germany's operational air strength at the time. He actually did gather approximately 800 planes.

Beginning December 1, Schwerdtfeger had daily contact with headquarters Kurfurst and Wolfsschanze, and each evening his simple response was: "Not yet." On December 14 he reported to Hitler then at the Adlerhorst, "Probably yes, confirmation tomorrow at noon." At noon on the 15th he reported to his two "prime customers": "Fog and/or persisting low-cloud deck with poor visibility underneath to be expected in the entire region, for 16-18 December."

At 5:30 a.m. on December 16, the command was given and the advance began—nearly 300,000 German soldiers against 85,000 defending the Allies lines. The front stretched seventy miles from Ecternach in the south to Monshau in the north. At the forefront

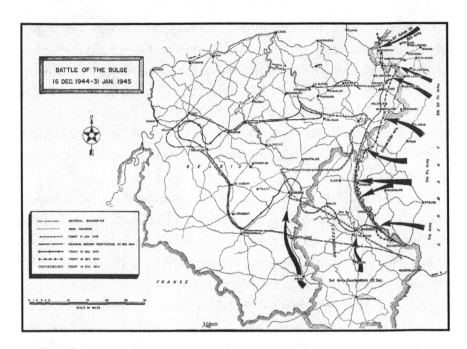

were the 2000 troops of Skorzeny's Operation Greif with their ten captured Sherman tanks, sixty German tanks crudely disguised as American tanks, and an additional eighty American and English vehicles.

Stateside, ticker tape reports from reporters based in Britain, mainly from the Associated Press, splashed headlines about Von Rundstedt's surprising and bold offense. It was not known until after the war that it was truly Hitler's drive, initiative, and dogged determination that made the Ardennes Offensive a reality. Von Rundstedt was a loyal soldier of the Reich, but also believed that military officers should not become involved in politics. He had been relieved of his command after Germany's defeat at Normandy in June of 1944. At that time, he had advised Hitler to negotiate a peace with the Allies. He is said to have been aware of efforts to assassinate Hitler in 1943 and 1944 but declined to participate in any of the plots. After the Valkyrie attempt on Hitler's life in June of 1944, Von Rundstedt was assigned to head the "Court of Honor," which investigated the alleged participants in the plot. The efforts of that court resulted in the execution of 4,980 people accused of knowledge or participation in the plots to kill Hitler.

To all the world at the time, the Fuhrer's active and aggressive involvement in the planning and execution of the Ardennes Offensive was unknown and would remain that way until the war had ended, he was dead, and his generals were talking to the victors. The actual reality of the buildup and orders for execution had been carefully protected through clandestine Nazi secrecy. It was not picked up by the Allies' top-secret ULTRA, a previously accurate insight to the Germans' plans and movements.

"In any event the fighting during the autumn followed the pattern I had personally prescribed. We remained on the offensive and weakened ourselves where necessary to maintain those offensives. This plan gave the German opportunity to launch his attack against a weak portion of our lines. If giving him that chance is to be condemned by historians, their condemnation should be directed at me alone."

— Dwight David Eisenhower

Chapter 3

EISENHOWER'S VERSAILLES (SITUATION)

DECEMBER 16 BEGAN as a good day for General Dwight D. Eisenhower. He was up for his normal 6:00 breakfast of sausage and grits in the charming setting of the Trianon palace at Versailles, the Supreme Headquarters of Allied Expeditionary Forces (SHAEF). The day was overcast and bitterly cold, but that would not dampen his spirits. Two days earlier Congress had passed a bill authorizing a new rank, "General of the Army." He had been informed that he and General Omar Bradley would be receiving that fifth star on December 20, four days after George Marshall and two days after MacArthur. Hap Arnold received his fifth star on December 21. To all appearances and despite the stubborn and dogged determination of the Huns, the war was going in favor of the Allies. Battles had been hard won, with tremendous cost to the men and women of the military and to the country as a whole. But victory was in sight and a certain optimism had caught all who were not wet and freezing on the front lines. As Eisenhower was finish-

*General Dwight David
Eisenhower*

ing his meal and reviewing his morning mail, he found a note from Field Marshal Montgomery requesting holiday leave and requesting payment on a bet the two had made fourteen months earlier that the war would be ended by Christmas 1944. Ike quipped to an aide that he would pay up, but not before Christmas.

*Air Marshal Sir Arthur
Tedder*

The rest of the planned order of the day was a celebration. Eisenhower's personal aide, Sgt. Mickey McKeogh, was marrying Sgt. Pearlie Hargrave of the Women's Army Corps. The ceremony was held in the Louis XIV chapel at Versailles. Eisenhower hosted the champagne reception in his quarters at Saint-Germain. It was quite an event, and all were in good spirits. During the party Eisenhower was contacted by SHAEF's chief intelligence

Major General Kenneth Strong

officer, Major General Kenneth Strong, of the need to review some troublesome developments at the front.

At 2:00 p.m. Eisenhower had scheduled a meeting in his map room to discuss the critical shortage of infantry replacements in Europe. Generals Strong, Bradley, Bedell Smith and Major General Harold R. Bull were present. Representing Air Command were Air Marshal Sir Arthur Tedder, Eisenhower's deputy commander at SHAEF, and General Carl Spaatz, the senior American airman in Europe. Montgomery was playing golf at Eindhoven, Holland, with a visiting Welsh professional. Much to his later regret, he had filed an intelligence report early in the morning that read:

> "The enemy is at present fighting a defensive campaign on all fronts; his situation is such that he cannot stage major offensive operations. Furthermore, at all costs he has to prevent the war from entering a mobile phase; he has not the transport or petrol that would be necessary for mobile operations..."

General Strong, while admitting that information from the Ardennes was sketchy and fragmentary, reported that there were indications

General Carl "Tooey" Spaatz

of a German advance. Bradley dismissed them as a diversion intended to distract his efforts to advance to the Ruhr Valley dams. Strong warned them to not underestimate the Germans, but soon the meeting adjourned and all proceeded to a celebratory dinner honoring Eisenhower on his promotion to General of the Army. It was an evening of scotch whiskey and cigars. During the evening, additional incomplete, but very distressing messages continued to come in from the Ardennes front. Eventually Bradley became concerned enough that he decided to return to Luxembourg City, driving because conditions in the air were impossible.

Reports also came to Eisenhower about the missing plane of the immensely popular band leader 35-year-old Glenn Miller. Miller had left from the RAF Twinwood Farm in Clapham, Bedfordshire, on December 15, flying through the dense fog from England to Paris for a planned concert for the troops there. The wreckage of his single-engine UC-64 Norseman aircraft was never found and was presumed lost over the English Channel.

Popular musician and director
Glenn Miller

It is clear the attitude of Allied Command on December 16, 1944 was based on an optimistic conviction that the steady progress of advancement toward Berlin that began with the hard-fought progress since D-Day would continue. The Germans had retreated to the protection of the West Wall, the Siegfried Line. Even so, Aachen, Charlemagne's ancient capital, had been secured by the Allies on October 21 after a brutal fight with extensive losses on both sides. Fighting in the unforgiving Hurtgen Forest was continuing, but with punishing and slow progress. Intelligence had reported a Wehrmacht buildup west of the Rhine, Hitler's *Wacht Am Rhein,* and the Allies interpreted it as a move that they would have made themselves, establishing a strong and fortified defense. They even dismissed a leak intercepted by the Allies' top-secret ULTRA deciphering and intel system on November 15 when the Japanese ambassador messaged to the emperor of Japan indicating that Hitler had promised him a German attack in the West.

Oblivious to the nighttime, fog-covered, radio-silent advancement of men, equipment, supplies, and ammunition that had been quietly moved through the Schnee Eifel to the stagnated combat front, the relatively sparsely defended Allied line awoke with a shock as Nazi guns began with an overwhelming barrage along the length of the front from Monschau to Ecternach, at exactly 5:30 a.m. on Saturday, December 16.

The success of Hitler's unexpected advance and the marginal weather conditions left the US troops on the ground with minimal aerial support. Not expecting the offensive, the top Allied tactical air commanders met on December 16 in Verviers, Belgium, approximately thirty miles from the front. They had gathered to plan for their own upcoming ground offensive and were caught by surprise as news of the German attack reached them. In England, the Eighth Air Force, despite the extremely poor weather conditions, had dispatched 236 B-17s in the morning of the 16th to attack the marshalling yard in Stuttgart and nearby Bietingheim, though only 115 successfully made it to the target and back. At Versailles, Field Marshal Montgomery was reminding General Eisenhower that he owed him five pounds on his bet made the prior year that the war would be over by Christmas. As the day and evening advanced, news of the renewed German offensive began to filter in to those at SHAEF Headquarters. Some incredulity on the part of members of Eisenhower's staff led to a delayed response. The day of

Eisenhower's promotion to five-star general ended with a doubling of security at the palace and added security for Eisenhower personally based on a report that there could be enemy commandos in the area.

The first day of Hitler's Ardennes Offensive came to a close, and the Allied leaders were still uncertain as to whether it was a local skirmish or a major campaign. It was not until Sunday the 17th that they came to the realization of what was going on. As reports of the advance reached the headquarters at Versailles, so did confusing reports of the mischief of some of Skorzeny's imposter troops. On Monday the 18th General Eisenhower, when the German advance had claimed an area approximately forty miles deep and thirty miles wide into Allied-held territory, ordered Patton to redirect his Third Army to the north to stop the German advance and drive them back to their previous position. Patton had preferred a more aggressive approach of cutting off the advancing troops from their supply lines, but acquiesced and began the task of restructuring his own communication and supply lines.

On that third day of the German advance a number of Skorzeny's imposters were captured. They intimated that their force was charged with eliminating several important personages in the Allied

Slaughtered American prisoners at Malmedy.

Command. Though this was found to be a false claim after the end of the war, it precipitated a sense of terror that filtered all the way to SHAEF Headquarters in Paris. Eisenhower was put into protective custody and was to remain there, much to his own consternation, for days. General Spaatz had SHAEF, the Air Command Headquarters, locked down with heightened security and his own personal guard augmented. Orders to do the same went out to all of the general staff on the continent. Fragmentary reports continued to come in from the rapidly broadening front of heavy shelling, enemy paratrooper drop, close combat, columns of tanks and artillery, mayhem caused by enemy terrorist rogues, severed communication lines, attacked retreating Allied units. They also slaughtered civilians and a unit of Allied troops at the village of Baugnez, just south of Malmedy. Slowly it became clear that this was no skirmish, no diversion, but rather a major and unexpected offensive assault. As Spaatz later admitted to General Arnold, commander of the USAAF, "The offensive undertaken by the Germans on December 16th undoubtedly caught us off balance."

Yet there was still no definitive aerial assessment of the magnitude of the German force or support. Weather conditions continued, just as Hitler had planned, to obscure the direction of the battles and advances, the strength of the forces, the available reserves and supplies, or the ultimate target the Germans were striving to capture. Ground intelligence was improving with the capture of combatants, the reports of fleeing civilians, and the decoding of information from the Germans' Enigma coded message system which was now carrying accurate battlefield information rather than the deceptive messages that had been used prior to conceal the true plan.

The bad weather that was key to Hitler's surprise was also his nemesis. His people on the ground quickly found that the movement of heavy equipment and advancing troops was, in some cases, hampered by difficult terrain, narrow lanes, melting sub-surfaces, rapidly extending supply lines, and dwindling supplies of fuel and munitions. Initial planning called for quick capture of Allied fuel stocks, a plan that was only partially successful. Captured prisoners were also a problem for the rapid advance. On the 17th SS Lt-Col Jochen Peiper's Task Force rumbled into view near Malmedy. A US field-artillery observation battery from the 7th Armored division found itself under enemy fire with no heavy

Lt Col Jochen Peiper

weapons or tank support and surrendered. The 125 men, after being searched, were taken to a nearby field under guard to await an escort to the rear. The SS troops continued to move on, leaving the captives under guard by two Mark IV tank crews. Machine guns of both tanks then opened fire on the prisoners. Though many fled into the woods, eighty-six of their comrades lay dead in the field, being slowly covered with a blanket of freshly falling snow.

Further away in the little hamlet of Wereth, eleven black American soldiers of the 333rd Field Artillery Battalion (Negro) were captured and summarily killed in cold blood by a recon party of the 9th SS Division.

Originally planned for the 16th but delayed to the early morning of the 17th because of bad weather and fuel shortages, the Germans attempted to execute Operation Stosser, the drop of 1,300 Fallschirmjager (paratroopers) seven miles north of Malmedy. The 112 Ju52 transport planes took off amid a powerful snowstorm, with strong winds and extensive low cloud cover. Many went off-course and men were dropped far afield from the intended drop zone. The strong winds also carried even those in the drop zone far afield and to extremely rough landings. Only 300 or so managed to assemble but were unable to harass the Allies with their planned guerrilla-like actions. Though their dispersal over such a broad region created additional confusion for the Allies, who believed a major division-sized jump had taken place and took action to secure their rear instead of sending troops off to the front to face the main German thrust.

The weather and problem of determining the actual identities of who was on the ground severely hampered Ninth Air Force bomber operations, but they did put up over 1,000 fighters from bases on the continent. Despite the soupy air they flew armed reconnaissance, defensive patrols, and attacks on bridges and gun positions. The IX and XIX Tactical Air Commands also were in the air to support ground forces and in a battle to hold the Saarlautern bridgehead. During the night of the 17th/18th, RAF Bomber Command hit several targets with 523 aircraft; 486 of them bombed the city of Duisburg, causing heavy damage, and three of the attacking planes were lost. Accustomed to flying by radar, an additional 317 Lancasters and 13 Mosquitos made a carpet sweep from the city center of Ulm to industrial and railway areas. Simultaneously, 280 Lancasters and eight Mosquitos hit the old center of Munich, doing extensive damage to it and to railway targets. The Hermann Goering benzene facility at Hallendorf and a number of other targets of opportunity were also severely damaged.

General Spaatz urgently shifted his attention from strategic concerns to tactics that would support the foundering ground forces. Weather had become his major enemy. The Eighth Air Force heavy bombers and fighters in England were socked in and mostly unable to fly. In order to provide at least some additional air support to Allied ground troops, he directed two of the Eighth's fighter groups to move immediately to the Continent, if they could find proper air fields. They were placed under operational control of General Hoyt Vandenberg. Additionally, he put the Eight's 2nd Air Division at Vandenberg's disposal to act as a "fire brigade" for direct call up without contacting USSTAF or SHAEF. The 2nd Air Division was designated because it specialized in Gee-H radar bombing, which had a 300-mile range, employing an airborne transmitter and two ground beacons to fix a target's position. It had a bombing accuracy much superior to the H2X system alone and was the best available countermeasure to the continuing vile weather conditions.

Continuing thick ground fog in England made bomber takeoffs and landings extremely treacherous. Lt. Mac McCauley, a pilot with the 385th Bomb Group, described conditions this way: "Fog rolled in over the battlefield and airpower was grounded. We read the news, knowing that bombers could be rushed in to change the flow of German ground forces. The fog was so heavy we didn't see fifty feet. Ice was forming on all bushes, etc. Day after day went by and still the fog hung thickly over the land." Nonetheless, the Eighth was able to send out missions on December 18 and again on the 19th. On the 18th only 411 of the 985 planes sent up actually bombed their assigned targets, all using radar. Targets included rail marshalling yards in Cologne, Koblenz, Kaiserslautern, Mainz, and Bonn. On the 19th these were all rail lines supplying the German offensive in the Ardennes, though the bulk of men, materiels, and supplies had all passed through them and into the forests, valleys, and roadways of the Eifel Mountains prior to the 16th. The Ninth Air Force was able to send a handful of fighters to slow the spearhead of the Nazi advance that day also. They were able to swoop down on the SS Panzer column led by Lt. Col. Jochen Peiper which was responsible for the massacre of surrendered US soldiers near Malmedy. The Thunderbolts of the Ninth inflicted sufficient damage to impede the armor advance. Fuel supplies were critically short for the advancing Wehrmacht from the onset and this bombing did interrupt the limited available resupply, though the German plan officially earmarked captured Allied fuel as the means to continue their offensive drive. One B-17 and three of their P-51 fighter escorts were lost on this mission.

During the nights of the 16th/17th and 17th/18th bombers were dispatched over France, Holland, and Germany to drop leaflets. On the morning of the 19th 328 bombers were sent to attack the Koblenz and Ehrang marshalling yards. Marginal weather dictated that they targeted with radar. In the early morning ice, one B-24 of the 93rd Bomb Group crashed on takeoff at Alburgh, Norfolk, killing all nine crewmen aboard. Attacks on the formation claimed two additional bomber crewmen during the mission. P-47s from the 78th Fighter Group flew out of Duxford and provided escort to the heavy bombers. Three of their forty-five aircraft were shot down, though all the pilots were safely recovered. Sixty-two of these aircraft from the 446th Bomb Group hit other tactical targets including the town of Kyllburg and its rail line and rail tunnel entrance. Their bombing utilized the Gee-H locating system to penetrate the thick cloud cover. The fog and cloud cover became so dense that the returning aircraft had to be diverted to landing strips on the west coast in Wales.

Though it seemed impossible — but just as predicted by Hitler's weatherman — conditions deteriorated further from the 20th to the 22nd and totally grounded the East Anglia based Eighth Air Force. The increasingly restless and frustrated fliers caught up on their laundry and letter writing in their fog-shrouded Quonset huts and grew anxious for action as they heard disturbing news reports of the advancing Hun.

On the 23rd 403 radar-equipped bombers were dispatched to the marshalling yards at Ehrang, Kaiserslautern, and Homburg and the communications centers in Junkerauth, Ahrweiler, and Dahlem. Nearly half of them sustained significant damage from the concentrated ground flak and Luftwaffe fighters. One flier was killed in action and another seriously injured. Seven fliers from the 94th Bomb Group were missing, but later recovered. Several crews returning to base reported some limited visibility at a few of the target areas. Six hundred and thirty-six fighters were dispatched. Most provided fighter escort to the heavy bombers, but 183 were sent to sweep the Bonn area. The escort fighters followed the highly successful procedures introduced by General Jimmy Doolittle and based on the advance sweeping moves developed by fighter ace Col. "Hub" Zemke, sweeping ahead of the formation and then pursuing targets of opportunity at the front after delivering their bombers to their assigned target areas. Seven US fighters were lost and seventy-five German aircraft were claimed downed in the attacks on the 23rd.

The shroud of fog and snow cover was making things as nearly impossible on the ground in Belgium as it was in the air. General Anthony McAullife, surrounded at Bastogne, had just told the threatening Germans "NUTS!" when they demanded his surrender. General George Patton had wheeled his forces to the north to relieve the situation but was frustrated with the difficulty of weather and combat conditions. According to the chronicle of the 102nd Infantry Division, more recently repeated in Bill O'Reilly's book, *Killing Patton*, on the 23rd General Patton made his headquarters in a geriatric home in Luxembourg City known as *Fondation Pescatore*. That morning he took his typically controversial outspokenness to the home's medieval chapel. Kneeling before the altar, the irascible commander removed his helmet with

General George S. Patton

its three stars and poured his heart out in prayer as only he could do. It is reported that he prayed:

> *"Sir, this is Patton talking. The last fourteen days have been straight hell. Rain, snow, more rain, more snow — and I'm beginning to wonder what's going on in Your headquarters. Whose side are You on, anyway?*
>
> *"For three years my chaplains have been explaining that this is a religious war. This, they tell me, is the Crusades all over again, except that we're riding tanks instead of chargers. They insist that we are here to annihilate the Germans and the godless Hitler so that religious freedom may return to Europe. Up until now I have gone along with them, for You have given us Your unreserved cooperation. Clear skies and a calm sea in Africa made the landings highly successful and helped us to eliminate Rommel. Sicily was comparatively easy and You supplied excellent weather for our armored dash across France, the greatest military victory that You have thus far allowed me. You have often given me excellent guidance in difficult command decisions and You have led German units into traps that made their elimination fairly simple.*
>
> *"But now, You've changed horses in midstream. You seem to have given von Rundstedt every break in the book and frankly, he's been beating the hell out of us. My army is neither trained nor equipped for winter warfare. And as You know this weather is more suitable for Eskimos than for southern cavalrymen.*
>
> *"But now, Sir, I can't help but feel that I have offended You in some way. That suddenly You have lost all sympathy for our cause. That You are throwing in with von Rundstedt and his paper-hanging-god, Hitler. You know with me telling You that our situation is desperate. Sure, I can tell my staff that everything is going according to plan, but there's no use telling You that my 101ˢᵗ Airborne is holding out against tremendous odds in*

Bastogne, and that this continual storm is making it impossible to supply them even from the air. I've sent Hugh Gaffey, one of my ablest generals, with his 4th Armored Division, north toward that all-important road center to relieve the encircled garrison and he's finding Your weather more difficult than he is the Krauts.

"I don't like to complain unreasonably, but my soldiers from the Meuse to Echternach are suffering tortures of the damned. Today I visited several hospitals, all full of frostbite cases, and the wounded are dying in the fields because they cannot be brought back for medical care.

"But this isn't the worst of the situation. Lack of visibility, continued rains, have completely grounded my air force. My technique of battle calls for close-in fighter-bomber support, and if my planes can't fly, how can I use them as aerial artillery? Not only is this a deplorable situation, but worse yet, my reconnaissance planes haven't been in the air for fourteen days and I haven't the faintest idea of what is going on behind the German lines.

"Damn it, Sir, I can't fight a shadow. Without Your cooperation from a weather standpoint I am deprived of accurate disposition of the German armies and how in hell can I be intelligent in my attack? All of this probably sounds unreasonable to You, but I have lost all patience with Your chaplains who insist that this is a typical Ardennes winter, and that I must have faith.

"Faith and patience be damned! You have just got to make up Your mind whose side You're on. You must come to my assistance, so that I may dispatch the entire German Army as a birthday present to Your Prince of Peace.

"Sir, I have never been an unreasonable man; I am not going to ask You for the impossible. I do not even insist upon a miracle, for all I request is four days of clear weather.

"Give me four clear days so that my planes can fly, so that my fighter-bombers can bomb and strafe, so that my reconnaissance *may pick out targets for my magnificent artillery. Give me four days of sunshine to dry this mud, so that my tanks roll, so that ammunition and rations may be taken to my hungry, ill-equipped infantry, I need these four days to send von Rundstedt and his godless army to their Valhalla. I am sick of this unnecessary butchery of American youth, and in exchange for four days of fighting weather, I will deliver You enough Krauts to keep Your bookkeepers months behind their work,*

Amen."

Shortly afterward he summoned Brig. General Monsignor James O'Neill, chief chaplain of the Third Army, and ordered him to fashion a simpler prayer to serve as Patton's Christmas card to his troops. That card was distributed to all of the troops under Patton's command a few days before Christmas and read:

"Almighty and most merciful Father, we humbly beseech Thee, of Thy great goodness, to restrain these immoderate rains with which we have had to contend. Grant us fair weather for battle. Graciously hearken to us as soldiers who call upon Thee that, armed with Thy power, we may advance from victory to victory, and crush the oppression and wickedness of our enemies and establish Thy justice among men and nations."

Whether Patton or his men had anything to do with it or not, weather forecasts for the coming day gave all a new optimism. A high-pressure zone over the Russian front, called a "Russian High" by meteorologists, was pushing to the west and clearing skies that had been opaque for days. As blue skies from the east began to replace Hitler's protective clouds, Supreme Allied Commander Eisenhower looked up and ordered a "maximum effort" response.

As bad weather conditions had persisted, many of the aircraft and their crews that flew in the adverse weather from the 19th to the 23rd of December had not been able to land at their home bases and were out of position for the maximum effort mission planned for the 24th. The 303rd Bomb Group stationed at Molesworth, for example, dispatched forty-two available B-17s from the scattered airfields where they landed on 23 December. Only seven took off from their home base, thirty-five went from Bassingbourn, four from Poddington, four from Snetterton Heath, and two from Knettishall. An additional two aircraft were dispatched to fly with the 92nd Bomb Group from Poddington, and six others flew with 3rd Bomb Division Groups. In an effort to fly anything flyable, some 303rd crews were flying planes of other units, and crews of other units were flying 303rd assigned aircraft. Some planes flew with crews from a variety of units. Some formations were "composite formations" made up from aircraft and crews of unrelated units.

*"It does not do to leave a live dragon out of your
calculations, if you live near him."*

— **J.R.R. Tolkien**, *The Hobbit*

Chapter 4

HIGH WYCOMBE
THE PLAN (SITUATION)

SPAATZ RELAYED EISENHOWER'S command from his headquarters in Paris to Doolittle in England. Every available aircraft was to fly. Every airman in Britain had waited for this moment. Ground and air crews had been marking time, unable even to train in the foul conditions. But the story was different for those responsible for command, intelligence, operations, and logistics. Staffing Eighth Air Force Headquarters in High Wycombe, they worked long hours poring over mountains of available information, decrypted messages from enemy communication, years of aerial observation, debriefing from captive soldiers, reports from ground forces, prior mission reports, and more. They were shocked at the news and speed of the Ardennes Offensive, as was most of the Allied command. Prior to December 16, the planners of High

Wycombe had focused on strategic targets aimed at eliminating the long-term and sustaining support of the German war effort. Ball bearing plants, aircraft plants, submarine facilities, weapons and ammunition plants, and most importantly, synthetic petroleum refineries and storage were their regular and primary targets. For the second time in seven months, the entire Eighth shifted from their strategic mission to tactical support of troops on the ground. The first was D-Day, June 2, 1944.

Despite the initial confusion, fragmented intel, and fluid situation on the ground, the planners began to pull a significant aerial counteroffensive together, and they did it "by the book." At this stage of the war SHAEF had pulled together an orderly system of command, control, and procedures for all activities, including mission planning. As Air Force Colonel William R. Carter pointed out on the 45th anniversary of the Battle of the Bulge: "On 31 January 1943, President Franklin D. Roosevelt met with Prime Minister Winston Churchill at Casablanca, Morocco. At this conference the Anglo-American leaders and their staffs defined the alliance's grand strategy, established the Combined Chiefs of Staff, and agreed on both a strategic bombing and tactical support policy." That policy became US War Department doctrine on 21 July 1943 in Field Manuel 100-20. It was that directive that guided the 8th Air Force Mission Planners during the 3rd week of December 1944.

FM 100-20 for air power employment spelled out:

"First Priority. To gain the necessary degree of air superiority. This will be accomplished by attacks against aircraft in the air and on the ground and against those installations that the enemy requires for the application of air power.

"Second Priority. To prevent the movement of hostile troops and supplies into the theater of operations or within the theater (air interdiction).

"Third Priority. To participate in a combined effort of air and ground forces, in the battle area, to gain objectives on the immediate front of the ground forces (close cooperation)."

The policy goes into great detail on the desirability for the introduction of air power to disrupt the orderly operations and air defense in the theater to prevent the mobilization and strategic concentration of the enemy's field forces. It observes that only total destruction of the enemy's aviation can gain and maintain complete control of the air and also acknowledges that this is "seldom possible." It proscribes centralized command and control of air power along with adequate communications for liaison.

The resulting plan ("Mission 760") called for a "Maximum Effort" attack utilizing all available flying resources.

The planners at High Wycombe pored over the available pre-attack intelligence and pieced it together, increasing intelligence reports, maps of the combat area, rail systems, communication links, and Luftwaffe support bases. Hoping against hope for relief from on high, they developed a plan for maximum effort response. They established three priorities for the initial response:

1. To rapidly gain the necessary degree of air superiority, first by overpowering Luftwaffe forces supporting the offensive. That included those in the air and on the ground, as well as landing and refueling capability. The objective was to take quick and incapacitating action against those installations providing support to the Wehrmacht on the ground.

2. To provide direct air interdiction intended to prevent the movement of hostile troops and supplies into or within the fluid theater of operations.

3. To provide close cooperation in a combined effort of Allied air and ground forces in the battle area to assist in gaining the objectives of the ground forces at the immediate front.

The targets of their plan included eleven Luftwaffe aerodromes thought to be actively involved in supporting the Ardennes Offensive. These were identified as the operations at Babenhausen, Gross Ostheim, Zellhausen, Biblis, Darmstadt, Frankfurt-Rheine, Nidda, Ettinghausen, Kirchgons, Giessen, and Merzhausen. The next category of targets was all major rail centers and marshalling yards supplying the German offensive, including those at Pforzheim and Kaiserslautern. And finally, "communication centers," those locations where rail and roadways were essential for

VIII Bomber Command Mission Planning

the movement of reinforcements, equipment, ammunition, and supplies to support the rapidly advancing Nazi ground troops. These included Haildraum, Koblenz, Ruwer, Pfalzel, Wittlich, Eller, Cochem, Bitburg, Mayen, Ahrweiler, Rheinbach, Euskirchen, Daun, Gerolstein, Wetteldorf, and Schoenecken. Allowances were also made for the attack of Targets of Opportunity in the vicinities of the various primary and secondary targets.

In keeping with a tactic frequently practiced with the 8th Air Force, a feint mission (Mission 759) was also planned. This one, designed to confuse German Intelligence, would take a formation of B-24 bombers to the German coastal battery at La Pallice in La Rochelle, France.

Routing for the planned Mission 760 called for the assemblage of an unprecedented vanguard of 2,034 heavy bombers over England, setting across the Channel in an extended trail of group formations across the Channel to Ostend, Belgium, then passing south of Liege, Belgium, over the Siegfried Line into Germany, vectoring over the known German buildup in the Eifel Mountains.

At the 1015 hours weather briefing at VIII Bomber Command at High Wycombe (code named *Pinetree*), it was determined that a high-pressure mass from the east, a "Russian Front," was finally beginning to clear the skies over northern Europe. That forecast report would be

Mission 759 target: La Pallice battery, La Rochelle, France

repeated at 1600 hours and 2200 hours before the mission would be cleared for takeoff. But plenty needed to be done in preparation if this largest of all air missions was to be accomplished. The deputy commander of operations and his staff selected the suitable targets and established their priority. They were then reviewed at an operational conference early in the evening on the 23rd. The three Bomb Division headquarters had already been given advance warning of the impending "maximum effort" operation. All units were on alert to prepare aircraft and brief personnel after the first briefing that morning. Once the Combat Wings received the targets and ordnance requirements, they began to plan their segment of the mission in detail. Their 2,222 specialists studied the target identifications, plotted routes and times, and specified altitudes. In consultation with VIII Fighter Command, they arranged fighter support for the heavy bombers.

Earlier in the day each group had received their alert by way of a scrambled telephone message on a secret line in the Group's Operations' message center. Late in the day teletype machines were humming to thirty-nine different Bomb Group stations and sixteen different Fighter Group stations in East Anglia and north of London. As the evening came, so came pages and pages of detailed flight plans, formation order, and target information by unit. Sent as a SECRET message, all were identified as Field Order No. 1446A and establishing Zero Hour as 1100 B.S.T. given that the winter solstice was on the 22nd, making Christmas Eve one of the shortest days of the year. Suddenly each station snapped into action after their week of boredom, anxious anticipation, and expectant inactivity. All this information passed to the watch officer in his windowless, gas-proof, constantly manned Group Operations building. His duty clerk immediately notified the commanding officer, the air executive, the S-3 group operations officer, the S-2 Intelligence Section, the group navigator and the bombardier officers, the weather office, Flying Control, ordnance and armament sections, engineering office, the signals and photographic units, and the mess hall, motor pool, and Charge of Quarters on each squadron living site. The duty officer informed the guard room, told the base telephone exchange to restrict calls, and requested the Military Police detachment to post MPs at the doors of Operations and War Room. At the barracks CQs raised the red flag, restricting personnel to the base. At some stations a red light was lit over the bars at the officer's and NCO's clubs, shutting off the supply of spirits.

Meanwhile target folders were prepared with the files of the Intelligence Section containing all necessary intelligence to date for briefing officers and combat personnel. Maps, photographs, and other relevant matter, including "flak charts" and "mission flimsies" were prepared in the war room. In Operations, the route to the target was plotted on a large wall map. The group bombardier's office obtained information from Intelligence, navigators, and the weather officer to assess specific target conditions as well as speeds, drift, and heading data computed for bombsight settings for the attack altitude. When the final version of Field Order No. 1446A was transmitted after the 2200 hours' weather check, it was approximately twelve to thirteen feet long as it emerged from the teletype machine.

As the earliest warnings of FO 1446A had begun to filter through the chains of command across the fields of East Anglia, Colonel Nick Perkins, General Frederick Castle's chief of staff at the 4th Combat Wing Headquarters, was busy in the Operations Room processing the incoming messages and preparing for the coming day's largest mission to date for the 8th Air Force and for the 4th Combat Wing that was assigned to lead the attack. At the time the headquarters of the 4th Combat Wing was located in Bury St. Edmunds, the home of the 94th Bomb Group, a group then Colonel Castle had commanded from June of 1943 until April of 1944 when he became commander of the 4th Wing. He was promoted to the rank of brigadier general on November 20, 1944, just thirty-four days before the Christmas Eve mission.

When the division weather officer informed him that the fog might lift at last, Perkins began staffing for a maximum force mission, and he assigned Lt. Col. Robert D. MacDonald to lead the wing as command pilot and himself to lead the second group. He realized then that if General Castle knew this, he would take the lead himself. So, he told the people in the Ops Room that if the general came in, they should keep busy and not volunteer information about the mission unless they were asked a direct question. Given the scope of the mission, they all knew what Castle would do, even though his doctor had recently noted that he was exhausted and recommended that he get a little rest.

Then Perkins got word that the 4th Combat Wing's 3rd Division was assigned to lead this largest ever mission on the following day. He recalled later: "Shortly General Castle walked in looking very tired and said his driver had just let him out at Ops where he only wanted to say he was home from a visit to his bomb groups and on his way to bed. He asked if we were stood down again, and Perkins said, 'No — we might be able to get off.' Castle responded, 'Fine. It's about time because we have to stop that breakthrough. I'll see them off in the morning, but right now I'm going to bed.'"

To the relief of Perkins and his staff, Castle walked out after saying good night. But he didn't walk far, because in less than a minute he stuck his head in the door and asked who was leading the division. Perkins had to say it was the 4th Wing. He then came all the way in and asked who was leading the 8th Air Force, and Perkins had to say the 3rd Division. Castle thought a minute and said, "I'm sorry, Mac, I'm going to have to take your place tomorrow."

While England slept, the Germans were busy overhead. At approximately 0500 hours forty-five German V1 rockets were launched from Heinkel He111 bombers flying over the North Sea before returning to their home base. Aimed at Manchester, only seven came close to striking

German V-1 rocket

their intended target. Of the others, fourteen fell in the North Sea, the remaining twenty-four striking across the countryside from Manchester to the eastern coast. Forty-two people were killed in the attack and 109 were injured, fifty-one of them seriously. Chris Lucas of Didsbury recalled, "I was five and in a shelter with my family when one went over and hit just down the road." Kevin Regan, also an eyewitness, stated, "Christmas Eve 1944, our farm at Scammenden had no gas, electricity, or water supply other than the wells and river. The searchlights were the only glow, piercing the sky on the distant horizon. Their bombers were occasionally illuminated like dancing fish. Five ballistic missiles flew overhead. I fell into the grass and froze, what on God's earth is this, witchcraft, fire in the sky — Manchester must be the target..."

The rockets of that early morning created destruction up to a mile around their impact points. They also left canisters of propaganda for the survivors. This particular attack left paper blowing in the wind that included pages of *Signal* magazine that talked of the collusion of Russia and the United States in the dissolution of Europe.

As that Christmas Eve attack on Manchester was being staged to the north, Brigadier General Frederick W. Castle was driven from Bury St. Edmunds down to Lavenham, the station of the 487th Bomb Group. There two lead pilots, Lt. Robert Harriman of the 838th Squadron and Lt. John Edwards of the 839th Squadron, tossed a coin to determine who would fly with the general. Harriman won

the toss and was assigned the
lead position with Castle in the
right seat as air commander.
Edwards would be deputy lead
with Capt. Mayfield R. Shilling
of the 487th BG as deputy air
commander.

Ground crews and armor-
ers had been busy at Lavenham
and 8th Air Force bases across
East Anglia throughout the
long night, readying their aircraft for this enormous mission.
"Every flyable aircraft" included support planes not normally
included in combat formations

Capt. Mayfield R. Shilling

in addition to an assortment of "Weary Willies." Flying crews got a
5:30 a.m. wake-up and began the ritual of an oxygen-mask-accom-
modating clean shave, preparing their flight attire, breakfast, and a
series of briefings before moving to their aircraft's hard stand with
their equipment in preparation for takeoff and formation to meet at
1100 hours Zero Hour.

With carefully choreographed precision, the twenty-three combat groups of thirty-six aircraft each of the First Force (the Third
Division) formed a formation as trained, rising from the end of the
runways at Lavenham promptly at 0900 in perfect weather conditions. Both Harriman and Castle were in relatively new B-17Gs
designated for lead crews and fully equipped with the latest in-
novations at the time, including the H2X "Mickey" radar systems.
Harriman and Castle's plane was called "Treble Four." It was a
newer craft without a nickname but was identified by the last three
numbers of its serial number: 44-8444. Once airborne their first

8th Air Force Ground Crew

Pre-Mission Briefing

action involved flying to 7,000 feet and holding a racetrack pattern as the rest of the lead formation fell in place behind them. There they held while the other formations followed the same procedure at other altitudes. Similar formations were rising from the forty heavy bomber stations across the British countryside. The roar of engines from these rising behemoths shook the villages as they took flight, breaking the quiet anticipation that the bad weather of the previous days leading up to Christmas had brought. Civilian children and adults across the East Anglia countryside looked to the skies as they heard the roar of 2,046 heavy bombers and 853 fighters taking flight in the clearing skies.

Once all were airborne and in place, the pilot 1/Lt. Robert W. Harriman and Air Leader Brig. General Frederick W. Castle led every flyable aircraft in the 8th Air Force. The 1st Force headed toward Felixstowe on the coast of East Anglia and began their journey across the Channel from there. Similarly, the 2nd Force flew in order to Clacton, just south of Felixstowe for their journey to the Continent. The B-24s of the Third Force followed a similar procedure but headed to Great Yarmouth to the north for their departure point from England as they crossed the Channel. The mission commander led an impressive trail of aircraft, bombs, and more than 20,000 airmen in the largest formation of aerial bombers in history. Though the weather in the forming area was generally fine, some of the elements of the 4th Wing were delayed and did not reach their various rendezvous points on time. As a result, the leading formations were approximately fifteen minutes behind schedule on their climb across the Channel and past Control Point 2 over Ostend and into Belgium.

This mammoth armada was passing over and continuing its climb from 7,000 feet as it left Control Point 1 over Felixstowe, Clacton, and Great Yarmouth on the coast, climbing to 22,000 feet when it arrived at the planned escort rendezvous point at Control

Point 3 southwest of Liege, Belgium. As they were beginning their journey, an ominous Luftwaffe message intercepted by the Signal Corps included a call for all available German fighters to the Belgium location of the US bomber formation. German intelligence knew they were coming.

For most of the groups the formation was routine and orderly. But for a few the icing conditions and ground fog were severe enough to be a problem. A B-17 from the 91st Bomb Group crashed after takeoff from Bassingbourn. The only injury was a broken leg suffered by T/Sgt Vivian R. Chowing. The crew survived. At Poddington a 92nd Bomb Group B-17 crashed on takeoff, killing six, including a new pilot, Robert Seeber of the 327th Squadron. Seeber was attempting an instrument takeoff with minimal visibility. The heavy fog prevented a clear view of the trees about 200 yards to the left of the runway at its end. Seeber began to turn to get on course before elevation was attained, encountered prop wash from the plane in front of him, and crashed into the treetops. His burning aircraft exploded about two minutes later. The remote and heavily wooded site of the crash hampered access by the ambulances. Lt. Charles H. Nesbit, equipment officer of the 325th Squadron, ran to the site of the crash and courageously pulled several of the crew members from the wreckage, ignoring the risk of further bomb explosions. Sadly, the three men he rescued died later from their injuries. Only Seeber, copilot Lt. William H. McQuinn, and engineer Sgt. William J. Brockmeyer survived the crash. At one point Nesbit was within 100 feet of a bomb when it exploded among the wreckage. He miraculously escaped injury or death by dropping to the ground.

Two B-17s from the 398th Bomb Group crashed, killing two; 457th Bomb Group B-17 crashed taking off from Glatton, killing one. At the 398th Bomb Group's station in Nuthampstead, as the planes were maintaining thirty-second intervals on takeoff, there were two crashes. In the first, pilot Donald D. Grinter hit a tree at the end of the runway in the fog due to icing on the wings. The plane was travelling at 125 mph under full weight and caught fire, killing the bombardier, Lt. Dick Herrin, and a navigator newly assigned to the crew. Copilot Jim White suffered a broken leg and was pulled from the wreckage before the plane burst into flames.

The 78th FG at Duxford and 339th FG at Fowlmere were both fogged in and unable to fly as scheduled. The 339th FG had been assigned to accompany the last four combat groups of the 1st Force from the rendezvous point through the target and exit. The 78th FG had been assigned to perform a supporting sweep in the Third Force target area at zero plus 178 minutes.

The skies had been busy over both Belgium and Luxembourg that first clear morning in days. The 9th Air Force with its medium bombers and fighters, plus fighters from tactical groups supporting combat troops on the ground, were out in strength as soon as conditions were suitable for flight. Headquarters of the 9th Air Force were located in Luxembourg City on December 15, less than an hour from Vianden on the Our River, an attack point of the advancing German troops in their surprise advance on December 16.

Early that Christmas Eve, the US Tactical Air Force, which had been moving along and supporting the ground troop advance since D-Day, was active continuing the bombing and strafing of Germany troops and equipment, bridges, railways, and supplies that were essential to the Germans' Ardennes offensive. American troops on the ground were ecstatic that their air support was finally able to resume activities as the sky began to clear on December 23. The same blue-skied weather pattern continued on the 24th.

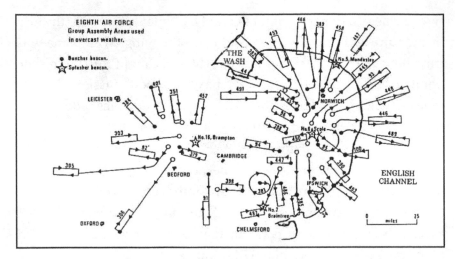

System of splashers and bunchers that enabled each unit forma-
tion to gather after takeoff, gaining altitude while flying in a
rectangular pattern prior to peeling off in a straight line at the
assigned altitude to cross the Channel.

As the more than 2,080 aircraft and nearly 21,000 men of the
massive formation of the 8th Air Force's mission 760 were forming up over England and moving across the Channel, the tactical
air forces already operating on the continent were flying their over
2,700 sorties of the day.

There was a slight delay in the formation of heavy bombers over
England, causing the lead box with General Castle's plane to depart the signal over Felixstowe and enter airspace over the Channel
about fifteen minutes late. Once over water, the crews of each of the
aircraft performed their standard pre-bombing checks. The bomb
bay was opened and closed. Every gun in the front, waist, ball turret, and tail was test fired. Inter- and intraplane communication was
checked. Radio contact was made with MEW control (Microwave
Early Warning Radar), which was operating under the call-sign
"NUTHOUSE" and had recently relocated its radar control base

across the English Channel to the village of Eys in Holland, about fifteen miles east of Maastricht. The positioning of aircraft within the formation was checked and tightened, the tail gunner in each craft giving visual feedback to the formation command pilot. The crew, except for the pilot and navigators, settled in for a quiet moment as the beautiful blue sky and a few puffy white clouds covered the horizon, a welcome sight after the days of winter gloom. Despite the freezing cold, it was a moment of relief from the tension of the morning, a brief time for reflection, a quick prayer, a joke or two to relieve the stress.

A most serious problem for the mission that was about to be revealed was the failure of 55th, 357th, and 479th fighter escorts to be with the lead formation at the rendezvous point east of Namur, Control Point 3. That control point was about twenty-five miles west of Liege in friendly territory. The thirty-four P51s of the "A" Group of the 55th FG led by Col. Crowell had taken off from Wormingford at 1100 hours, zero hour for the mission. They rendezvoused at 1200 hours with the bomber stream "at Brussels" according to their after-mission report, rather than the designated location ten miles northeast of Namur. At 1105 Lt. Col. Dregne of the 357th FG "B" Group took flight from Leiston with twenty-five P51s. They were north of Namur at 24,000 feet at 1149 hours yet they were not present at 1229 when General Castle's lead formation was attacked just twenty-four miles east of there at 1229 hours. The A Group, led by Maj. Peterson, did not take off from Leiston until 1130 and rendezvoused with the bomber stream at about 1212 hours, though at some point back of the lead which was about to be accosted by the enemy. The A and B groups of the 479th FG both reported a rendezvous with the bomber stream at 1200 hours, at 25,000 feet above Brussels for the A group and 17,000 feet above Bruges for the B group. NUTHOUSE vectored the A group forward at 1225 hours to assist the lead formation, but all the damage was done before they arrived. They sighted the struggling B-17s in the distance as they approached, but the fight was over before they arrived.

Chapter 5

FREDERICK WALKER CASTLE

General Frederick Castle

TO FULLY UNDERSTAND Frederick Castle, it is helpful to consider the words of his lifetime friend and classmate at West Point, General W.H. Sterling Wright. Wright had been stationed in Europe as cavalry officer during World War II and participated in the D-day attack. In letters held by his son Walter Wright of Savannah, Georgia, he describes Castle as "someone who—even in his youth—said and did the right things. He was not political, but rather was knowledgeable and insightful. Freddy Castle was golden and he knew it. That keen sense of awareness brought him to this day." Castle was considered brilliant by those who knew him. He was not only intelligent and hardworking, but he was well connected. His father was a West Point graduate and a classmate of Hap Arnold, who went on to become an aviation pioneer and chief of the Army Air Corps. Arnold was also young Frederick Castle's godfather. Before World War II broke out, the young Castle was working for the Sperry Corporation in the development of aircraft equipment for the military. He became one of the civilians selected by Ira Eaker to establish the 8th Air Force presence in England.

One can only speculate about what was going through General Frederick Castle's mind at the spearhead of this enormous formation of bombs and bombers. As things progressed from the challenges of takeoff and forming, with Lt. Robert Harriman piloting the plane, the relative calm over the Channel gave Castle a brief mental break before Ostend appeared on the coast to the east. Perhaps he gave quick thought to the thirty-day pass in his pocket and what he might do in his first return home since flying with General Ira Eaker in February of 1942, as one of the seven pioneers of Eighth Bomber Command in England. That group was occasionally referred to as "Eaker's amateurs" in reference to their lack of experience in building anything on the scale of what the "Mighty Eighth" was to become. Or was he reliving his prior twenty-nine bombing missions? Or his days as commander of the 94th Bomb Group, where rebuilding the unit was the order of the day? Perhaps, with the vista of the Belgium coast appearing on the horizon, he was carried back to his civilian days at the Sperry Corporation and efforts to develop a state-of-the-art bombsight, one that was surpassed by the Norden unit below him in the nose of the plane. Or did he hear the cadences of his days at West Point urging him on? Perhaps it was the voices of his proud father or his proud godfather, General Hap Arnold, encouraging him as they always had, congratulating him on his rapid rise to brigadier general on November 20th.

Suddenly the reality of the moment came back into focus and Castle's mind snapped into focused attention. The navigators marked arrival over land at Ostend, Belgium, on planned course, though late. They set a course to a beacon at CP3, the rendezvous point for the fighters who would accompany them to their eventual target, the Babenhausen aerodrome. They reached CP3 at 1223 hours. This escort meeting point was southeast of Brussels and slightly southwest of Liege. It was all friendly territory according to the best intel they had available. They had clear contact with "NUTHOUSE," the MEW radar command station northeast of them in Eys, Holland. They were unaware, however, that their presence had also been detected by German Intelligence. An intercepted message indicated that a German observation point spotted the vanguard of the formation as it had crossed into Belgium at

LTS. HARRIMAN, ROWE, PROCOPIO, MACARTY, BIRI.
LT. WILKINSON, S/SGT. HUDSON, MYSELF, T/SGT. SWAIN

Ostend and detected that it was without fighter protection as it flew into Belgium.

Prior to the sighting of the 8th Air Force, the skies of southern Belgium and all of Luxembourg had been busy throughout the morning hours as fighters of both the Allied 9th Air Force tactical forces and the Luftwaffe were busy in the region, each providing support to ground troops on their respective sides of the ongoing battle below. Bridges, roadways, railways, equipment, choke points, and troops were the ready targets for the fighters working the ground battles like attacking hornets seeking out targets on the ground and pouncing on them.

The fighters of the 8th had a different agenda. They were assigned to accompany and protect the heavy bombers as they made their way to their assigned targets. Their planned rendezvous with the formation was to be at Control Point 3 defined in Field Order No. 1446 A as just north of Namur, Belgium, at 50°35'E and 5°00'N, approximately twenty-six miles southwest of Liege, Belgium. General Castle's lead plane crossed that point approximately sixteen to seventeen minutes later than the planned 12:07, but his assigned escort fighters from the 357th Fighter Group had not arrived and were nowhere in sight. Reports of the 357th filed at the end of the mission indicate that the B contingent of the 357th led by Lt. Col. Irwin H. Dregne entered Belgium air space at 1149 hours and rendezvoused with the first three groups of the First Force (Castle's lead) at 1212 hours, but that does not coincide with the rest of the generally accepted timing of the morning's tragedy. It is more likely that they met the bomber stream at that time, but were far behind the leading formation, call sign Vinegrove 1-1. The A contingent's reports from flight leader Major Peterson indicated that his planes did not reach the coast of Belgium until 1217 hours, entering at and more than ninety miles from the rendezvous point. Similarly, the fighters of the 479th and 55th fighter groups met the bomber formation at approximately 1200 hours, but over Brussels, not fifty-seven miles southeast of there, where the lead formation was about to be brutally attacked.

Perhaps assuming that the fighter escort was already ahead of the delayed formation, Castle directed his pilot, 23-year-old 1/Lt. Robert Harriman, to pick up speed in an effort to catch up with the originally scheduled time for rendezvous. Harriman was a seasoned and respected pilot who had arrived at Lavenham in May of 1944 and had been flying regularly as a lead pilot. Originally from Madison, Wisconsin, he had been a football standout in high school and junior college, enlisting shortly after Pearl Harbor. As a lead pilot he was known for running a tight ship with a disciplined crew, according to his bombardier, Paul Biri. Like General Castle, Harriman also had plans for a visit home after this mission. His fiancée, Barbara Weiner, was anxiously awaiting him for their long-planned wedding.

As the plane with its heavy load of weapons and fuel began the quick acceleration, a mechanical problem showed itself with the number one engine, which began to throw oil. By about 1229, Gen. Castle over the town of Amay called over the VHF radio that *Treble 4* would be aborting because of the engine oil problem. The lead formation had already reached their assigned 22,000-foot altitude. Harriman banked down and to the left. Unexpectedly, some of the formation had missed the prior radio message and began to follow him. He quickly pulled back into the formation and attempted to resume the lead. It was then that the first German fighters began to appear. Initially, they passed through the formation without firing. The C or low formation was already a mile behind, having not caught up with the prior acceleration. Three minutes after the first attempt, Castle's plane made a second abort move, and Capt. Mayfield Shilling's deputy lead plane, piloted by 1/Lt. John Edwards, took over the lead of the 487th and the 8th Air Force bomber stream. Later Edwards reported that the last he saw of General Castle was him sitting in the right seat and focused on a map, apparently searching for a safe place to take the plane down.

Within seconds a single Me109 made a pass at 44-8444 from the two o'clock direction, firing at the aborting plane and hitting radar navigator or "Mickey operator," 1/Lt. Bruno Procopio, who was located with his APS-15 radar set across from the radio operator T/Sgt Lawrence Swain, on the starboard side of the fuselage. Immediately three additional Me109s appeared from the three o'clock direction and pounced on Castle's plane with a barrage of cannon and machine gun fire. This attack set the number one and two engines on fire.

Now with very serious problems, a command came over the interphone to bail out and Harriman told Bombardier Paul Biri to jettison the bomb load. Biri replied that their position was still over Allied-held Belgium and there were likely Allied troops and Belgian civilians below. Even

Bombardier Lt. Paul Biri

though release of the bomb load would have given the damaged plane more maneuverability, Castle agreed, and the bombs were not released.

Displaced from the co-pilot's seat by General Castle, Lt. Claude Rowe was flying as tail gunner, a common procedure for lead crews. There he was also responsible for observing and reporting the condition of the trailing formation. Rowe was wounded in the cannon attack, bailed out, but was apparently hit again during his parachute descent. He was found about five miles from the wreckage of the plane. A local civilian witness reported that he had seen an attacking German fighter fire at Rowe as his parachute drifted down. He was recovered on the ground, but died on the scene from his wounds. 1/Lt. Procopio, the radar navigator who was hit in the initial attack, also bailed out; he was recovered, though he died at the military hospital in Liege. T/Sgt Lawrence Swain, the radio operator/waist gunner, bailed out, but he was found dead on the ground without a parachute. Cpt. Edmund Auer, pilotage navigator, and T/Sgt Quentin Jeffers bailed out and survived, though Auer severely injured his left knee. S/Sgt Lowell Hudson, waist gunner and the first to bail out, landed in a tree more than six miles from the final wreckage and survived. He was hanging by his chute in the tree near Terwagne with burns on his face and contusions on his right foot when local citizen Jules Lejeune arrived. Not knowing if he was in enemy or friendly territory, a cautious Hudson pulled out his handgun and held his friendly rescuer at bay until US Military jeeps arrived.

There was some drama in the plane as Castle, on the flight deck, fought to control it and directed Harriman to bail out. Bombardier 1/Lt. Paul Biri was the only member of the rest of the crew still in the plane. Harriman was unable to locate his parachute or any spare. Biri was at the front access door and preparing to jump when Harriman asked him to wait, so they both could jump using the single chute, though this was extremely unpractical given their combined size and that of the opening. Immediately enemy fire to the right-wing auxiliary fuel tank—the "Tokyo tank"—caused it to explode violently, tearing off the end of the right wing and putting the plane into a spin at 12,000 feet. It also propelled Biri, who was wearing his chute, out of the front access door of the craft. Once the broken fuselage began to erratically roll, it was impossible for Castle to continue to maintain any control of the aircraft and neither Harriman nor Castle could bail out. Both were killed instantly at point of impact. As the remaining front end of the plane rotated, the bomb load detonated, spreading the wreckage over 200 yards and starting a fire in the dense wooded area near the Chateau d'Englebermont, a castle that the US 518th Military Police Battalion was using as a mobile headquarters in the fluid Battle of the Bulge fighting.

An eyewitness on the ground, Mr. Rogister, reported "a tremendous aerial battle began in the direction of Xhos (from Fraiture)…" Suddenly a Fortress made a steep, 180-degree turn to the left while heavily trailing smoke, and then several white mushrooms appeared – parachutes; some of the crew had bailed out six, and then the plane went into a tailspin and exploded, but another chute opened as the plane came apart. All of this happened very quickly. A part of the fuselage fell at Baugnee, and a wing at the cemetery of Nandrin. After several seconds, there was a violent explosion. The B-17 had fallen over an area of several hundred meters near the castle of d'Englebermont." (5013N-0528E) This was about five miles from where Rowe's body had been found. Biri came down closest to the final wreckage, suffering an injured knee as he hit the ground. In his statement during the incident investigation, he indicated he had been taken in by members of the Nyrink family of La Croix Andre. He and McCarty were later picked up by American troops of the 125th AA Battalion and taken to a hospital in Liege.

The entire tragic drama took less than twenty-one minutes. General Castle's first abort call was made at 12:29. The first fly-by of a Me109 occurred at 12:30. Castle's second abort call was made at 12:32. The first Me109 firing pass happened at the same time. The final firing pass, hitting the fuel tank, occurred at 12:31. Approximately thirteen excruciating minutes later two great men and their aircraft were gone.

The enemy aircraft involved in this first attack are believed to be from the Luftwaffe's JG3 and were vectored to the Liege area in an unusual move that far ahead of the front lines by their fighter controller at Horhausen, located just 13 miles east of the Rhine

River crossing at Remagen. according to subsequent analysis by Major Robert H. Hodges. The Germans had ample radar coverage of the area and then clear optical visibility upon arriving to locate the vanguard of the formation and single out Castle's troubled lead plane as it left the formation. Long before Castle's formation reached Control Point 3 (5035N 0500E) and discovered his fighter protection was not yet there, the Luftwaffe was already in motion to attack him. A message intercepted by ULTRA included a call for all available German fighters to the Belgium location of the US bomber formation as the mammoth armada was leaving its 7,000 feet altitude at the coast of England and beginning its climb to 22,000 feet over the English Channel. The Germans were ready to pounce while the US fighter escort was beginning to scout the area.

The severed tail section of General Castle's downed plane, Treble Four, and his dog tag found in the wreckage.

*Every gun in the front echelons was firing,
turrets turning. Aircraft were falling, burning all
around us. The sky itself seemed to shake."*

— **1/LT James Bradford**

Chapter 6

SEVENTEEN MINUTES OF HELL
AND
HEROES OF THE REST OF THE
INITIAL ATTACK

GENERAL CASTLE'S HEROIC and self-sacrificing action has come to be the iconic event of battle. The violent and sudden death of this 35-year-old bright star, one of only five general officers killed during the European war, was met with sorrow and tears all the way from Belgium to Washington, DC. It was days before his death was confirmed, an uncertainty even felt all the way up to Commanding General "Hap" Arnold, a lifelong friend of Castle's father as well as Frederick Castle's godfather. Without taking away anything from the gravity of this event, it is equally important to recognize that similar crises were playing out almost simultaneously. As the battle continued, seven additional bombers were lost, with numerous crew members injured or killed in action. There were twenty-nine deaths over Belgium in addition to General Castle's. The entire formation—though with some difficulty—was continuing to move eastward into the flak fields that had advanced with Hitler's Ardennes Offensive, into territory thought to be "safe" earlier in the week.

The pack of four Me 109s that took out General Castle's plane was accompanied by an estimated fifty fighters who were intent on ravaging the composite low element.

1229 Hours

At 12:29, the same time that Castle's plane above and ahead was experiencing oil leakage problems in its number one engine and out of sight of the Castle and Harriman crew, the first enemy contact was beginning below and behind them. The first hit was 2/Lt William J. Waldron's plane *Weary Willie*, flying in the number nine position on the left side of the low formation. The tail gunner, S/Sgt James P. Naughton, reported a "company front" formation of FW-190s attacking from the tail. The entire plane was riddled with holes in this first pass. The number three engine on the right wing was aflame and there was a fire in the bomb bay. The interphone was shot out. The bombardier, 2/Lt Russell C. Neu, could see the glitter and sparkle of exploding cannon shells set with proximity switches through the plane's plexiglass nose and lowered the chin turret gun controls, ready for use. He took out an FW190 directly in front of him. And then he realized that his own ship was beginning to nose down. He grabbed his chest pack chute and yelled to the navigator, F/O Joseph Shuster, to do the same. Waldron took off his oxygen mask and gave the order to bail out to all within earshot and still alive while struggling to keep the plane level. Immediately there was a bright flash and the plane began to spin out of control. The centrifugal force pinned Neu to the floor. In the later investigation, Waldron said that he had yelled to Shuster while the plane was falling, but before the big flash and subsequent spin. At that time Shuster appeared to be dazed but unhurt.

Waldron made his way to the galley-way and there saw Shuster, S/Sgt Benedict Andrews, the engineer, and 2/Lt Oscar Eshleman, the copilot, all immobilized by the centrifugal force. Isley had already bailed out. Waldron attempted to help the remaining three move to the exit door, but without success. With the next explosion, he was blown out of the plane. At the same time, so was Neu from the front hatch. Apparently, the tail gunner, S/Sgt James Naughton, the ball turret gunner, S/Sgt Reuben Baganz, and the radio operator, George Ferenchak, were already dead or seriously wounded.

The plane came down near Chateau de Warnmont in Rouvreux, Sprigmont, Belgium, approximately nine minutes after it was initially hit. 1/Lt Neu and Waldron parachuted safely and were recovered. Isley had numerous injuries, was taken to the local field hospital, and then medevacked to McGuire General Hospital in Richmond, Virginia, where he fully recovered.

1232 Hours

Three minutes later and a little to the north and east of Waldron's downed plane was the B-17 flown by 22-year-old 1/Lt Ira L. Ball. According to the plane's bombardier, 1/Lt John C. Broom, one of the two survivors of this crew, the mission was shaping up to be a "milk run" when just south of Liege several Me109s streaked out of the sun, each firing away with their four 20mm cannons. They made one pass hitting Ball's plane, which was flying in the number five position on the right-hand side of the formation. The first attack shot away the plane's rudder control. They also struck and damaged the formation's lead aircraft flown by 1/Lt Lloyd Reed.

The tail gunner on this flight was not a usual crewman, but rather 22-year-old 1/Lt Cuno V. Becker, the armament officer of the 836th Bomb Squadron of the 487th Bomb Group (Heavy) stationed in Lavenham. Like General Castle, Becker did not need to be on this mission, but had volunteered to be part of this significant attack. Broom recounts that immediately after the initial attack Becker spotted about fifty more Me109s approaching from the rear. He yelled into the interphone, "They are coming at us company front—there are so many of them—what should I do?" The first pilot, Ball, had his headset switched to Flight Control at the moment. Copilot 1/Lt Gordon R. Tomeo responded, "Pick out the one you think is aiming at you and shoot him down." In the second attack, there was an explosion and the smell of gas and smoke filled the plane. The number two engine was on fire, and also either number

Lt. Richmond C. Young of the 838th Squadron's plane with Sgt. William "Henry" Hughey manning the ball turret.

three or four. The navigator, 1/Lt Harold Sperber, yelled into the interphone, but heard no response. He could see that the bombardier, John Broom, had removed his oxygen mask and was putting his chute on. Sperber then put his own chute on and moved to the escape hatch. He pulled the handle and it came off in his hand as the door remained closed. He kicked the door open and bailed out. The bombardier followed him out. Both survived. The rest of the crew except for Becker followed the badly damaged plane, landing in the Ambleve River near Aywaille. They all perished. The tail section separated from the main body of the plane and Lt. Becker rode it 21,000 feet down into a nearby stone quarry. He survived the fall but died of his wounds two days later at the Allied hospital in Herbesthal near Liege.

1234 Hours

Sometime between 1228 hours and 1234 hours, Major Lloyd W. Nash, air leader for the 836th Bomb Squadron, flying with Pilot 1/LT Lloyd Reed and as air commander for the low element, was hit by an object at the same time the plane's interphone was taken out of service. Amid the noise and action of the air battle, Nash was seen beating his right shoulder and pointing to the right cockpit window. Reed motioned him to get out of his seat so he could see the trouble. Nash had been attempting to call in the delayed fighter escort for the formation. Nash became excited and went down in the tunnel toward where the radio station and navigator were located. Navigator James Bradford later stated that they had seen General Castle's plane fall from the lead element, get pummeled by German fighters, have the crew bail out and then go down. He also saw 1/Lt Robert Densmore's plane take a hit and then pull out from the number three position of formation on Reed's left wing. Bradford said, "Every gun in the front echelons was firing, turrets turning. Aircraft were falling, burning all around us. The sky itself seemed to shake."

In a new frontal attack the number three engine of the lead plane was hit and smoking. Soon there was a fire there and in the waist section. As the number three engine quit, Reed said in a calm voice to the crew's headsets, "Okay, troops, this it is!" 2/Lt Fred Dumler, the bombardier, proceeded to jettison the bomb load and disable the bombsight. Navigators Hatfield and Bradford set to destroying maps and logs.

Crew co-pilot 2/Lt John Virgin, who gave up his seat to Major Nash and was flying as tail gunner/spotter, bailed out from the back of the plane. As Lloyd Reed struggled to control the disabled plane, the rest of the crew donned their chutes and proceeded to play "Last Man Out." The entire crew safely parachuted except for Major Lloyd Nash. He was not located and was officially Missing in Action until early February of 1945. At that time his frozen body was found in the snow in a stone quarry east of Comblain-au-Pont and just south of Fraiture Belgium by quarrymen returning to work after the Germans' Ardennes Offensive had been rebuffed. It was handed over to the American Forces in the area who identified Nash despite the serious damage to his head in his fall.

It has never been determined whether Nash's chute malfunctioned or was shot down by enemy fire. The details of his recovery were not fully known until 1999 when a group of 487th Bomb Group members and their families made a trip to Fraiture to participate in a memorial to those who fell on 24 Dec 1944. Nash's daughter, Anita, who was one year old at the time of his death, met local Belgian residents who were familiar with the story—some of them were present at the stone quarry when the body was discovered—and they provided detail of its recovery. The young man who came from the crowd and volunteered to translate for Anita Nash said he was privileged to help her out in honor of the brave men of the

American Air Force. He told her that in December of 1944 the re-treating Germans were rounding up and executing the old men and the young boys in the area. He said that the Americans had saved his grandfather.

The plane flown by 1/Lt Robert Densmore in the number three position on the left wing of the Reed/Nash lead aircraft was able to abort after being hit by what Densmore thought was flak. There are a number of reports in the documents of the Luftwaffe attack that day that reference the surprise sighting of flak, though they tended to be by planes clearly over German-held territory.

Of course, the front had moved rapidly to the west since the German offensive had begun at 0530 hrs. on the 16th of December. The Germans had moved a tremendous force of men and equip-ment, including flak guns. On the 23rd and 24th of December, they had solid control of Vielsalm, Trois Ponts, Stavelot, and La Gleize, Belgium. Vielsalm is less than ten miles east of Fraiture, where most of the aerial action was taking place. To the north, Trois Ponts is only fifteen miles away and La Gleize a mere twenty. It is entirely possible that German flak cannons were active along this front as reported by pilots and bombardiers in the lead formation. But it is unlikely that the Germans would put their own attacking fighters at risk.

There are numerous reports that the attacking Luftwaffe fight-ers were shooting from their 20mm cannons. Henry Hughey, ball turret gunner in 1/Lt. Young's plane on the left wing of Harriman/Castle, reported "flashing lights" coming from the attackers. Paul Tomney, togglier/nose gunner on Densmore's plane, reported that the attacking German fighters were using timed 20mm shells that exploded in white puffs in front of the plane, giving the impression of flak.

The initial fighter attack damaged the number one engine on Densmore's plane and he began to lose power. He couldn't increase it or decrease it from the throttle setting. Then he lost a second engine and decided he needed to abort. There was an alternate emergency field in France and he instructed the navigator to plot the course to it. As he dropped to a lower altitude the number one engine began to respond properly. With three engines operating, Densmore revised course, jettisoned his bomb load over Germany, and headed for his home base at Lavenham, England, landing there safely later in the afternoon.

1236 Hours

At approximately 1236 hours, seven minutes after it reported it was pulling out of the formation, General Castle's plane went down. After its crash and explosion, it was eerily alone and remote from the intense drama still playing out in the sky above the smoldering remains of *Treble 4*. The fractured and strewn wreckage was located in four pieces each about a half mile from the next. They were north of Hody near the Chateau d'Englebermont, a chateau being used by the 516th Military Police Battalion. Also, in the area were members of the 7th Armored Division, a group that had been in close combat with the advancing Germans until their successful victory at the nearby Baraque d'Frature, also known as "Parker Junction" in memory of 589th Field Artillery Battalion Major Arthur C. Parker III, who successfully warded off the advancing Germans there only days earlier on the 19th. Had they not been successful in their standoff, many of the victims of the first attack on the 24th would have fallen behind enemy lines on the 24th.

Members of Parker's 7th Armored Division unit and the military police located some human remains in the wreckage shortly after the crash. Yet a full examination and review did not take place until December 28 when Majors Ralph S. Hayes and James W. Brooks, medical officers of the 487th Bomb Group, arrived from Lavenham to complete a comprehensive analysis and report. Additional remains from the two crew members, including General Castle's dog tags, remained within the fractured B-17 shell in the snowy woods. All that were found were sent to the American cemetery at Henri Chapelle.

After Castle's plane had left the formation, the deputy lead aircraft piloted by Lt. John Edwards and under the control of Captain Mayfield R. Shilling regrouped the remains of the scattered lead formation and entered German territory through heavy ground flak fire. Pilotage navigator 1/Lt A.C. Wilkinson plotted the original planned course that was to take the First Force north of Wiesbaden and Frankfurt on a feint attack of central Germany before making a ninety-degree turn to the south in the area near Wetzlar and headed for the Initial Point for a bomb run.

1238 Hours

Pilot 2/Lt Kenneth Lang's plane was flying in the number eleven position of the ill-fated low element of the 487th Bomb Group's lead formation and was the sixth ship of that besieged grouping to be taken out of service by the repeated and vicious German attacks. Chuck Haskett, the tail gunner, recalls that the first attack came from the 12:00 direction and he couldn't see it until the Me109s flew past his position in the tail. Though the plane seemed to continue to fly levelly despite the rumbling of guns from the turrets and waist, he suspected that the pilot, Kenneth Lang, and the copilot, Howard Miller, were seriously injured in that first flyby. He did hear Miller's voice over the interphone and assumed that it was he who was still holding the plane under control and preventing it from going into a spiral fall with both left engines out.

The navigator, FO Samuel Alvine, moved to the cheek guns when he first became aware of the onslaught, but they were frozen. The ship was full of holes everywhere he looked. There was no longer a window in the nose. Somehow the bombardier, 2/Lt George Lang, avoided being hit in this fusillade. Alvine's navigator seat was stuck in the catwalk. Hearing the bailout order, he tore it out by sheer force, crawled down and pulled the pins on the forward escape hatch, and rammed it out with his feet when it failed to move. He had his chest pack on, but ripped off his oxygen mask, flak helmet, and suit. He sat briefly looking at the ground, his legs dangling in the hatchway. Then he grabbed the crossbar and hung by it. Finally, he let go, grabbing the side of the ship before the slipstream tore him loose. As he checked his status, he realized he had left his gloves and his hands were freezing. He realized he had also left his pistol, so he was without a weapon. He looked around and saw wings and planes falling everywhere all in a ball of fire. There were quite a few chutes and a fighter diving straight for the ground, exploding on impact.

The Germans then regrouped en masse from the rear of the formation and came again in a company front attack. Grabbed by his own adrenaline, Haskett focused on the plane that was coming at him, and began blazing with both barrels, without a concern that they would overheat. He yelled, "I got him!" as his attacking opponent fell from the sky. At that time, he heard the ball turret gunner, Bob Yowan, call on the interphone to Don Kausrud, the waist gunner, "I'm hit!" There was no response from Kausrud. Haskett noted a line of shell holes along the lower left side of the fuselage. They extended to the plastic window near the right side of his face and shattered

Sgt. Bob Yowan, Ball Turret
Gunner

it. He thought, *this is a bad dream; it happens to other people, not to me.* Jim Weber, the flight engineer, called out, "Hit the silk, boys, she's burning like hell." And he knew then something was wrong with the pilot, the one who should have been giving the order to abandon ship.

A phosphorus round had hit the turret, and eighteen-year-old Yowan could smell his flesh burning. He had no idea how badly he was hit or how he was going to get himself out of the damaged turret. He hadn't heard the order to bail out. Somehow, he managed to crank the turret to line up with the fuselage and run the guns to the down position so he could open the door. He ripped off his oxygen hose and disconnected his throat mike as he came up into the waist of the plane. There was no response from anyone. He couldn't see the waist gunners or the radioman. There was fire in the bomb bay area — with a full bomb load — and on one wing, though the plane was holding level. Yowan fumbled with his parachute, but finally secured it, pulled the escape door handle, and dropped into the wind. He counted to three and pulled the rip cord. As he drifted down, he saw that the air battle that had done so much violent damage had moved on to the east. Yowan was drifting in and out from lack of oxygen but recalled the beautiful blue skies and puffy white clouds in a sudden quiet absent of cannon fire. He landed on the ground with his chute hanging above him caught in a tree. A little groggy, he saw a crowd of children, women, and men gathering and calling out, "American, American!" Suddenly he feared he had fallen in German-held territory and things would not go well for him. They brought a stretcher, identified themselves as Belgians, and took him to a nearby house. Soon a doctor arrived and administered morphine to alleviate the pain of his badly damaged hip and thigh. He was soon medevacked, first to Liege, then to Paris, then to the US, being carried by German POW litter carriers along the way.

Sgt. Charles Haskett, tail gunner, heard Weber's call to bail out just before the interphone went dead. He also heard a partial last word from the copilot, Howard Miller, who was apparently holding the plane steady after the pilot, Kenneth Lang, was incapacitated. As soon as Haskett left the plane, he was caught in the slipstream and turned for a loop. Struggling, he was able to secure the hooks on his chute, but then made a delayed opening, almost waiting too long. He ended up making a hard hit on the frozen ground, breaking his ankle and slamming his tailbone and back. Hurting badly, he was overcome with fear and confused, knowing how close they had been to enemy territory. He expected someone to come up and shoot him or take him prisoner. He crawled up on his parachute, lit a cigarette, and calmly began to smoke it. Soon he concluded no one had seen him. He fashioned a crude crutch, telling himself he was going to head home. He headed west, avoiding sounds of gunfire or sounds of civilization. Initially he saw many parts of aircraft falling around him. He also saw one other parachute. On Christmas day, he was found by four men from a Ranger battalion. They verified that he was, in fact, an American (Germans in US uniforms and on US equipment had been roaming the area since the beginning of the Ardennes Offensive on December 16.) He was taken by jeep to a small American aid station in the town of Aywaille.

Kenneth Lang's crew lost four members that day: Lang himself, his copilot Howard Miller, Waist Gunner Donald Kausrud, and Radio Operator/Gunner Donald Huck. As late as March 15, 1945, an error in the original Missing Aircraft Report listed Huck as the tail gunner rather than waist gunner and showed him as MIA. In March the status of Kausrud was changed from missing in action to killed in action. In another error, a Washington Headquarters document dated April 11, 1945 shows five crewmen who "have since returned to military control." That list includes the deceased pilot, Kenneth W. Lang. It was not until September that the confusion regarding Huck was cleared up and his family was notified. Similarly, the fates of Kenneth Lang and Howard Miller, much to the chagrin of their families, were not fully resolved until that same late date.

1240 Hours

The plane piloted by 1/Lt Willard J. Curtiss was flying in the number six position in the low formation of the left wing of Charles Kulp and just behind Robert Densmore's original position. It is believed that he closed ranks and moved to the number three position when Densmore aborted six minutes earlier. Curtiss was an Idaho farm boy who signed up for the army when he was twenty. He had already completed his required thirty missions but was on base and volunteered to join this major one.

Sgt. Ralph R. Barajas, normally the tail gunner, was flying as engineer. He had also completed thirty missions and was officially on his second tour. This was his third flight with the Curtiss crew and he was impressed with how cool Curtiss was as a pilot. Barajas was in the process of delivering flak vests in the cockpit. Then he returned to the turret, connecting his earphones, oxygen, and heated suit. It was then that he heard a loud noise and saw dust flying all around. He spotted a large hole in the right horizontal stabilizer and thought they had been hit by flak. Immediately he saw a Me109 climbing at nine o'clock. Then there were German fighters everywhere, mainly FW190s. They made individual passes and Lang's plane went down in the first attack. Barajas was firing as much as he could from the top turret. Eventually he burned out the barrel of his right gun, so he gave what he could with the left.

The Germans swiftly gathered together at nine o'clock, swung in smooth formation to seven o'clock, and approached from six o'clock in a company front formation. They attacked with full force. Barajas could see all four engines were aflame. 1/Lt Edward Ghezzi, the navigator, was shouting about the fire. The radio room was also on fire. Curtiss pulled the ship out of formation to the left about 500 feet. He called out calmly, "Put your chutes on and stand by." Barajas was scared. He, like the cool-headed pilot, had seen too many B-17s with a full fuel load and thirty-two hundred-pound bombs blow up in his thirty-plus missions. The plane began losing altitude with the number three engine hit and the number four engine failing. There was another attack, shaking the plane and filling the flight deck with smoke and debris. Curtiss gave the order to bail out and began to put the plane on autopilot. That is the last that Collins saw of him.

On hearing the command, the ball turret gunner, S/Sgt Robert C. Blackwell, exploded out of the turret. He and Barajas both grabbed chutes, and Blackwell kicked out the escape door. Barajas went first, Blackwell almost pushing him out. It was peaceful as they escaped the battle; then they heard the scream of their aircraft as it dropped to the ground. When it hit the ground and exploded, they were at about 15,000 feet, and the blast made their chutes pop and bounce in the air. Barajas hit the side of a cliff, landing in some fir trees. The whole area was covered with frozen, heavy mist. A man on the road below him started shouting. Suspecting he was about to be taken POW, Barajas reached for his forty-five in its shoulder holster when he realized it was back in Lavenham hanging at the head of his bunk.

The plane had crashed in Comblain-au-Pont, just southeast of Fraiture, Belgium, with the pilot Willard Curtiss riding it down. No one knows what happened in those last minutes that prevented him from escaping. The radio operator, S/Sgt Salvatore Saporito, and Tail Gunner T/Sgt Frank Callaghan were both killed, probably by enemy fire during the attacks. The survivors were Copilot 1/Lt Thomas Collins, Navigator 1/Lt Edward Ghezzi, Bombardier 1/Lt James Merritt, Engineer Sgt Ralph Barajas, Ball Turret Gunner

S/Sgt Robert Blackwell, Waist Gunner S/Sgt Samuel Pagac, and Tail Gunner T/Sgt Frank Callaghan, though Collins, Merritt, Ghezzi, and Barajas suffered minor injuries in their fall. Blackwell was injured and evacuated to Brussels for treatment. Both Pagac and Blackwell quickly made it back to Lavenham and resumed flying.

Curtiss, Saporito, and Callaghan were all initially reported as Missing In Action. Given the confusion of the battle zone and the focused combat to drive the Germans back, it was months before the fate of Curtiss, Saporito, and Callaghan was resolved. For the Callaghan family in Denver, this was a second loss. Their other son James died on the USS *Arizona* during the Japanese attack on Pearl Harbor.

The military file on Lt Curtiss contains months of troubled correspondence with his mother beginning with the notification on March 21 that he had been killed and identified. Mrs. Clara Curtiss began in April of 1945 asking how she might get particulars regarding the change from MIA to KIA "as none were given." In May of 1945 she was informed that the decision was made on the basis of a burial report dated March 30, 1945. Her repeated requests for more information were regularly shuttled from one office to the next for response. In November of 1945 she was supplied a listing of all of his thirty-two missions by date and target. In January of 1946 she wrote "…what really took his life, was he found in the plane or did his parachute fail to open?" She received a letter three weeks later that her question was being referred to the adjutant general's office for response. August 22, 1946, she and her husband were given the very basic details contained in the Missing Air Crew report completed in February of 1945. Three years after his death, Willard Curtiss' grieving parents had his remains repatriated to Lewiston, Idaho. Salvatore Saporito's remains were repatriated in November 1947. Frank Callaghan is buried at Henri-Chapelle American Cemetery in Belgium.

1246 Hours

The crew of the plane piloted by 1/Lt Howard A. Turnquist was flying *Miss Behavin* in the "tail end Charlie" position. That number thirteen spot in low formation was frequently referred to as the "coffin position." On the flight deck they had a perfect view of the carnage facing them as five of the planes in the low formation fell from the sky and another aborted and turned back. They were in the path of the fifty-plus enemy fighters systematically destroying their formation and killing their brothers in arms.

On the second enemy pass shells exploded right through the middle of their airplane and started a fire that quickly engulfed the entire right side, seriously burning the copilot, 2/Lt Thomas Chatterton. Waist Gunner Neil Matz was the first to bail out. Knowing that he was likely not going to make it due to the severity of his injuries, Chatterton stayed at the controls while Turnquist grabbed his chute and prepared to bail out. He was caught on the escape hatch as he jumped and couldn't move either in or out of the plane. The bombardier, 2/Lt Richard Ceder, knowing he had to clear the escape hatch before he could bail out, grabbed Turnquist by the straps of his parachute, pulling him back in and then dropping him out the escape hatch. Turnquist, now free, pulled the rip cord on his chute. It streamed out, but failed to blossom, leaving Turnquist in an uncontrolled free fall.

Before leaving, Matz thought that he saw the radio operator S/Sgt Stanley Kleinman lying on the floor, a victim of the same fire that claimed Chatterton. But somehow Kleinman successfully made it to the emergency exit with his parachute as did Sgt David Machauer, the ball turret gunner.

Ceder followed Turnquist out and survived. Chatterton, no longer able to keep the burning and bullet-riddled craft aloft, rode it down along with the tail gunner, S/Sgt Jefferson Gregory, and

Engineer T/Sgt Warren Stanton. Both Gregory and Stanton were likely killed during the initial attacks.

Miss Behavin crashed with its full bomb load and what fuel had not been incinerated on the way down just south of Sprimont, not far from the area of active ground combat. The remains of Chatterton were eventually returned to the Rock Island National Cemetery, far from the home of his wife and young son in Siletz, Oregon. This brave copilot shares a grave with Warren Stanton, his flight engineer. Jefferson Gregory was laid to rest at Henri-Chapelle American Cemetery in Belgium.

The six surviving aircraft of the beleaguered low formation tightened ranks and followed the lead and high components across the enemy front and into Germany to continue their assigned mission, the destruction of the airfield at Babenhausen. They were followed by a fourth composite low-low component made up of planes from the 487th and the 385th Bomb Groups. This configuration gave the first formation of Mission 760 fifty-four aircraft before the first enemy attack just south of Liege.

1330 Hours

The lead plane of the extra low-low composite component of sixteen aircraft was *Mutzie B,* piloted by 1/Lt Robert Kraker. Apparently hit in the first attack, Kraker was forced to abort when problems began to develop with his number three propeller, which required it to be feathered, followed by trouble with the number two engine. Kraker took the plane down to a lower altitude, and the number two engine began to operate as planned again. At that point he decided he could make it back to Lavenham and left the formation. Over the Channel about five minutes out on a heading for Felixstowe, the number one engine blew up. Kraker turned the plane back toward the Belgium coast. The bomb load was jettisoned shortly after the engine exploded and the wing continued to burn. Kraker gave the order to prepare to bail out. The navigator, 1/Lt Scott Roberts, told the radio operator, T/Sgt Gordon Thoroman, to stand by for the bailout order. The fire continued to get worse on the wing and about two miles inland in Belgium the bailout order was given. There was no response from the men in the waist. They had bailed out over the Channel four minutes previous. Copilot 2/Lt Braden Souders was the last one to jump. He landed in the water about a mile out from the shore. Seeing four chutes stretched out in a trail, he swam to the shore. The other four, Mickey Operator Morris Schmulewitz, Radio Operator Gordon Thoroman, Engineer William McClendon, and Waist Gunner Robert Nash came down about eight miles out in the Channel. Rescue boats and Mosquitos were sent out from Ostend to look for the chutes, but without luck. The four airmen who were the first to bail out were never recovered. Kraker's plane was forced to do a belly landing, the six remaining crewmen all surviving.

The Luftwaffe
0700 Hours – 1246 Hours

The Luftwaffe had been busy on December 23 as the weather over the Ardennes Offensive cleared before it did over England. In their aggressive stance, they sent up 500 fighters and only 200 to 300 appear to have made it to the battlefield. Ninth Air Force and the British #2 Group kept the air battle tilted in their direction. The Germans finished the day with the loss of sixty-three of their pilots and another thirty-five wounded. That same day Goring ordered his air force to stand down wherever possible to conserve fuel in light of the broad shortage that had begun to stall the German war effort.

Despite the issues on the previous day, German mechanics had worked through the night and readied 700 to 800 fighters for combat. Knowing that the long-planned no-fly weather was about to end, the Germans anticipated that the Allies would take advantage of the predicted crystal-clear weather. From 0800 to 0905 hours, the Luftwaffe mustered 105 fighters from Frankfurt, Darmstadt, Dortmund, and Duisburg/Essen in the morning and sent them to the battlefront southeast of Liege. It was no wonder that Luftwaffe radar controllers sighted the enormous American bomber stream approaching a few hours later. They were able to quickly vector a contingent of fighters to the Liege area. The first to arrive was one of the most experienced Sturmgruppen IV/JG3 who had been in readiness at Gutersloh since 7 a.m. Gutersloh is a small town in North Rhine-Westphalia with a Luftwaffe aerodrome that had been home to Juffer JU-88 bombers, but recently it became a base for JG3 fighters as Germany began the withdrawal from the eastern front and prepared for the Ardennes Offensive. Though relatively close to the battleground of the Bulge, it was not among the list of targeted bases, the order of the day for the Mission 760 plan.

German radar intelligence had quickly observed that the bomber stream was without fighter escort and scrambled a formation of thirty fighters departing Gutersloh at 9:30 a.m. They proceeded unmolested until they located the first three boxes of B-17s just crossing the Meuse River in Belgium and traveling southeast of Liege. Within minutes the formation from JG3 was joined by fighters from I/JG 27 and JG6 flying out of Delmenhorst. Both of these units had been on freelance fighter patrol between Malmedy and Aachen before joining the fray. During the Battle of the Bulge JG27 was officially stationed at Grossenhain on the other side of Germany just north of Dresden. They were temporarily billeted at Rheine, a base close to the advancing Ardennes Offensive and strategically located to participate in Hitler's planned Operation Bodenplatte and scheduled for New Year's Day. The identification of JG27 was found through interrogation of captured pilot Uffz. Paul Borth. He stated that his unit had taken off from the bombed-out airfield at Quakenbruck in Lower Saxony at 11:20 the morning of the attack. Quakenbruck was also not a target or even close to the targets of the 8th's mission of the day. The Germans had carefully drawn their attacking forces from northern bases that would not be molested in the target areas of Mission 760.

Borth was on his fifth mission and had gone out on his first with only twenty-five hours of training in the Focke-Wulf 190 a few days earlier. He was one of twenty German pilots of JG3 reported killed or missing in the dramatic battle with the B-17 formation. Another was Lt. Franz Ruhl, who wore the Knight's Cross and was commander of the 4th Staffel of JG3. JG6 reported thirteen pilots lost including the commander of its ten Staffel, Oblt. Weyl, one of the declining number of experienced Luftwaffe pilots and veteran of twenty-seven prior victories. JG27 reported three pilots lost or missing.

Aggressive return fire from the gunners of the 487th Bomb Group took down a number of the attackers. Two who were captured near Liege were Fw. Wilhelm Hopfensitz and Obgefr. Hubert Hirschfelder. Hopfensitz was on his second pass at a B-17 when he was taken down by the tail gunner of one seventy feet below him. He had earlier sent another B-17 from the formation spiraling to the ground. Hirschfelder was also taken out by the tailgunner of a B-17 he was pursuing. US interrogators of these two young pilots noted that their morale was "exceedingly high...a typical example of the familiar bone-headed Nazi youth." Another POW, Uffz. Kurt Mollerke, when captured, arrogantly told his captors that "von Rundstedt's offensive would succeed and force the Allies to accept a compromise peace." Though only twenty years old, he was the veteran of fifty-five prior missions.

Another Luftwaffe pilot captured near Liege was Uffz Karl

Kapteina, a member of Sturm Gruppe IV/(Sturm)JG3, a group that practiced the "Sturm" attack known to the Americans as the "Company Front Attack." Kapteina had participated in a similar successful attack on 23 December south of Bonn. This was his second. On the 24th his unit took off from Gutersloh at 1115. There were thirty-five fighters in his group, and they were joined by others over the Mohne Dam near Dortmund. There was no Allied activity visible there, and the formation was instructed to fly directly to the front line in southeastern Belgium. Once on their way they were receiving a running commentary about the position of the Americans over the radio so that they were able to fly directly toward them. When they arrived at the area between Liege and Bastogne, they began to circle, awaiting their prey. Much to Kapteina's surprise, the first plane that flew toward them was a Me109, part of the earlier group sent to the area. With a precision maneuver, they were immediately 700 feet above and 2,600 feet behind the targeted US squadrons. The commander radioed, "We're attacking," and they gave full throttle and lowered their noses. They had selected the formation on the extreme left. Kapteina was apprehensive of his own squadron partner, a man named Ott, fearing that he might ram him in this tight attack formation. Kapteina said later:

"Then I took aim at my first opponent. After the first burst I had destroyed his tail turret. Then I fired with all I had at the wings. By now I had got so close that bits of his tail section were flying past my ears. The kite was on fire all over. The undercarriage dropped out, then the machine went down over its port wing. Whether the crew had been able to save themselves I could not tell. On breaking off I saw my comrade Hopfensitz go down, trailing white smoke. After a dive of 1,600 feet I took a look at the formation we had attacked. All that was left was a burning bunch of disintegrating machines, from which two intact ones sheared off to port. These too must be downed! I got excited and started to climb again, which was easy after my speed in the dive."

Kapteina and another Fw190 began pursuing the remaining planes. They watched three crew members bail out from the closest one before they even fired a shot. The rest followed after the B-17 had been raked by the Fw190. Kapteina's next foe began to take wild evasive action. Kapteina closed in and gave a short burst with his guns. Observing his hits, he followed up with his cannons. The entire B-17 was on fire; then the port outer wing broke off and the plane went down. At the same time Kapteina's rudder and elevator took a hit. He had no control as he flew by the crashing American bomber. There was a banging in his engine and his cockpit filled with smoke with flames coming out of the right footrest. He struggled to release his harness and finally jettisoned the cockpit roof. The resulting draft covered him in flames. He was terribly burned and in pain. He was going in and out of consciousness when he tripped the parachute button and was violently pulled from the burning aircraft plummeting to the ground. He was found by American soldiers and spent the rest of the war in hospitals in Belgium, France, and England.

Evidence in the ground battle and in the air has shown that the advancing Germans in the Ardennes were definitely feeling the pressures brought about by Allied Air Force successes of the previous months. SS Colonel Otto Skorzeny's "Greif" unit was to race ahead of the main force to the river Meuse disguised with American and British equipment and uniforms, sowing confusion and disinformation. Lacking sufficient fuel reserves to sustain their advance, their first task was to find and capture Allied fuel reserves, without which they could not move.

After his capture at the end of the war, Gerd von Rundstedt, the commander of western operations for the Wehrmacht, told interrogators that three factors defeated Germany in the West. "First, the unheard-of air superiority of your air force made all movement in daytime impossible; second, the lack of fuel so the Panzers and Luftwaffe were unable to move; third, the destruction of railway communications which prevented every single train from crossing the Rhine, which robbed us of our mobility and ability to reinforce." Other accounts point out the shortage of armaments that also came both from the isolation of raw materials for armaments and the rail capacity for moving ammunition to the front. Additionally, though the Luftwaffe had a steady supply of aircraft from Albert Speer's manufacturing miracle, it was sorely short of trained and experienced pilots as a result of the serious losses they suffered throughout 1944. They were sending up "green" fighter pilots with, in some cases, as little as 150 hours of flight training. At the time of Mission 760 the Luftwaffe was desperate to regain the air superiority over the Allies that it had lost earlier in the year.

The Germans had already begun to feel the impact of the fuel shortage resulting from the Allies repeated bombing of synthetic oil facilities. Additionally, repeated pummeling and destruction of key rail connections and marshalling yards slowed or prevented the movement of fuel, equipment, and reinforcements. As for the Luftwaffe, repeated air battles had left them with a shortage of trained, experienced pilots. They were fighting feverishly to regain the air superiority they had lost months earlier, but beginning to doubt that was possible, despite the Fuhrer's conviction to the contrary.

8ᵗʰ Air Force Fighter Groups
0700 Hours - 1700 Hours
"Little Friends Where Are You"

The First Force was six and a half minutes late in crossing the Channel and sixteen to seventeen minutes late in reaching the planned rendezvous point—indicated as "CP3" or

"5035N-0500E" on the Field Order No. 1446A for the mission of the day, Mission 760. That location is seven miles north of the city of Andenne, Belgium, and nine miles north of Namur, both cities on the Meuse River. Andenne was also one of the targeted cities for Skorzeny's original planned attack. General Castle's lead ship should have been over that point by 1207. He arrived there at 1223. The amended mission plan called for the 357th, 55th, and 479th Fighter Groups to be there at 1213, but they were nowhere to be seen. Andenne was roughly twenty miles from the tight combat fronts with advancing German troops on the ground at the time. The post mission reports submitted by each of the assigned fighter escort units do not contain references to the CP3 location, a location that would be very specific to a bomber's navigator on the mission. The freewheeling fighters, relying on instruments, but more so visual evidence of other aircraft, submitted post mission reports of their physical rendezvous with the bomber stream, which at the time extended from the German border all the way back 186 miles to Felixstowe, England. The reports show the following:

357th Fighter Group: Rendezvous with last 4 Groups of the First Force at 1230 at **Brussels** at 25,000 feet.

55th Fighter Group: Rendezvous at **Brussels** at 1200 at 20,000 feet with "VINEGROVE 1-4, 1-5,1-1-6" (these are the radio call signs for Air Leaders of the 4th, 5th, and 6th components of the formation)

479th Fighter Group "A Group": Rendezvous at **Brussels** at 1200 at 25,000 feet. "B Group": Rendezvous at **Bruges** at 1200 at 17,000 feet

Clearly none of these reported rendezvous points are as indicated in the Field Order, and none of them are up to the specific CP3 location. Each of these fighter groups may have made visual contact with the bomber stream, but an estimated thirty-five miles back from the lead component of that stream headed by General Castle's aircraft with the designation "VINEGROVE 1," the component within minutes of the surprise attack by forty to fifty Luftwaffe fighters.

Of the first three escort fighters, only the report from the 479th Fighter Group indicates anything was amiss. They show radio notification just after their rendezvous over Brussels of "gaggles of bogies reported SE Liege and group split to investigate." There is no similar note from either of the two fighter groups assigned to escort the lead formation of the massive armada.

The 353rd Fighter Group was originally assigned to rendezvous with fourteenth through twentieth combat group formations at Control Point 3 (5035N-0500E) at 1222. They apparently arrived there as scheduled and were immediately vectored by "NUTHOUSE" (MEW Command) to the lead combat group that was then under attack. It would seem that they were the fighter group that drove the attacking Luftwaffe away from the remnant of that 487th Bomb Group formation. Notes in the 353rd FG mission report state, "Arrived too late to save some bombers," and "Earlier R/V would have prevented several bomber losses and resulted in more E/A destroyed." Likewise, the B group of the 479th Fighter Group, somehow misplaced at Bruges, was vectored by "NUTHOUSE" at 1225 to help the first box, which was under attack by "40 E/A." But the bulk of the action was over before they arrived. The A group did report a single FW190 attacking B-17s in the distance as they approached. Though it had shot down four B-17s, the late arriving relief was able to shoot it down. Members of the 479th bounced four FW190s, which rolled over. One failed to pull out, crashed, and burned.

The "Oakland Summary – FO1446A – Dec 24, 1944," prepared after the mission, covers the highlights of the day, but seems to miss significant details that clarify what was going on during the initial confrontation with the enemy. There are also some inconsistencies between it and extant unit reports for the day. It states: "Hostile attacks were concentrated on VINEGROVE 1-1 & 1-2 and took place SW of Liege as bombers were coming in, before scheduled R/Vs." Yet the fighter units claimed earlier rendezvous points north and west of General Castle's location at the time of the initial enemy attack, a location that approximates the planned mission rendezvous point. Estimates vary, but it is likely that the fighter escorts were as much as five to seven minutes away from the initial contact of German fighters with the lead formation.

As all this drama was unfolding between CP3 and the location of the ground battlefront, the lead, high, remnant of the low, and composite low formations of the lead group were pulling themselves together and continuing their assigned mission. Though the German fighter attacks seemed to diminish, the lead group experienced considerable ground flak as soon as they began to cross enemy positions. Dawes Lott, the crew navigator of John Edwards/ Mayfield Shilling's new lead aircraft but flying as gunner on this mission, was hit in the shoulder. Luckily, he was protected by his flak suit and not seriously injured. The partially scat-

Capt. Mayfield Shilling

tered formation regrouped and proceeded on track to their intended targets. Edward's plane was manned with 1/Lt A.C. Wilkenson, assigned as pilotage navigator to the deputy lead for this mission.

He was a skilled and experienced navigator normally assigned to 1/Lt Kulp's crew. Kulp's plane was one of the few survivors of the low component.

Also manning John Edwards' plane were Copilot Gerard Gauthier, Bombardier Don Kilburg, Radar Operator Saul "Rube" Goldberg, Engineer William Renner, Radio Operator Grover McDuff, and Tail Gunner Sherwin Bosse. Cpt. Mayfield Shilling, as deputy mission leader, was flying in the right seat. It was customary, in situations like this, for the displaced copilot to move to the tail gunner position and take responsibility for keeping the trailing formation in tight order. Gauthier, one of the larger men on the crew, preferred to serve as a waist gunner and deferred to Sgt. Sherwin Bosse, a skilled lead tail gunner. Many years later, Bosse claimed that he was actively involved in the shooting as the Germans flew through the formation. He also proudly claimed that he had fired at a parachuting Luftwaffe pilot after seeing the Germans doing the same to the descending parachutes of the Americans. He felt no remorse for following the Germans' own procedure.

Shortly after entering enemy-held territory, the lead box was finally joined by fighters from the 55th and 357th Fighter Groups. Traveling in excess of 180 mph, by 1230 hours the reconstituted formation was in the area of Daun, Germany, about sixty miles east of the original combat location. NUTHOUSE Command had radioed "Rats—Heinie Rats—approaching the first box of big friends from the northeast." Responding fighters of the 55th FG approached from the southwest and observed enemy aircraft in the distance. As they approached, the Germans scattered, but about fifteen remained. Four of them formed up for another attack on the B-17 formation. Soon fighters from the 357th FG were also on hand to protect the bomber stream. A fierce aerial dogfight erupted between the opposing groups of fighters. In the high-speed confusion, 2/Lt Kenneth Mix of the 55th FG flying *Miss Marilyn* dropped in pursuit of three lone Fw190s at 10,000 feet. Unseen by him, a group of P-51s from the 357th FG were also dropping to engage the same enemy aircraft. 1/Lt Wendell Helwig of the 357th flying *Big Beautiful Doll* dropped through the 55th Group, colliding with Mix, crashing his engine into Mix's fuselage, tearing off the right wing, part of the tail assembly, and part of the left wing. Both planes burst into flames, and there was no sign of parachutes.

The tragic end for Mix and Helwig and the delay of both the 55th and 357th Fighter Groups in reaching the lead formations is difficult to understand without considering the transition in the interpretation of "fighter escort" that had taken place in the previous twelve months. There had long been a debate at the highest levels of command, all the way up to Lt. General Hap Arnold in Washington, as to the nature of the B-17 "Flying Fortress" and its ability to defend itself, especially when flying in formation. In January of 1944 the legendary Lt. General Jimmie Doolittle, who had received the Medal of Honor in 1942 for his incredible and heroic attack on Japan, replaced General Ira Eaker. Eaker had been an advocate of the self-sufficiency of the well-armed Fortress, as was Arnold. Doolittle was a pilot's pilot. After long resistance, long-range P-51 fighters were introduced in December of '43 and the following January. Doolittle's idea of fighter escort went beyond fighters hovering near bombers. In fact, he preferred to consider the bomber stream "bait" for killing enemy fighters. And as the fighter "escort" accompanied the bomber formation, Doolittle expected it to take out miscellaneous targets of opportunity along the way to target and back home. Occasionally this meant farmers' equipment and livestock.

Doolittle understood that military selection, training, and task had determined some significant differences between fighter pilots and bomber pilots. Success for a bomber pilot was to come back alive with an intact and loyal crew. The fighter pilot was motivated to come back from a "good hunt." The bomber pilot needed personal physical strength, especially when at the controls of a B-24, whereas the primary need for the fighter pilot was rapid eye-hand coordination. Good judgment, emotional stamina, dependability, success in leading teams, and discipline were essential for the successful bomber pilot. Whereas, the fighter pilot needed to be an aggressive, bold individual with a zest for battle. One Air Force study concluded a high degree of cockiness was essential for a successful fighter pilot.

The plan of execution under Doolittle's command was designed to make the most of these differences. While there is little available documentation to prove the case, it is possibly the reason that fighters from the 357th, 55th, and 479th fighter groups were not "escorting" the lead formation when the unexpected Luftwaffe attack took place over friendly territory. By all accounts they were in the region, near the bomber stream, at the assigned time. They were just not in the presence of the lead formation at the critical juncture. Perhaps some of this was due to Doolittle's release of the tether between the bombers and their escorts. The "little friends" had been given some freedom to "ride the range" looking for opportunities and risks. Intelligence had not identified the Luftwaffe attack force that had appeared suddenly from the northeast until it was too late.

Likewise, the tragedy of the collision of Mix and Helwig was one more example of the freewheeling aggressiveness, zest for battle, and cockiness encouraged among the fighter groups. The top speed of the P51 Mustang had been pushed to 460 miles per hour as compared to the B17-G, which had a maximum speed of 287 and a cruising speed of 182 miles per hour. The P51 maximum speeds were also faster than the Focke-Wulf 190, which was capable of 426 mph in the D-9 model flown in the last year of the war. Certainly, the risk-taking fighter pilots were flying with a confidence that they could be where they wanted to be when they wanted to be there.

Though the sky on 24 December was clear and visibility was long, intel was primitive and not all-inclusive. Pilots Mix and Helwig lost at a high-speed dogfight game.

The scene similar to the first fatal attack of the day was best and most dramatically described by John Killen in his book *A History of the Luftwaffe: 1915–1945*:

"To fly with those massed squadrons, the huge, staggered formations of majestic Fortresses or Liberators deploying hundreds of defensive guns, was to venture into a man-made inferno created by packs of Fw190s, Bf 109s and Ju88s, attacking in waves through the smoking, crisscross lines of tracer. 'Fighters at twelve o'clock, high!' —and the guns from every bomber would be firing together, the knife-edged wings of the German fighters stabbing orange flame as they came in for head-on attacks, closing to point-blank range and then breaking gracefully away through the bomber formations, still firing. To stand behind the pilot and copilot of a B-17, with all guns pounding away and the pungent smell of burnt cordite filling the cockpit, was to stand poised on the brink of a nightmare; to glimpse awful scenes jumping into sight and then vanishing in a moment, like the flickering images on a cinema screen. Beyond that reeling glassed cabin, bombers would be dropping out of the formation in flames, coming apart at the seams like old battered toys or breaking quickly and neatly into two pieces spilling men out into space like peas from a dry pod."

Shaken and pockmarked with multiple holes from both fighter and flak attack, the lead formation of the First Force (3rd Division) bomber stream continued steadily through patches of flak, but with minimal Luftwaffe interference after these initial attacks.

They made their planned turns at 5012N-0621 over Prum and 5008N-0805E north of Mainz and they unknowingly passed a significant unseen potential target of opportunity near Bad Nauheim, Hitler's Adlerhorst bunker.

Thirty-six minutes after the carnage of the first Luftwaffe attack, the 390th Bomb Group on their way to Zellhausen, when they began to experience extensive and very accurate ground antiaircraft activity. Just north of Gerolstein and in the space of a minute two B-17s were blown out of the sky. The first was piloted by 1/Lt Robert Fackelman. The aircraft was hit with two separate pieces of flak. The first tore the skin from the left wing, and the other hit the number one engine, putting the burning plane into an uncontrolled steep left bank as it crashed to the ground. The waist gunner, ball turret gunner, bombardier, and navigator were all able to bail out, but were quickly apprehended by the Germans. They were held as POW until they were liberated on April 29 by the advancing Allies. The other five crew members perished in the crash and resulting explosion. Copilot John Clark in a trailing plane in the low formation of the 100th Bomb Group witnessed the two aircraft going down and said: "Since the flak was unexpected and uncharted, it was thought to come from one of the larger German Tiger tanks. We were all scrambling to put on flak jackets, and to maintain formation while dodging aircraft parts raining down from above."

The second 390th aircraft hit by the same antiaircraft guns was piloted by 2/Lt Paul Herring. The copilot and waist gunner were killed in action. The remaining crew members were rounded up with the members of the Fackelman crew and, like them, were liberated on April 29. Ironically, the area of these very effective antiaircraft guns was in the region of Gerolstein, an area scheduled for attack later in the day by the third attack force under the master plan for Mission 760.

There was one more tragic loss shortly after the formation

passed Hitler's bunker. A plane piloted by 2/Lt Lawrence Vogt of the 385th Bomb Group was apparently hit by ground antiaircraft fire shortly after making the turn at the pre-IP point and on the way to bomb the Gross Ostheim aerodrome. The hit caused the plane, which had been flying in the number four position in the low section of the 385th's E squadron, to lose control and continue to fly but very erratically. First it dove out of formation; then it rose rapidly and into the number two propeller on lead craft in the squad being piloted by Lt. Weltman. The propeller cut Vogt's plane in two at the waist section. Weltman was able to gain control of his plane and continue the mission. As the two sections of Vogt's plane fell away, no parachutes were sighted and the front section with a full bomb load exploded on impact. Miraculously, the tail gunner, Sgt Calvin Rhodes, was able to escape the severed tail section with his chute and survive. He spent the rest of the war at Dulag-Luft Wetzlar. All the rest of the nine crew members—Pilot Lawrence Vogt, Copilot James Anding, Navigator Victor Hammonds, Ball Turret Gunner Roy Capwell, Gunner Harry Sevick, Gunner Richard Rudd, Togglier Clifford Canterbury, and Waist Gunner William Johnson—were killed.

Despite the tragedies, for the majority of nearly 2,000 planes with close to 20,000 airmen in the nearly 300-mile formation following them, the trip to their designated Initial Points (IP) resembled a "milk run."

"Do you believe, mein Fuhrer, that we can still win the war?"

—Christa Schroeder

Chapter 7

THE MISSED TARGET OF OPPORTUNITY

UNKNOWINGLY, THE PATH of the First Attack Force flew on all sides of Hitler's secret and fortified retreat behind the Castle Ziegenberg, General von Rundstedt's headquarters. The opera-

tives of Hitler's Ardennes Offensive had been at the secret underground bunker in strength on December 12, receiving their instructions from the Fuhrer before returning to their respective components of his bold and unexpected offensive attack. By Christmas Eve

General Alfred Jodl, Chief of Staff Heinz Guderian, Adolf Hitler, and General Wilhelm Keitel

and much to the dismay of Allied Command, the German attack had successfully reclaimed a large swathe of ground in Belgium lost in their retreat since D-day. They had successfully achieved a salient some forty miles into Allied-held territory. When his generals returned to the front to initiate their surprise attack, Hitler and his immediate entourage of "household command" — secretaries, doctors, and his personal valet — remained at the camouflaged Adlerhorst bunker while Hitler kept in close contact with the events at the front. In addition to his personal staff, Hitler's "household command" also included Generalfeldmarshall Wilhelm Keitel and Generaloberst Alfred Jodl. While both had been key to the planning of the Ardennes Offensive, neither Keitel nor Jodl had any actual combat experience. They were broadly seen by field officers as sycophants who tended to encourage Hitler's optimistic illusions. For his part, Hitler was said to view Keitel as "an unthinking assistant who would blindly do his bidding."

At approximately 2:30 in the afternoon on this day of blue skies and long visibility, a stream of more than 700 B-17s flying in tight formation at 22,000 feet passed within a few miles of Hitler's Adlerhorst bunker, which was disguised on the surface as a quaint country village near Bad Nauheim. Hitler had been at Adlerhorst since first arriving on December 11. On the afternoon of 24 December he was standing under the trees near the open with his long-term and trusted secretary Christa Schroeder and another personal secretary, Gerda "Dara" Christian. They were watching a seemingly unending formation of

Camouflage for "Adlerhorst" bunker

US bombers as it passed just to the north of them and 22,000 feet high in the beautifully clear sky. In her memoirs, Schroeder recalls that clear sunny day and asking, "Do you believe, mein Fuhrer, that we can still win the war?" Hitler replied to her, "We have to."

His simple response to Christa Schroeder and Dara Christian was far different from the euphoria he communicated in the first days of the offensive when his forces stepped off with surprise and quick advance just as planned, making significant progress in driving the Allies back across southern Belgium

Adolf Hitler with secretaries Christa Schroeder and Dara Christian on his 50th birthday.

and Luxembourg. According to Albert Speer, Hitler had said in November that he was "staking everything" on this offensive. He added, "If it does not succeed, I no longer see any possibility for ending the war well...but we will come through."

The memoirs of Heinz Linge, Hitler's personal valet, recount that Hitler was seriously ill toward the end of the war, a fact concealed from most of his staff. Linge privately delivered the medicines Hitler's doctor provided. He observed that Hitler was amazingly energized after giving the order to begin the Ardennes Offensive. But Linge observed him days later fall back in to dismal weakness and pain, his face with a grayish pallor, his gait stooped and shuffling, his left side trembling, as it became clear that his bold attack was failing. Hitler and his closest staff had stayed at the Adlerhorst from December 12 until the middle of January in order to monitor the offensive. On Christmas Eve, it became clear to him that his initial hopes were dashed. Linge notes that when they were alone together, Hitler's public image that "everything is in order" deteriorated to lethargy and depression.

Linge's memoirs may overestimate the confidence between himself and his Fuhrer and underestimate the perceptions of those others who were close to Hitler. A number of the commanders who attended his secret meeting on December 12 observed what Linge thought they had not: his gray pallor, his labored gait and shuffling, his apparent signs of Parkinson's disease. Those who had known him noted serious premature aging of this 55-year-old man.

It was clear to Hitler that he had problems with his military staff and particularly with Goering and his own Luftwaffe, which was at the moment long in new equipment thanks to Albert Speer's manufacturing success, but short on experienced pilots as a result of continuing combat losses. They were also hampered by serious shortages of fuel resulting from the relentless Allied aerial campaign on his synthetic fuel plants and the campaign that was crippling rail traffic and the movement of fuel, ordnance, equipment, and personnel to the front. He had begun with bold ambition, made incredible aggressive advances, but had already lost them in France, Russia, North Africa, and Italy. And he had pulled his eastern defenses back to support his western offense. Things were not going well.

Those who were loyal to Hitler were won over by his personality and his strident leadership for the Fatherland. But his façade had long been at odds with the reality. From his earliest days, he had experienced a variety of physical problems and what many who knew him would consider personality disorders. In 1936, Hitler was introduced to Dr. Theodor Morell, the first doctor whose treatment provided him relief from his chronic digestive problems. Despite their success for Hitler, Morell's methods were considered unorthodox. Yet Hitler was sold, and Morell continued his bizarre treatments up until Hitler's suicide. After the war, Speer said Morell "was not an out-and-out quack — rather a bit of a screwball obsessed with making money." There were those of the inner circle who were convinced that Morell's years of injections of strange and experimental substances into Hitler's veins were pure quackery. Among other things, Morell's records indicated that der Fuhrer was regularly treated with the methamphetamine Pervitin, cocaine, and Eukodal (oxycodone). There were some likely chemical causes for Hitler's renowned mood and energy swings, swings that were certainly observed by those other than his valet.

As the Ardennes Offensive stalled and then went into retreat, so did Hitler. He knew he had played his last card.

Sadly, the Allies did not have sufficient secret intelligence available to know where Hitler was, what he was thinking, and how distressed he was physically. Perhaps, if they did, they could have targeted him in the Adlerhorst and ended the war four months earlier. The bomb tonnage that flew overhead as he watched on Christmas Eve would have certainly made short work of his "Eagles' Nest." But on 24 December, he was Adolf Hitler, an unobserved observer, quietly watching the progress of the largest aerial bomb attack in history. The conclusion already reached by many of his military leaders, as evidenced by the murder attempts prior to Claus von Stauffenberg's significant, but failed attempt at the Wolfshanse in July of 1944, is that many established German military and political leaders were ready to be rid of Hitler if only that were possible. After it became clear that the continuing advance of the Allies toward Berlin was inevitable, Hitler made the decision to leave Ziegenberg and return to his underground bunker near the Reich Chancellery in the capital. In the middle of January Hitler and his retinue boarded his private train and returned to Berlin for the beginning of the end.

"...between our entry into the war and the German surrender, our fighter planes had won superiority over the Luftwaffe and our bombers had penetrated every defense which the German had raised against them."
— Dwight David Eisenhower

Chapter 8

THE TARGETS OF THE FIRST ATTACK FORCE

THE FIRST ATTACK Force (the 3rd Bomb Division) proceeded on its planned course with some ground flak interference, but absent additional fighter problems after the initial surprise attack over Belgium. The route to the five of their six assigned targets took them in a rectangular route slightly north of Hitler's Adlerhorst bunker, then northeast of it and finally southeast of it as they entered their bomb runs. The lead targets were identified to be tactical in nature and intended to cripple fighter support for the Ardennes Offensive. In retrospect, it appears that the weather that Hitler was counting on had blinded Allied Intelligence to the actual locations of Hitler's air power. Prior to the Ardennes Offensive, it was generally accepted the Allies' air forces had achieved air superiority over the Germans, though that was before the extensive movement of personnel and equipment from the Nazis' eastern front as the Russians advanced.

Though the Allies had significant information at their disposal from ULTRA intercepts, the reorganization and movement of Luftwaffe units had become quite fluid after D-Day. Many air bases on the Continent were considerably less formal and built up than the Allied bases in England. Manned fighters were exceptionally mobile and many of the German bases were simply grass fields with camouflaged stands for their aircraft. Not all included paved runways. There were sixty-nine operational Luftwaffe bases in the west in 1944. Fifteen of those bases were considered major Sturm bases, bases equipped to accommodate *Sturmgruppen*, an elite corps of volunteer pilots flying up-armored Fw 190s solely devoted to the destruction of bombers by whatever means necessary. Gutersloh, the home base of 16/JG3 in December of 1944, was one of these bases. 1/JG3 arrived in Gutersloh on 16 December as part of the Ardennes Offensive buildup plan. The unit had been upgraded to the FW190A aircraft and Sturm training in early 1944. It spent five days flying out of Dreux, France, turning the D-Day invasion, but then went to Bavaria and Austria, before heading back north and west to Gutersloh in December. This was the unit's tenth station in six months. 1/JG3 also played a part in the Luftwaffe surprise Operation Bodenplatte attack on 1 January 1945. Gutersloh, the source of the morning's attack, was not on the 8th's target list for the day. This was either great luck or good intelligence on the part of the Nazis.

Babenhausen Air Base 1330 hrs.
Effective: 96 Bomb Tonnage: 325.3

The lead formation for Mission 760 was comprised primarily of aircraft from the 487th Bomb Group, "The Gentlemen From Hell," stationed at Lavenham, though aircraft from the 385th Bomb Group filled out the lead formation, and planes from the 94th Bomb Group filled out the composite low formation. Its assigned target was the aerodrome in Babenhausen and the task of "post holing" the runway/landing strip. After the surprise attack, southeast of Liege, Belgium, and the destruction of General Frederick Castle's lead aircraft, Deputy Air Leader Captain Mayfield Shilling took command in the plane piloted by 1/Lt John Edwards and moved to the lead position. Shilling, a Texan, was the operations officer for the 838th

Lt. John Edward's Crew: (front) William Renner, Sherwin Bosse, Grover McDuff; (back) Gerard Gauthier, Jack Pippin, John Edwards, Dawes Lott, Don Kilburg, Saul Goldberg

Bomb Squadron. He had enlisted with a year of college in January of 1942 and arrived at England in September of 1943 as a copilot, the position he flew for Beirne Lay, a pilot.

Lay had returned to the States in 1943 to oversee the training of the 490th BG training in Salt Lake City, Utah. On February 28th he assumed command of the 487th, training in Alamogordo, New Mexico. He was the group's commanding officer from February to May of 1944, bringing his command to Lavenham, England, in April of 1944. Lay had been a pilot and an author prior to the outbreak of the war and penned the book *I Wanted Wings*. That book was turned into a movie in 1940 by Paramount Pictures and was the inspiration for enlistment by many of the airmen in his command. Lay was also flying and was shot down over France on May 11, 1944, the fourth mission of his command. A group commander would have been a choice capture for the Germans, but Lay was successfully hidden away by the French underground. During the D-Day invasion he was brought out of hiding and returned to Lavenham. He detailed his adventure in another book titled *I've Had It: The Survival of a Bomb Group Commander*. After the war, he and Sy Bartlett coauthored the famed book *12:00 High*, which later became an Academy Award winning film.

John Edwards, who piloted Shilling's plane, hailed from Due West, South Carolina, where he had been an outstanding and popular college athlete at Erskine University. He arrived at Lavenham in August of 1944 and quickly distinguished himself as an excellent pilot. Edwards was known more for his skill under pressure and his popularity with his crew, both officers and enlisted, rather than his strict adherence to military conventions. After his initial missions, he was promoted to lead pilot status and his original crew was modified with the addition of Navigator Jack Pippin, Bombardier Don Kilburg, Radar Operator Saul Goldberg, replacing Navigator Robert King Jr., Armorer Gunner Henry Montgomery, and Gunner Oliver Olivieri. Copilot Gerard Gauthier, Navigator Dawes Lott, Engineer William Renner, Gunner Sherwin Bosse, and Radio Operator Grover McDuff remained from Edwards' original crew. The restructured crew quickly gelled and performed well. They were a team, John Edward's team, just as much as a military crew. For the mission to Babenhausen Navigator A. C. Wilkerson, a member of Charles Kulp's crew from the 836th Bomb Squad and known as one of the finest navigators in the 487th BG, was added to Edwards' crew as the deputy lead navigator.

Edwards' plane had sustained considerable damage in the chaos of the attack that took Castle and seven planes of the low squadron down, but none of that damage prevented continuation with the mission, and the crew was quickly back on course and tightening up the formation behind them. At the time, they were unaware that the Battle of the Bulge was raging below them. They were shocked by the attack that had claimed General Castle and seven planes of their low squadron and they were confused by the barrage of flak that was hitting them from ground antiaircraft cannons and soaring toward them from supposedly friendly territory. Eventually they were beyond the German installations at the front and coursing as planned with few interruptions until they made the turn before the IP too quickly. Air Leader Harriman notified the formation that they were going to make the IP good anyway. He echeloned to the left. There was not interference at the IP; they peeled off by squadron, making a visual run on the primary target.

On approach the visibility was hindered by ground haze and the angle of sun. Bombardier Kilburg checked his data and maintained the course using the PFF equipment until the target was clearly sighted. He had approximately a minute for visual synchronization and then it was bombs away. The rest of the formation dropped on Kilburg's lead. The bombs of the lead squadron fell at 1415 hours, approximately forty-five minutes off the original plan, postholing the right two-thirds of the air field. A few bombs fell over the trees at the west end of the field. The high squadron postholed the left third of the field, thus blanketing the entire field. There was no resistance from the ground nor was there any resistance from fighters. There was also no sighting of German aircraft on the ground.

The Babenhausen aerodrome was the center of a cluster of Luftwaffe fighter bases southeast of Frankfurt that were believed to be supporting the Ardennes Offensive. In late 1944, it was home to III/JG4, though it has also been identified as a base for JG11. Given the mobility of fighter aircraft, it was one of the many spots where Luftwaffe fighters could rely on for refueling, repair, reloading, or for safe haven. On this day, the bombers of the 487th blanketed the entire field from 22,500 feet, leveling the airstrip structure and any aircraft that may have been concealed on the ground. It is known that the remnant of III/JG4 did not claim another Allied aircraft for the remainder of the war.

Babenhausen strike photo.

The job done, 1/Lt John Edwards took over with the help of his navigators and turned for home, following the planned exit route. Landing back at Lavenham, shaken, but happy to be home, the crew counted more than 150 holes in the skin of their plane, evidence of the initial Luftwaffe attack. Dawes Lott, the crew navigator who was working as a gunner, had been hit by flak in that early confrontation, but suffered only minor injury because of the protection of his flak jacket. It was a night for celebrating life as well as Christmas. There were drinks all around when they returned for their debriefing. Kilburg went on to Christmas midnight Mass from the debriefing celebration but was told in the morning that he was standing when he should have been kneeling and kneeling when he should have been sitting. All were alerted that there would be a repeat mission in the morning on Christmas Day but were relieved to find that it had been canceled.

Babenhausen is located between Frankfurt and Aschaffenburg, about sixteen miles from Frankfurt and nine miles from Aschaffenburg. It is roughly thirty miles south-southeast of Adlerhorst, where Adolf Hitler had been watching the flyover of this massive formation with the 487th Bomb Group in the lead. Babenhausen had been selected as a target because it was known as a base used throughout 1944 to intercept bomber formations heading to and from strategic targets to the east. It was also known to have been the home base of Sturmgruppen units through the recent months, including the 1V/JG3 that was involved in the initial attack on this mission, but was then operating out of Gutersloh in the north. It was also located close enough to provide aerial support to Hitler's Ardennes Offensive. Mission analysis indicated that the day's bombing made the landing field unusable for three days after Christmas Eve in addition to destruction of facilities. The nearby Babenhausen Kaserne, though it was the home of the Wehrmacht's 36th Field Artillery Regiment, was not targeted. A few months later the victorious Allies deployed it as a POW camp.

Babenhausen was a town of about 3,000 people in 1940. The planes of the 487th BG and the 94th Bomb Group dropped 325.3 tons of bombs, mainly as 100-pound bombs, with most falling on to the landing field and a few veering over the trees at the west end of the field and onto a rail siding. The trip back to Lavenham was uneventful, though weather conditions over East Anglia continued to deteriorate as the evening approached. Fifty aircraft from the 401st Bomb Group were unable to land at their home base in Deenethorpe and were diverted to Lavenham. At the end of the day, all bases were alerted for another "maximum effort mission" on Christmas Day, though that order was later rescinded.

The 487th losses for the day were significant. At the end of the day, the 3rd Bomb Division reported eight aircraft from their division missing in action, and they were all from the 487th Bomb Group. Those from the 487th Bomb Group alone accounted for nearly one-third of the aircraft and crews lost for the day. Eleven others limped back but were damaged beyond repair. At the time fifteen airmen were confirmed as killed in action, twenty-one wounded in action, and another seventy-six missing in action. Almost half of those killed and wounded in action that day came from the 487th Bomb Group. Though there is some confusion in the surviving records, the claims of enemy aircraft destroyed, probably destroyed, or damaged (18-5-1) were all attributed to 3rd Bomb Division and the pre-bombing confrontation over Belgium and the western German border, the "kills" of the 487th Bomb Group, and the fighters who finally reached and engaged with them. The combat action of the day clearly belonged to the 487th Bomb Group, the spearhead of the largest aerial bomb mission in history. The bombing damage to the Babenhausen airstrip was evaluated as "excellent."

Pilot John Edwards, Bombardier Donald Kilburg, and Navigator A.C. Wilkerson were each awarded the Distinguished Flying Cross for their actions this day from the formation recovery after the enemy attack through the targeting at Babenhausen.

The forty-six planes of the 487th Bomb Group that pummeled the Babenhausen Air Base were immediately followed by fifty planes of the 94th Bomb Group, General Castle's old unit, stationed at Rougham Air Base, Station 468 at Bury St. Edmunds. Castle had been commander of the 94th BG from May of 1943 to April of 1944 when he became the commander of the 4th Combat Wing. One of Ira Eaker's "Eaker's Amateurs," he had gained experience and respect of the men in his command. And they were proud to follow his lead on Christmas Eve. As one young radio operator/gunner said, "He was tough but quiet, firm, and fair. He was the GI's general, a man to follow."

The lead aircraft of the 94th's formation had a unique view of the attack on the lead formation ahead of them. They reported twenty-five rather than the forty to fifty German fighters reported by the men under attack. They looked on in horror as the battle ahead of them progressed. They reported that the fighters from both sides appeared and engaged in a fearsome dogfight. They looked on in horror as the fighter escort made contact and for a period of twenty minutes the sky was aglow with the fire of battle. Though it is not supported by missing aircraft reports, Eugene Beggs, engineer on Delbert Main's crew of the 94th, reported fighters from both sides going down. B-17s were seen in various degrees of distress. Beggs also recalled seeing all but four aircraft of the low squadron going down during the attack.

The 94th BG reported experiencing some light and inaccurate flak on the approach to their bomb run, one that they completed without incident. They began their run eight minutes after the 487th BG and from an altitude of 23,500 feet. On the return trip, some crew members reported seeing the snowy caps of the Swiss Alps as they flew over Nuremberg and Stuttgart at 21,000 feet in clear skies. They safely made it back to Bury St. Edmunds, only to find that a fast-moving front was rapidly obscuring the island. Rougham Air Base was one of the few bases open and it was reporting bare minimums. By the time the returning 94th landed and parked, they were notified to prepare for other incoming groups seeking safe haven. Final count revealed that there were over 150 aircraft in the space allocated for seventy. Chaplain Joe Collins reported, "Some seventy-seven planes from other bases landed at Rougham. They were coming in long after dark—practically out of gas. The tower was a busy, noisy place—pilots pleading to land, tired and out of gas." The base was bedlam trying to find sleeping quarters for more than 700 extra men.

Later, Father Collins was called to a nearby crash site where a plane piloted by 2/Lt. Donald K. Lathrum of the 327th Squadron from the 92nd Bomb Group crash-landed after being detoured to Bury St. Edmunds, hit a tree, and burst into flames. Eight men were killed in the crash, with only the tail gunner surviving.

Repairs at the Babenhausen airfield began immediately. The grass runway had never been paved and was chewed up with bomb craters. The Luftwaffe had a workforce of 111 convicts from the nearby prison at Rodgau who were used as forced laborers on the field. Working around the clock, they had a landing and flight strip serviceable within four days. This was the first bombing of Babenhausen during the war, but there were follow-up attacks in February and March of 1945. Twice in February the 8th Air Force returned to bomb the rail junction and the garrison. In March the British returned with 75 B-26 Marauders, again rendering the airfield unserviceable, but experiencing considerable flak resistance. By March 25, Babenhausen was captured by advancing Allied forces.

Gross Ostheim Air Base 1330 hrs.
Effective 60 Bomb Tonnage 223.8
Pforzheim Marshalling Yard
Effective 37 Bomb Tonnage 101.6

The Initial Point (IP) for the Babenhausen attack also served for the bombardier setup point for the targets at Gross Ostheim, Zelhausen, and Biblis, a World War II version of "shock and awe" bombing. Planners for the mission had carefully timed these targets for the first two to be at the same time as bombs away at Babenhausen. The Biblis attack was to be eighteen minutes later.

Gross Ostheim was an assemblage of neighboring villages located about ten miles southwest of Aschaffenburg. The actual target was located about three miles west northwest of Gross Ostheim in an area known as Ringheim, the site of an ancient mill that had been converted to a Luftwaffe aerodrome. Camouflaged to prevent easy detection from above, it was a grassy landing strip surrounded by hard stands covered with camouflage and buildings in the style of a rural German village. From 1935–45, the site was utilized for the development of radioactive and non-radioactive beam or ray weapons. The runway was a grass surface equipped with a flare path for night landings. There were no formal hangars or workshops, but the airfield was served by a branch of the main Aschaffenburg-Eberbach rail line. There was a dispersal area in the woods to the northwest with more than thirty aircraft bays.

On Christmas Eve 1944, the landing strip was also being used by III./JG 11. It was targeted on Christmas Eve 1944 for the 385th Bomb Group, "Van's Valients" out of Great Ashfield and the 486th Bomb Group out of Sudbury. The attacking formations were the 4th Combat Wing's D,E, and F groups comprised of the 385th, 388th, 447th, and 486 Bomb Groups. There were some difficulties in the initial ordering of the groups and uncertainty as the groups tried to assume their proper position in the bomb stream. This became a problem as the force approached the IP and suddenly the 4F groups from the 486th Bomb Group began passing other groups, cutting off the 4A, 4C, And 4E groups. It "S"ed across in front of the 385th Bomb Group squadrons and then cut them out of the division column just prior to the IP.

After the formation issues, a series of events and happenstance made it a confusing and disappointing day for the 486th. The sixty B-17 Fortresses of the 486th reached the coast of Belgium at or before their scheduled time, and they crossed the area southeast of Liege after the sky was cleared of bandits, but the tragedy that had unfolded there minutes earlier was now confined to the ground. Though a few German fighters were sighted, escort fighter cover quickly dispelled them. The 300-mile formation sailed past the Adlerhorst, where Hitler and his staff were looking up in dismay, and successfully reached their IP, where the bombardiers of each squadron took over control of their ship and initiated their bomb run. They had only experienced occasional and inaccurate flak fire up from the ground except for the 385th plane that was downed. At the IP, a right turn was made and the group peeled off into squadron formation

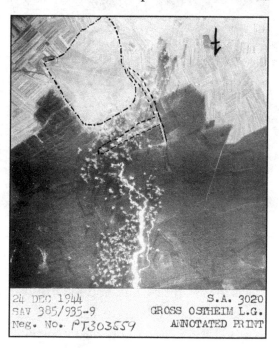

Gross Ostheim strike photo

to make a visual bomb run on the primary target. A thick haze, sun glare, and camouflage made it difficult for the A squadron to spot the target on time. The high and low formations of the A squadron proceeded to a selected IP for the secondary target, the marshalling yard at Pforzheim, about seventy miles southwest of Gross Ostheim. For those who bombed Gross Ostheim, results were considered only fair, and the field itself remain serviceable.

Pforzheim had not been high on the Allies' target list for most of the war. It was renowned for the manufacture of jewelry and watch making. As the war progressed it was concluded that the home shops of the old city were making precision instruments with wartime application, specifically fuses for V1 and V2 rockets. It was also considered as a transport point for German military. Typical of German cities, train station and the rail marshalling yard were located in the center of town. Planes of the 486th that failed to make the primary target headed for the marshalling yard at Pforzheim. The plane piloted by Hubert

Pforzheim strike photo

Hartsoe was hit by flak and fell out of the formation. He was able to make it safely back to base. The fifty-three planes of the 486th targeted the marshalling yard. On review, their results were rated as "poor" in their coverage of the yard itself. On February 24th of

1945, the British returned to Pforzheim and leveled the old city. Eighty-three percent of the town's buildings were destroyed and more than 31 percent of the population was killed.

On Christmas Eve the B formation had followed the A over the primary target, but it failed to drop any bombs because the lead plane's bombsight salvo switch malfunctioned. It followed the squadrons of the 486th that went on to Pforzheim. The C Squadron experienced a different problem. In their flight over the primary target, their release of the bomb load was approximately forty-five seconds late because the bomb bay doors were not fully open. One plane left the formation early and attacked a target of opportunity. All the others proceeded to Pforzheim.

The D squadron had more problems. As they reached the IP, the "Mickey" (H2X ground scanning radar navigational device) failed to set, and a visual run on the primary target was planned. Just before the time of release, the bombardier's gyro tumbled and he was unable to complete the run. This squadron joined the C group in their return, and their full bomb load was returned to base. The squadrons returned to Sudbury from 1650 to 1750 hours without incident. For the 486th Bomb Group it was a long, frustrating day with marginal effectiveness for the group. Fifty-three aircraft were airborne, thirteen aborted, three sustained major battle damage, and sixteen sustained minor damage. Later evaluation showed that the bombing that had been done was "poor."

Zellhausen Air Base 1330 hrs.
Effective 85 Bomb Tonnage 313.1

Zellhausen is located less than five miles from Babenhausen and its bombing run began from the same IP as was determined for Babenhausen. A branch rail line served the grass airstrip complete with storage for ammunition and fuel along with pumping capability for fuel. During the last year of the war, the base was occupied by a transport group flying He111s. These transports flew air supply missions for German enclaves including the supply for Hitler's Ardennes Offensive. It had fourteen aircraft hardstands in place and six more under construction. There was a small hangar, a main barrack complex, and a station headquarters and flight operations office. Prior to Christmas Eve, the field had been approved for installation of a pierced steel mat runway. That was to take ten days of halted air operations and the efforts of 200 men. The commencement of the Ardennes Offensive delayed that project as the base was flying supplies to the staging units west of the Rhine. It was also accommodating units of II/JG11.

The airstrip at Zellhausen was assigned target to the 390th Bomb Group out of Framingham, the group known as "Wittan's Wallopers." They were accompanied by aircraft from the 100th and 447th Bomb Groups.

The 390th A Squadron flew lead of the 13th A group leading the 13th Wing. On the bomb attack, the lead bombardier had the same complaint that had been heard at many targets for the day, namely that the mission planners had not factored in the low position of the sun on one of the shortest days of

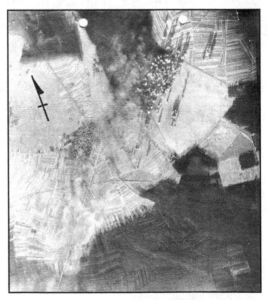

Zellhausen strike photo

the year. The C Squadron, flying the low formation, had already lost two aircraft upon entering Germany, both Fackelman's and Herring's planes and crews. They later discovered that the squadron lead aircraft had sustained damage to both its number two and number three engines in that same attack that took the two planes down. Two hours later the number three prop ran away and could not be feathered. It was impossible to maintain formation, so the lead was turned over to the deputy. One other aircraft of the unit, piloted by Lt. Peter E. Stene, was also shot by flak and aborted before the bomb run, but successfully made it back to Framlingham. Sadly, Lt. Stene died returning from a mission over Frankfurt on February 17. After taking what was considered insignificant damage during the attack, two engines caught fire and exploded on the return run, just twenty-four miles northwest of Ostend. The entire crew perished with the exception of the Mickey operator, who successfully bailed out and was rescued at sea.

The D Squadron of the 390th flew as lead squadron for the 13th B group. Takeoff and assembly went as briefed. But the last few groups of the division lead wing and the 13th Wing bunched up considerably, causing a broadening of the division column, considerable "S"ing, and little flexibility for maneuvering. Improper positioning created problems of excessive prop wash. The bunching up, coupled with quite a bit of uncharted flak, presented difficulties. At one point two groups of the 4th Wing fell in between the 390th D group and the 13th A group, causing them to fly a course slightly north of the briefed course. Despite this, they made their IP good and the bomb run was good. The bombardier changed the IP to the left when he noted the right side of the target was already well hit. The rendezvous point was made and the group reassembled for a smooth division column for the return as briefed.

The 390th E Squadron, flying as high squadron of the 13th B, ran into a very different problem on the bomb run. The Vickers unit of the top turret caught fire and caused the cockpit to fill with smoke. The pilot had the elevator turned off on the AFCE, because it wasn't functioning well. When the cockpit became filled with smoke, he hit the wheel as he reached for the window and caused the bombsight gyro to topple. This caused an error in bomb release. The withdrawal was flown as briefed which included the opportunity to maneuver around known flak areas and the use of chaff made of narrow strips of stiff aluminum foil about three feet long and bent into a V. It floats slowly to the ground when dropped and tricks radar-aiming devices into thinking it is seeing real airplanes. The flak bursts end up well below the actual flier.

Pilot Martin Presswood of the 570th Bomb Squadron of the 390th BG and from Texarkana, Texas, said, "As I climb into bed tonight, I have a deep down good feeling knowing that I helped our ground troops in a small way today. I fall asleep wondering if our soldiers on the 'Bulge' front battle lines are getting any sleep tonight."

The field was heavily damaged by eighty-five attacking B-17 Fortresses. Bombing was evaluated as "excellent" and the airstrip was totally inoperable for three days after the attack.

Biblis Air Base 1348 hrs.
Effective 100 Bomb Tonnage 325.8
Kaiserslautern Marshalling Yard
Effective 24 Bomb Tonnage 87.4

The village of Biblis is located approximately seven miles northeast of Worms and on the east side of the Rhine. The aerodrome there was built in 1936 with hangars and buildings designed to look like part of a large farming estate. It was well equipped with lighting to accommodate night flying when it was being used as a base for German fighters and jet aircraft making nocturnal attacks around Bastogne and behind the Allied lines in Belgium. The grass landing strip had one large and two small hangars in the woods off the eastern boundary. A small barracks camp and numerous scattered huts were in the woods off the north boundary to provide accommodations. There were storage buildings adjacent to the hangars in the woods. On the north side, there was a rail spur that served the landing area. There were dispersal areas to the east and to the north with two open aircraft shelters and twenty-six aircraft parking hardstands. Some had paved taxiways, especially off the east boundary. In late December and into January 1./JG 11 was stationed at Biblis.

The US visitors for the day on 24 December were from the 95th Bomb Group stationed at Horham and the famous 100th Bomb Group from Thorpe Abbots. There were also aircraft from the 384th Bomb Group assigned to composite formations. Their combined formation would form the 13(D) Combat Bombardment Group for the run to Biblis. The first squadron—the B Squadron—took off from Horham at 0845. They were also supplemented with sixteen aircraft from the 351st Bomb Group in the high squadron. The A Squadron began takeoff at 0852. And the C Squadron took off at 0904 hours. By 1010 hours they had assembled and moved to buncher number eleven, where wing assembly was completed at 1051 hours.

The wing 13th E group was comprised of the D and E squadrons of the 95th BG flying lead and high positions respectively and a squadron from the 100th BG flying in the low position. They began takeoff at 0910 hours and were joined by the low squadron at buncher number eleven. They passed Felixstowe at 1117 hours at 10,000 feet and made

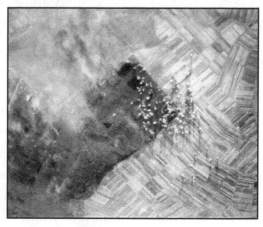

Biblis strike photo

the Belgian coast at 1154 hours.

Arthur Juhlin of the 100th BG recalled that they saw "bandits" shortly after passing Brussels, but "our fighters got them before they could make a pass at us." He also saw four "bandits" spin down in flames and crash. There were reports of a jet shadowing the formation, but staying out of range. Passing through the area where the initial attack had been executed by the Germans, they crossed over Malmedy and experienced a heavy and extremely accurate flak barrage. A number of the aircraft in their formation were hit and damaged, but they continued on to their assigned IP and made the approach to Biblis.

There was a default procedure for the lead plane. If it was not able to drop on target in the initial bomb run, it would make a diving turn to the left or right, lose approximately 1,000 to 2,000 feet in altitude with the squadron, and then regroup in tight formation and proceed to a secondary target. The lead in this case chose not to follow instructions. He made a standard rate 180-degree turn at constant altitude and air speed, returning to the initial point and making a second run on the Biblis target along the same identical flight path. The target aerodrome had several aircraft on the ground and was heavily protected with antiaircraft armament. Many planes in the attacking formation suffered damage during this second, but successful approach. Fighter escort had also strafed the field during the circling and second attack.

Kenneth Peters, a navigator with the 412nd Squad of 95th Bomb Group, wrote in his diary, "I was more scared than any time in my life. Flak very accurate and close. Several 95th men wounded! Note!-Was biggest raid in history of the world." Regarding damage to his own plane, he noted "hole in waist large enough to put my fist through. Glass in turret and Pilot's windshield was shattered plus other minors."

The F group for the 13th Wing was a composite of 95th Bomb Group aircraft and 384th Bomb Group aircraft that had been out on a mission on 23 December attacking railroad marshalling yards and bridges at Ehrang. Though thirty-five aircraft successfully completed that previous day's mission, weather conditions prevented them from returning to their home base at Grafton Underwood and they were diverted to Horham, the home of the 95th Bomb Group.

As this F formation approached Biblis, the target was visible to the naked eye through the haze and smoke, but the lead bombardier could not pick it up in the bombsight due to the glare from flying directly into the sun. He called for the formation to proceed to the secondary target, Kaiserslautern's marshalling yards. Though they were making a PFF run, the conditions were clear, and the lead bombardier picked up the target visually three minutes before the release point and bombed visually.

Kaiserslautern, thirty-six miles southwest of Biblis. As was typical at the time, the railyards were located near the Hauptbanhof, the main rail station located in the center of the city. Kaiserslautern was an important rail nexus, connecting Saarbrucken on the west with Mannheim, Stuttgart, Darmstadt, and Frankfurt—all locations involved in the supply of men, materiel, and armaments for Hitler's Ardennes Offensive. They were also essential for his future defense of Germany's western wall in the face of Allied advancement.

Though many planes suffered damage, only one was unable to return to base in England. *Lucky Lady*, of the 95th Bomb Group, piloted by Lt. Glenn Purdy, was one of the planes hit during the second try at the bomb run. In the twelve-plane squadron, they were flying on the left wing of the low element, a position often laughingly referred to as the "purple heart corner." On the run to the target, the flak was heavy and extremely accurate. Several of the ships in Purdy's formation were hit, including his own. His radio operator, Sgt Edward Schneider, had a piece of flak pass between his legs, ripping his flying suit, leaving him shaken but not injuring him seriously.

About two minutes before "dropping," late in the bomb run, he received a near direct hit with the shell exploding just below and between the fuselage and the number three engine. There was a hole ripped in the fuselage near the floor by his left foot. The hydraulic lines in the area were severed and pink hydraulic fluid was spraying all over. He peeled the plane off to the left, not realizing the plane was on fire until a crew member called in on the interphone shouting that the left wing was on fire. He immediately went into a steep dive to blow out the fire. He was told later that he dove into a cloud bank which lit up brilliantly with the flames, causing other squadron members to report that his plane had blown up.

The fire blew out in a dive of about 10,000 feet. Purdy was able to pull out of the dive and feather the three engines that had been damaged by the flak. He concluded the fire was burning oil from a severed line and not gasoline. Only his number two engine was still functioning. He turned the turbo charger on this engine from maximum to "war emergency." Though he had been trained that this was a setting that could only be sustained for two minutes without ruining the engine, the single engine stayed wide open until the plane's full ditching.

In order to reduce weight, the crew was instructed to toss out anything that was loose — ammunition, flak suits, fifty-caliber machine guns, etc. Adjusting the flaps for maximum lift, by trial and error, he was able to finally stabilize their descent at about fifty feet per minute at an air speed that was just slightly above the stalling point. William McEwen, the navigator, was busy plotting the shortest course out of enemy territory based on the morning's briefing on the latest status of front-line positions.

The crew was given the option of bailing out of the crippled plane over enemy territory or riding it down with Purdy and his copilot, Theodore Harris, in hopes of making the unlikely crossover to friendly territory in France. In the end *Lucky Lady* glided to the ground in a landing that sounded like someone had dropped a load of metal dishpans. *Lucky Lady* was finished, but her lucky crew was welcomed by the US Army. There is no Missing Air Craft Report (MACR) because she crash-landed in Allied-held territory. Within a week the crew members of the *Lucky Lady* were all back at their base in Horham, and on January 9 they resumed flying missions in a new aircraft.

One of the planes from the 100th Bomb Group piloted by Gerald Brown that had gone on to the Kaiserslautern attack rather than circle around Biblis lost one engine to flak over the target. They also had eight bombs hung up in the rack. Returning to England, the bombardier Tony Lentz attempted to free the wedged bombs, but was only able to free four. The decision was made to land at Thorpe Abbotts with the remaining four. Touching the runway, they realized the flak attack had destroyed the left tire. The flat tire caused the plane to veer into the mud where the B-17 became stuck with a wing still across the runway. The next plane coming in struck the wing and nearly tore it off. But it cleared the path sufficiently that the following planes could land.

A formation of six planes of the group that diverted from the Biblis run headed to Heilbronn on the Neckar river, about twenty-eight miles northeast of Pforzheim. This target of opportunity, though one the farthest from the Ardennes Offensive front, contained a large marshalling yard, standing rail stock, and bridges critical to the east-west movement within Germany.

In the final analysis, the field at Biblis was heavily damaged and put out of service for the following four days. Four Fw190s from I/JG 11 were hit on the ground, one totally destroyed and three others heavily damaged. After-mission photos did show that in addition to serious damage to the target runway and buildings, there were extensive concentrations of errant explosives outside of the perimeters of the field.

Kaiserslautern Marshalling Yard

The Kaiserslautern railroad marshalling yard was hit by a formation of twenty-four aircraft from the 100th Bomb Group that had inadvertently overrun Biblis and located the marshalling yard as a target of opportunity.

Result of a marshalling yard bomb attack.

Darmstadt Griesheim Air Base 1348 hrs.
Effective 189 Bomb Tonnage 234.2
Koblenz Marshalling Yard
Effective 35 Bomb Tonnage 640
Heilbronn (Haildraum)
Effective 6 Bomb Tonnage 18

The second largest contingent of the mission was sent to the Darmstadt Greisheim Air Base, a total of 189 planes composed of five different bomb groups attacked: the 388th from Knettishall, the 96th from Horham, 452nd from Deopham Green, the 493rd from

Debach, and the 401st from Deenethorpe. The target for the day was the Luftwaffe aerodrome located about three miles west southwest of the city center of Darmstadt and 1.5 miles southeast of the village of Griesheim.

Darmstadt itself had been the scene of repeated night raids by the Royal Air Force, the worst of which occurred on September 23/24, when a firebombing attack killed as many as 12,300 and rendered 66,000 in this city of 110,000 homeless. Darmstadt was not a large military town, but it was home to several key suppliers to the war effort, including the chemical works of Rohm & Haas and E. Merck. It also contained a metal production and fabrication industry as well as a major rail equipment repair yard. An old minor airport about halfway between the city and the Darmstadt Griesheim Air Base had been converted to flak positions and a signals station. The target airport had four paved runways, with fuel and ammunition dumps in wooded areas nearby. There were three medium hangars on the north boundary and another on the northeast boundary. All four had a concrete hangar apron. Behind the hangars were extensive workshops. There were also extensive barrack accommodations, station headquarters, administration buildings, offices, storage buildings, and sheds. The nearest rail connection was in Griesheim village. There were more than four open aircraft shelters along the southeast perimeter and a few light flak positions. There were also several earthen air-raid shelters. A variety of Luftwaffe units had used the air base throughout the war years, but in late 1944 it was known to be the home of 2/NJG 11, III/JG and 43/le.FlakAbt715. There were refueling points and ammunition storage on the north, southwest, and west boundaries of the landing field.

The A formation of the 45th Combat Bombardment Wing was made up of three squadrons from the 388th Bomb Group. The lead aircraft for the 388th A, B, and C squadrons took off from Knettishall between 0840 and 0844 hours. They assembled at buncher number

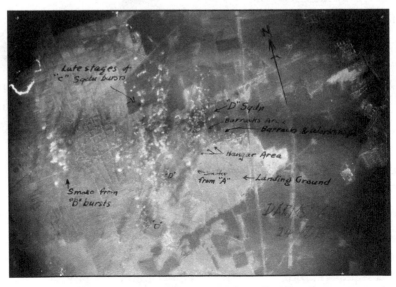

Darmstadt bombing attack strike photo.

ten using the instrument assembly procedure. The A Squadron leader remained at that altitude, while the B leader ascended to 10,500 feet and the C leader descended to 9,500 feet. Each of their squadrons fell in behind their respective leader. Once assembled the A Squadron led the wing, with the B Squadron falling in as the high element and the C Squadron as the low element. Heading for Felixstowe on the coast, they formed the beginning of the 45th Combat Bombardment Wing formation destined for Darmstadt.

Forming as the 45th Combat Bombing Wing B Group, the D and E squadrons of the 388th Bomb Group took off between 0854-0916, beginning assembly over buncher number ten with the D Squadron 13,000 feet and the E Squadron at 13,500 feet. Then the first major confusion of the morning's massive forming appears to have occurred. The low squadron of this group was to be supplied by the 96th Bomb Group D Squadron flying out of Snetterton Heath but it was not at buncher number ten for the planned assembly and departure. In the myriad of simultaneous movements happening all over East Anglia, the 96th Bomb Group squadron had mistakenly reported to the number nine buncher. In a quick correction, the 96th element caught up with the two 388 Bomb Group elements somewhere over Swaffham.

The C group of the 45th Combat Bombardment Wing was comprised of three squadrons of the 96th Bomb Group. They properly formed at buncher number nine and then moved to buncher number ten to fall into wing formation. Their formation was "good" though they had issues containing a tight formation. This group had some difficulty forming, with the A element lead ship and wingman being out of position. The forming was considered only "fair." Eventually the lead element of the Combat Bombardment Wing was about ten miles off the assigned course, though traveling parallel to it. This created problems of unnecessary exposure to flak emplacements. They experienced moderate, but accurate flak crossing over the combat line and again between Cologne and Frankfurt.

Later they encountered unexpected winds that caused them to be nearly a half hour late at the IP.

The D group of the 45th Combat Bombardment Wing was comprised of the A, B, and C squadrons of the 452nd Bomb Group from Deopham Green. As the A Squadron rose to their assigned positions, they discovered that elements of the 45th CBW C group were crowding their access to the assigned buncher. With some improvisation, they successfully assembled and joined the bomber stream as briefed. Similarly, the 452nd's B Squadron found B-24s from the third attack force forming at their same assigned altitude, creating a need for significant "S"ing to get into position without risking a collision. The C Squadron experienced similar problems in forming. The 96th Bomb Group circled over the 452nd Bomb Group field, interfering with the 452nd formation twice. Crew members noted that there was plenty of room for them to maneuver to the northwest of the field, but the air leader chose not to use it. Eventually they were joined by fifteen aircraft from the 401st Bomb Group. These planes and crews had been stranded at Deopham Green by weather since December 19th, when they were attempting to return to their home base at Deenethorpe. They followed the formation to Darmstadt airfield, but abandoned the target because of the ground haze and approach that had them flying into the sun. Instead they did a visual approach on the marshalling yards in the center of the city.

The next group of the 45th Combat Bombardment Wing, the E group, also came from the 452nd Bomb Group stationed at Deopham Green. It included the D, E, and F squadrons of the 452nd. The D Squadron consisted mostly of new crews and several war-weary ships resurrected for this greatest of all maximum effort missions. All three squadrons formed and joined the bomber stream without incident. They were joined by the E Squadron from the 493rd Bomb

Group as the low element. The lead and high squadrons failed to drop on the primary target. The low squadron from the 493rd Bomb Group dropped on the primary target, Darmstadt, visually with PFF assist. The two squadrons from the 452nd Bomb Group went on to bomb their target of last resort at Stuttgart. At that point the 493rd squadron sought and received permission to break from the formation and return to their home base. They made a routine return back to Debach.

The 45th Combat Bombardment Wing's last group, the F group, was truncated formation comprised of six aircraft, 388th forming the lead squadron and the 96th Bomb Group's F Squadron forming a low squadron. They assembled over the number nine buncher at 15,000 feet. Joining the bomber stream proved to be somewhat of a problem because of altitude difference. The F group started its climb to bombing altitude before the 45th A group reached the assembly altitude of the F group. In the congestion, the F group had to do considerable "S"ing and ended up approximately twelve miles north of the briefed course on the left of the IP due to all other groups taking too much interval in the fan-out.

As the components of this enormous assemblage of heavy bombers heading to Darmstadt crossed the battle line in Belgium, they began to experience moderate but very accurate flak. Some of them experienced more because of navigational deviation from the planned path. Between Cologne and Frankfurt, the lead plane piloted by H. W. Moore was hit and, while able to fly, was forced to abort and return to base. The deputy lead, piloted by 1/Lt Ramon Melton, reformed the group and continued on about five miles north of course. They continued on course next to the formation of the 13th Combat Bombardment Wing, which was about fifteen miles north of the course. As they converged at the Pre-IP the 13th Combat Bombardment Wing converged on course and made it necessary for the 45th A group to "S" left to get in proper division column.

There was minimal defense at the target, but they experienced two issues that affected the outcome of the entire mission for the 45th Combat Bombardment Wing. Despite the clear sky overhead, the Darmstadt field itself was covered with a ground haze. Combined with a flight plan that called heading directly into the setting sun on one of the shortest days of the year, these two problems made visual target identification extremely difficult.

Post-mission evaluation called the results "fair." Bombing at the target was mixed. The runway was only minimally damaged and was serviceable on the next day. The surrounding administrative, ammunition, and supply storage buildings, equipment and maintenance facilities received significant damage, however. Some damage was done to the rail connecting lines by the 388th Bomb Group, though through lines continued to operate. There was some serious damage at the small nearby air base at Griesheim.

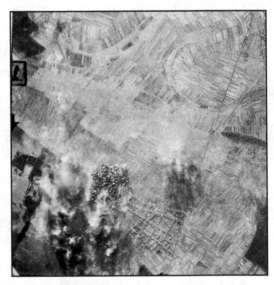

Griesheim bombing attack strike photo.

Navigator 1/Lt Lawrence Rasmussen of the 493rd Bomb Group, in an aircraft filling in a composite formation of the 45th Combat Bombardment Wing's E formation, noted that his plane had dropped 12,500-pound Navy incendiary explosive bombs on the Griesheim airfield, taking out hangars and installations on the north side of the field.

It was known that III./JG 4 had been using Darmstadt during December of 1944, though there was no evidence of damage to the unit on the day of the attack. Intelligence summaries from the day indicate that forty-five Me109s had been detected taking off from Darmstadt and Frankfurt areas that morning at 0800 hours, three hours before zero hour for Mission 760. Additional Me109s took off at 0835 hours, thirteen from Dortmund and twelve from the Duisburg/Essen area. At 0905 hours an additional thirty-five Me109s departed. All were understood to be active around Liege and to the south-southeast of Liege. This helps to explain why no enemy aircraft were seen on the ground or near the Darmstadt target.

Six aircraft from the Darmstadt attack are identified as continuing to another target of opportunity at "Heilbroon" or "Haildraum" (the records are unclear). The correct name of the target is Heilbronn, an ancient city on the Neckar River, located fifty-five miles south of Darmstadt. Heilbronn was known as a wine producer and source of salt (from underground mines) since the time of the Romans. But east/west rail lines and a large port on the Neckar River connected it to easy transport to the Rhine River and the battlefront on the west of the Rhine. During the Nazis' buildup for battle, though before the offensive began, the RAF conducted a major raid on Heilbronn. On the night of December 4, 1944, 80 percent of the central city was destroyed and over 7,000 people were killed. The rubble of the city was still piled high on 24 December when the formation of six aircraft from the 94th Combat Bombardment Wing, bombing visually, dropped eighteen tons of explosives on the cleanup effort.

The 8th Air Force planning dispatched 226 aircraft to Darmstadt target as part of Mission 760; 189 were ultimately effective, dropping 232.2 tons of explosives. Several planes turned back for a variety of mechanical issues. Others were damaged by flak after crossing the battle line on their way to the target. Some of those hit successfully made it back to friendly territory in Belgium or France. One, piloted by 1/Lt Jay Kenworthy of the 452nd Bomb Group, went down near the IP. The radio operator, T/Sgt Vincent Sullivan, was killed in the hit. The rest of the crew was taken prisoner.

The B Squadron from the 388th Bomb Group was missing one aircraft in action before the target. It was believed that this was the plane (44-8411) piloted by G.K. Thompson which was hit by flak over the combat front. The operations officer report for the day says, "A/C 44-8411 was hit by flak before the target and blew up. 6 chutes." This was incorrect. Thompson was able to feather the number one engine and then crash-landed into friendly territory with his whole crew surviving. The squadron had a second plane that was hit and pulled out of the formation. It was 43-38424, piloted by 1/Lt Casimer Sulkowski and also crash-landed in friendly territory.

Joe Capraro was a waist gunner with the 561st Squadron of the 388th Bomb Group flying with Pilot Douglas O'Brien in the low contingent of the F squadron. Capraro reflected years later: "We successfully dropped our bombs to help, and that was Christmas Eve. So, then we came back and we went to church. And the choir was singing 'Adeste Fideles.' Come All Ye Faithful. You know, I sat there in church and wondered — we went out and killed all those people and here we are singing about goodwill and peace toward men. But, that's the way it was. I was never really able to sing that song again."

Joe Capraro

Al Greenberg, a togglier with the 96th Bomb Group, recalled that the mission briefing was packed to the gills, including General

Archie Old, commander of the 45th Combat Bombardment Wing and a group of war correspondents. Greenberg's crew ended up flying the oldest ship in the squadron. As they pulled the safety pins on their bombs, they wrote "Merry Christmas" on one with a piece of fudge Greenberg had brought along on the mission. When he salvoed his bombs over the target, only the inside racks released. He didn't find out until after they had left the target and ended up dropping the remaining bombs over a river.

Daniel Freitas, a radio operator with the 401st Bomb Group, shared his story of a distraction from the bitter cold on Christmas Eve, his sixth mission. He was on one of the thirty-six planes supplied by his bomb group to complete the 94th Combat Bombardment Wing's B formation headed to Koblenz. 1/Lt John D. Gerber's crew flew on the aircraft tagged *Little Cheezer*. He was tense and the static on his liaison receiver required his full concentration to monitor and copy the radio code from his assigned frequencies. As they approached an identified flak area, Freitas donned his flak vest and helmet. The plane's intercom was operating sporadically, but he picked up some talk about engine problems. As they approached the IP, the pilot feathered the number one engine. For the next twenty-seven minutes they experienced moderate but accurate flak. To compound the tension, he could see six to eight Me 262 jets circling his formation.

As they reached the IP, he turned on the bomb strike camera and began to discharge chaff, to confuse the enemy's sighting radar. He was scared, hearing the thump of flak bursting around the plane, and he was saying his usual prayers. Then, opening one of the boxes of chaff he found a piece of chaff paper bearing a handwritten note. Suddenly the war seemed to stop, and his fear and concerns disappeared as he read the note:

"If you've not a girl friend to care where you roam: And if you've no wife waiting at home; If you'd care for a pen friend, man now is the time, to sit down and write Joy or Win." The note was signed by Miss Win Bevan and Miss Joy Chaplin. Both gave their complete address in Kent.

Thoughts of the two young ladies ran through his head, as he wondered what he would write to them. Coming out of the bomb run, the pilot interrupted his distracted thought. They were losing altitude and lagging behind the formation headed for home. They began tossing out any excess weight that they could. As they approached the English Channel, Freitas contacted Air Sea Rescue and they tracked the plane across the water. There were many aircraft in distress as they were, low on gas and searching for a landing field. Finally, they made an emergency landing at Great Massingham with a unanimous sigh of relief.

They were welcomed by the RAF and celebrated a fine English Christmas with them. Then Freitas and his crew huddled together in the back of an army truck for the six-hour ride back to East Anglia. Thoughts of Win and Joy rolled around in his head as they bumped along the road. Once back at Deenethorp he fired off a letter to each of them. Soon he was disappointed with their response. They had hoped their note would have been discovered by an airman stationed in Italy! He preserved their chaff note, referring to it often to preserve the memory of the two young English girls who made the air war temporarily stand still for him.

The 8th Air Force didn't only drop chaff and bombs on Germany that Christmas Eve; there were also two aircraft of the 388th Bomb Group dropping twenty containers of propaganda leaflets in the course of this mission in hopes that the citizenry would abandon support for the war and the Fuhrer.

The return trip to East Anglia was uneventful for the majority of the planes targeting Darmstadt, though a few landed in safe territory in Belgium and France because of a lack of fuel or flak damage. Once they returned, the weather over England had begun to deteriorate and many of them sought safe refuge at bases other than their own. Some like Pilot Haven Burningham's of the 457th used up every ounce of fuel and crash-landed near their home base.

The attack on the Darmstadt airfield was one of the largest and one of the most disappointing of the day. Though the attack on the installation's buildings and storage facilities was excellent, the attack on the landing field was very poor and left the field immediately serviceable. The attack on the central city rail station and marshalling yard made an impact, however.

Frankfurt Rhein Main Air Base 1402 hrs.
Effective 100 Bomb Tonnage 325.8

The Rhein Main air base just south of Frankfurt a Main was the target for 93rd Combat Bombardment Wing. The air base there, located in the center of the Frankfurt, Wiesbaden, Mainz, Offenbach, Hanau industrial/commercial area just east of the confluence of the heavily barge trafficked Rhine and Main rivers, was a hub for the protection of the region but also within flying distance for the support of the Ardennes Offensive. At the time of the attack, it was believed to be the station of IV/JG4, though it was also home to several supply, munitions, antiaircraft, ground transport, and ground defense and security organizations.

The 34th Bomb Group from Mendlesham formed the A group of the 93rd CBW formation with fifty-nine aircraft dispatched. Taking off at 0940 hours they gathered at buncher nineteen at 10,000 feet and then moved to buncher twenty-eight for group assembly. There were some issues with the wing assembly because the prior group was approximately 2,000 feet too high on assembly and climb. Unanticipated headwinds caused them to arrive twenty to twenty-five minutes late at the IP. Additionally, the prior group from the 45th Combat Bombardment Wing was twelve miles left of the briefed course and caused the 34th to do considerable "S"ing to stay behind them. Fighter support was marginal and pulled away early at the IP because they were running low on fuel. There was no enemy aircraft opposition to speak of.

The formation made the IP at 1500 hours and made a right turn onto the target for visual bombing at 1506 hours. They encountered one of the major problems of the day, very bad ground haze. The target was sighted at the very last minute of the run, requiring large corrections to put the lead and high squadrons over the target. The high squadron dropped thirty seconds before the lead. Yet the results were good, with no undercast and only meager flak at the target itself.

The rendezvous and return were uneventful, though four aircraft crashed on landing caused by the congestion of planes waiting to land, many because they had been diverted from their socked-in home bases. Landing intervals were seriously reduced and a number of aircraft were very nearly out of fuel. All crews survived and the four aircraft sustained moderate damage. One, flown by

Frankfurt-Rheine bombing attack strike photo.

William F. Latz, crashed due to serious battle damage. A number of Latz's crew members suffered minor injuries in the crash. Another, flown by Herbert Vick, also crash-landed, but without injuries. Two planes, one piloted by Gordon F. Barbaras and the other by Charles H. Ettelbrick, actually collided on the runway. Barbaras' plane destroyed a wing and stabilizer. All told, fourteen of the 34th Bomb Group's planes returned with battle damage, with five of them serious to major. One aircraft from the 34th had been on leaflet dropping detail, dropping ten containers of three different leaflet messages for the German populace.

The B group for the 93rd Combat Bomb Group was comprised by the 490th Bomb Group based in Eye. The B squadron of the 490th formed the high element of the formation. Forming over splasher number six, they left on time, but were delayed, having to awaiting aircraft joining the A group (34th Bomb Group) ahead of them. That formation was inadvertently fifteen miles north of the planned route. Jockeying for briefed positions caused the formation to do considerable "S"ing all the way to the IP. They encountered flak near Marche, Belgium, and at the target, but it was meager and inaccurate. The 34th overran the turn northwest of Frankfurt, a move that forced the 490th Wing to turn off to the left to get in trail on the bomb run from the IP to the target. Their lead squadron was so close to the 34th low at time of bombs away that they believed they hit slightly past the target. The high squadron, a visual run, dropped at 1506 hours and the bombardier reported results as "good." The low squadron dropped a minute later but hit long. One aircraft, 44-38340, passed over the target, but did not bomb because of a rack malfunction. This aircraft later bombed a target of opportunity at Darmstadt. Another aircraft, 43-38993, turned back before reaching the primary target because of flak damage to its number four engine. On its return it bombed a target of opportunity in Wiesbaden. All returned to Eye from the rendezvous point without incident.

The C group for the 93rd CBW was from the 493rd Bomb Group. They also fell prey to the congestion and location problems with the 34th Bomb Group lead and were out of the formation train much of the time. Formation was ragged. One aircraft experienced an engine failure and turned back just after entering enemy territory. The air leader reported thin fighter support along the way, but once enemy fighters appeared, their support was there on the spot. A sharp left turn coming out of the bomb run actually put them in front of the 490th Bomb Group they had been following. They experienced fairly accurate tracking flak over the target. The high formation from the 490th was trailing and hindering their movement. The low formation of the 490th was also trailing at the target but got away just in time for the 493rd Bomb Group's drop. The C group left the formation when they reached the coast and proceeded to buncher number twenty-seven, circling until they were called in by the base.

The D group for the 93rd CBW was a composite of the 493rd and the 490th Bomb Groups with the 490th flying in the low position. They experienced problems in assembly and with the "S"ing of the entire 93rd CBW formation. Over the combat front they experienced meager, but fairly accurate flak and noticed at least sixteen flak guns in place. They made the IP good, experienced no congestion at the target. They reported late timings due to increased trade winds.

Among the German units utilizing the Frankfurt Rhein aerodrome at the time of the Christmas Eve attack was a unit of the IV/ KG200 charged with the mission of "ferrying supplies to strongpoints." They also dropped spies and infiltrators behind Allied lines. Known as Kommando Olga, they had people on the ground at the time of the attack and after. One airman, Fahnenjunker-Feldwebel Heinz Hauck, was later captured and interrogated as a POW. In his testimony he stated: "An American raid on Christmas Eve wrecked the flying control building and two hangars, as well as destroying several aircraft. They came over during the afternoon. The warning went at two o'clock—we were just on the airfield. At three o'clock the alert was still on when suddenly they were there. I immediately threw myself down behind a tree. The first wave dropped their bombs somewhat wide of the mark. The second bomb carpet was right over us. Six waves passed over. I looked up and, seeing nothing, thought it was all over…Flak splinters were hissing—sss, sss—and I saw that everything around me was on fire, planes, the lot. That was where our machines had been. I was at the other end of the airfield where no bombs fell."

Another POW and wireless operator on Hauck's crew, Max Grossman, said, "Of the eight who died, four were from Kommando Olga: the Stabsfeldwebel and the Oberwerkmeister were in one of those slit trenches. They got buried and suffocated." Fw. Max Wittge, a third captured crew member, said: "The beam caved in and the dugout collapsed. We started shoveling and we got one of them out fairly quickly; at any rate we got his head free so he could breathe. A woman was still believed to be down there, but we never found her. Some of the huts containing Panzerfaust and signal ammunition were still burning. One of our four men had broken his right arm, his left leg and crushed his ribs. The other three were already dead." Wuttge continued: "Early the following morning members of the Volkssturm, Russian prisoners and all sorts of people came to clean up. It was just about 5 a.m. and another alert sounds. It kicks off right away, they're coming over the airfield, eight Mustangs. They strafed the field and everyone threw themselves into bomb craters. That was the only thing to do. They each dropped a bomb and machine-gunned us."

It took four days of work to make a single runway serviceable again. According to Hauck, the bombing disrupted planned planting of Dutch journalist Willem Copier, who had been trained to serve as a spy behind the Allied lines and had been trained for the project with the intent of dropping him by parachute. A month later, after a number of failed attempts, Copier and another agent by the name of Bennet were taken into the night sky by Hauck's crew over US-held Luxembourg. Copier jumped, but tangled line caused a series of problems. He lost his bag with transmitting equipment along with his clothes. He landed hard and seriously injured his leg. Bennet's chute never opened and he fell to his death. The plane was hit by a British fighter,

Frankfurt reconnaissance photo.

and its crew of four successfully bailed out, only to be rounded up and apprehended, finishing the war as POWs.

The northeastern two-fifths of the airfield was completely post-holed with small craters and was unserviceable, though the remainder of the landing ground appeared intact. The hangar and concrete apron sustained considerable damage. At least twenty-two aircraft, some dispersed into the woods, were sighted, though only two appeared to have been damaged.

Upon return to England, bad weather conditions forced planes from the 379th and 490th Bomb Groups to divert to Mendlesham, the home base of the 34th Bomb Group. There were four or five collisions that occurred on the runway due to very close landings as planes with critically low fuel levels rushed to land.

"Battle is the most magnificent competition in which a human being can indulge. It brings out all that is best; it removes all that is base. All men are afraid in battle. The coward is the one who lets his fear overcome his sense of duty. Duty is the essence of manhood."

—George S. Patton

Chapter 9

THE TARGETS OF THE SECOND ATTACK FORCE

THE SECOND ATTACK Force was assembled from the four Combat Bombardment Wings of the 1st Bombardment Division. The plan called for fourteen combat groups of thirty-six aircraft each. Their day began in similar fashion to that of the First Attack Force, though about forty-five minutes later and departing England over Clacton, about thirty miles southwest of Felixstowe. Just as the First Force, the roar of their engines and the drama of formation assembly excited the villages of their bases, especially after the cold quit of the prior week. But the Second Attack Force was not to have the smooth start that the First Attack Force did. Accidents, runway closures and displaced aircraft created serious issues in takeoff and assembly, making forming a serious challenge.

The 457th Bomb Group flying from Glatton supplied forty-five bombers to comprise the lead formation of the 94th Combat Bombardment Group's A formation. The A group commander was Captain William A. Doherty and the pilot was 1/Lt Donald L. Seesenguth. Despite the favorable weather in most of East Anglia, some areas around Glatton were still rough. Early in the morning two V-1 rockets dropped south of the base, apparently intended for a nearby munitions plant. The explosion shook the entire base and neighboring community. Briefings were completed as scheduled, but the weather delayed takeoff. Finally, at 1024 hours, the planes began to taxi to the runway. Six planes were airborne before Lt. Carl P. Sundbaum's plane crashed on takeoff, killing gunner S/Sgt Donald R. Peacock. The rest of the crew escaped before the plane blew up at the end of the fog-covered runway, rocking the base for the second time that morning.

With the runway closed, the eight aircraft that were in the air assembled on the Glatton buncher at 7,000 feet. They were joined by two additional aircraft that had been diverted to an alternate base returning from their previous mission on 19 December to the marshalling yard in Gemund, at the heart of the supply line to the Ardennes Offensive. When word of the takeoff accident and closure on the 24th was known, they were told the mission was scrubbed and directed to proceed to Ridgewell, the home base of the 381st Bomb Group. Moments later they were notified to stand by and they were directed to form with the 401st Bomb Group and to fly as a "high-high" squadron. In transit the formation was hit with heavy flak, the lead plane of the Doherty/Seesenguth plane was hit, and the plane in the number three position developed mechanical difficulties. This seven-plane remnant of the A group was unable to keep up with the 401st formation and proceeded on its own to the target, making a visual run and releasing their bomb load from 26,000 feet. They and their lead ship, which had found its own target of opportunity, returned individually to Glatton.

The 401st Bomb Group furnished thirty-six aircraft to the B group of the 94th Combat Bombardment Wing, heading to what was then an alternate target for them, the rail yards at Koblenz. Koblenz is located on the west bank of the Rhine river at the confluence of the Rhine and the Mosel. It served as a hub for the secret movement of men, equipment, and supplies, including the critically scarce supplies of fuel into the Ardennes mountains as Hitler was preparing for the Ardennes Offensive. Koblenz, when fully operating, also provided rail access from central and southern Germany to the critical regions of Bonn, Cologne, and Dusseldorf. It also established direct access to Mainz, Frankfurt, Mannheim, Stuttgart, and Munich, provided rail bridges over the Rhine and the Mosel were protected from attack. It had been critical to the buildup of the offense that the Allies failed to recognize before December 16, but it was also critical to the continued successful completion of Hitler's fanciful, but desperate plan.

They began their flight across the Channel about twelve minutes after the last unit of the First Force had departed and arriving at Ostend, Belgium, at 15,000 feet just minutes before the Luftwaffe was ravaging the mission's lead formation. Their formation fell into the long chain of 8th Air Force attack units and followed in formation until the area over Prum, where they left the path of the First Force and set out toward their own targets to the northeast and slightly away from the clear view of Hitler at his Adlerhorst hideaway. Just as with the First Force, their lead targets were identified to be tactical in nature and intended to cripple fighter support for the Ardennes Offensive. They were attacking air bases to the north, as opposed to the First Force's attacks in a quadrant south of Frankfurt. Yet their northernmost target was Giessen, a full eighty miles south of Gutersloh, the base that launched the morning's fighter attack that did so much damage to the American lead formation as it passed south of Liege, Belgium, just hours before.

The spearhead of the Second Attack Force was led by the 1st Combat Bombardment Wing's 381st Bomb Group based at Ridgewell. The Second Force formed in the same manner as the First Attack Force, but were routed to Clacton, just south of Felixstowe, the departure point for the First Force. They began to arrive at Claxton, crossing the Channel about forty-five minutes later than the First Force. Once over Europe their course was the same as the First Force route until they passed CP3. Then they plotted a northern route toward their assigned targets.

Later in the day when the Glatton runway was cleared, the thirty-four remaining aircraft from the 457th Bomb Group took off and assembled on the Glatton buncher, but no division assembly was accomplished. Because of the late takeoff, they were directed to proceed to the Channel and jettison their bombs in order to return to base by 1700 hours. All but one did as directed, executed a 180-degree turn and flew back to Glatton. The last aircraft proceeded across the Channel and found its own target of opportunity near Daun, before returning to base. Weather conditions in much of England were rapidly deteriorating and caused the returning 457th aircraft to land at Eye (490th BG) and Horham (95th BG)

The 401st Bomb Group was joined by thirty-two aircraft from the 384th taking off from its home base in Grafton Underwood and five aircraft from other fields. All thirty-seven were to join the formation en route. This column was proceeding in a very good formation until the lead aircraft aborted 150 miles from target at an altitude of 21,000 feet (4,000 feet below bombing altitude). When the lead found it necessary to abort, unable to make VHF contact with his deputy, he lowered his wheels as a signal. The high squadron lead took over the lead of the resulting two squadron combination. Lead and high squadron formation to the target was very poor.

Due to mechanical difficulties and flak evasion, the course was not as briefed from the IP to the target. Intensive accurate flak required evasive action, and the group started on a visual bomb run thirty-five degrees off the briefed magnetic heading. The lead bombardier synchronized on the MPI and then employed evasive action. When he placed sight on back of the target to refine corrections, he found the sight had become disengaged from the stabilizer. Since there was no time to replace the pin, he held the sight on target with his right hand and made small corrections with his left. When the indices crossed, he salvoed. All the other aircraft used a 75-foot inter setting. The high squadron bombed on the group leader, and strikes were seen in the target area. The use of 500-pound bombs left considerable damage to the busy marshalling yard.

The low squadron missed the turning point just before the IP, but with some maneuvering almost made it good. During the bomb run they had to make adjustments to sight the target, the Rhine river being the identifying checkpoint. Before the actual bomb run started, the nose of the lead plane was shot by flak. At bombs away, a smoke marker and a single bomb dropped, though the following ships dropped on the smoke bomb. The lead pilot was eventually able to drop his load and there was no explanation as to why the mechanism had not been working previously. All the planes in this formation had the luxury of spending the night at Lavenham on their return because of the inclement weather. There was one casualty for this event.

Ettinghausen 1414 hrs.
Effective 43 Bomb Tonnage 107.5

Disguised as a farm, the Luftwaffe field in Ettinghausen was located about ten miles east of Giessen. It was initially built in the late 1930s, first used for operational units and then by trainers and gliders. It was reactivated as a fighter field in November of 1944, just prior to the Ardennes Offensive. The runway was grass, but had two paved hardstands. There were two small portable hangar buildings off the southwest boundary and a small cluster of workshops off the northeast corner. A small group of barrack-type buildings was situated off the north corner and another off the southwest corner. There was a munitions dump located off the west boundary. A branch rail line serviced the northeast and northwest sides of the field. There were aircraft parked in the woods at times. III/JG2 was using the field in December of 1944. Ettinghausen is nineteen miles northeast of the bunker where Hitler was hiding at the Adlerhorst outside of Bad Nauheim.

On December 24th the airfield was an assigned target for the 381st Bomb Group, flying as the A Group of the 1st Combat Bombardment Wing under Flight Leader Col. Harry P. Leber. Leber was also the well-respected and combat experienced commander of the 381st. Takeoff and assembly were made without incident. The course flown to the target was as briefed, with some meager and inaccurate flak experienced at the battle line near Stavelot and St. Vith in Belgium. Bombing was visual and with very excellent results both for the landing strip and the surrounding structures. There were over 300 craters blanketing the landing ground except for a small portion in the northwest corner and adjacent the barracks area. They extended into the ammunition storage area and open

Ettinghausen bombing attack strike photo.

fields. There were scattered craters in the west and south dispersal areas. The two small hangars were destroyed. The follow-up reconnaissance determined that the field would be totally unusable without at least four days of serious repair and reconstruction. Though one ship aborted for mechanical reasons, the mission was accomplished without losses or casualties. Upon returning to Ridgewell from a routine and successful mission, they found their home base inundated with seventy-four visiting aircraft and crews unable to return to their own home bases because of the seriously deteriorating weather.

In addition to the crowd of aircraft back at the 381st's home station, a crew from BBC had come up from London to record statements from Col. Leber and Major Fullick, the lead bombardier. The recordings were a comfort for the war weary and were on the air several times during the following week.

Nidda 1414 hrs.
Effective 49 Bomb Tonnage 132.5

While the 1st Combat Bombardment Wing's 381st Bomb Group was attacking Ettinghausen, the 306th Bomb Group forming the D Group of the 40th Combat Bombardment Wing was attacking the airfield at Nidda, a facility only twenty miles north of Hitler's Adlerhorst bunker. This facility was similar to the one at Ettinghausen. It had a grass landing strip surrounded by buildings camouflaged to look like a farm. Built in the late 1930s, it was used in the campaign to France. But it was inactive from 1940 until it became a fighter station in September of 1944. There were no paved runways, but taxi tracks connected the dispersal areas to the landing area. There were fuel and ammunition points on the north, southwest, and western boundaries. There were two hangars and a separate very large repair hangar of the southwest corner, all camouflaged like the other structures on the property. A block of six very large buildings was directly behind the repair hangar, and these were likely workshops and stores warehouses belonging to the Luftpark. A branch rail line along the Nidda-Budingen rail line served the repair hangar and the edge of the landing area. There were also a barracks and mess plus some other small structures in this area.

In the dispersal area around the field there were seventeen parking spaces for aircraft cut into the edge of the woods along the northern boundary and another twenty-five at the edge of the woods along the western boundary. There were also flak towers and positions around the airfield, yet no flak was encountered by the attacking American forces. Nor were there

Nidda bombing attack strike photo.

any enemy aircraft observed. In late December 1944 the base was known to be used by II/JG2.

The lead squadron of the 40th CBW D Group came from the 306th Bomb Group and took off from Thurleigh at 0948 hours. It was joined by the low squadron which came from the 305th Bomb Group from Chelveston and was to be joined by the high squadron coming from the 92nd Bomb Group in Paddington. Assembly of the lead and low squadrons was accomplished over buncher twelve, but the high squadron was delayed by the fatal takeoff accident at Podington and failed to assemble. A message was received saying the A Group was late and the D Group made a 360-degree turn north of London and joined the air division formation, departing the English coast eight minutes late. They proceeded to the target and the high squadron followed, including a high-high component of three additional aircraft. Making a visual approach, the leader's bombs jammed and failed to release.

According to procedural changes in the prior year, only the lead ship in a formation had a Norden bombsight while the rest of the formation had a togglier who would drop his bombs on the lead's signal. On this day the deputy leader took over and made a second run, but his bombs also failed to release. Instead he dropped a signal flare and the rest of the formation bombed on that signal. All the planes bombing the primary target visually achieved good results, leaving the field and facilities heavily damaged. The two planes not dropping sought a target of opportunity. They found it in Linz am Rhein, a town on the east side of the Rhine just south of Remagen. There was a substantial system of rail tracks between the town and the river, and the bombs found their mark, yet, at the end of the attack only one of the planned 12 squadrons assigned to bomb Nidda hit their assigned target. Others proceeded to targets of opportunity, including the village of Bellersheim, 8 miles from Nidda and a target of minimal importance.

The delayed lone squadron from the 92nd Bomb Group was unable to locate its lead and low squadrons at control point one. Departing that point thirteen minutes late, it proceeded along the briefed route to the target alone, eventually dropping its bombs on a target of opportunity.

Unable to land at Thurleigh because of weather conditions, the returning formation landed at Bury St. Edmunds.

Giessen 1423 hrs.
Effective 74 Bomb Tonnage 185

Built originally in the 1930s, Giessen was originally a civilian airport. It was pulled into military service in 1932 and then built out as a full Luftwaffe air base in 1936. It was used almost exclusively for bombers until mid-1940. It had grass surface with concrete starting platforms on the east and west boundaries, paved hangar aprons, and a perimeter road that connected the hangars with the starting platforms. It was equipped for night landings. There were numerous refueling points, communications structures, and ammunition dumps, a compass swing, a machine gun registration range, and other amenities. There were seven hangars along the south boundary, including one large repair hangar, with workshops and stores buildings off the southwest corner of the airfield. The control tower was located between the hangars and the barrack blocks. There was also a branch rail line that served the airfield. Around the field were seven open aircraft shelters and four or five blast bays. Off the northeast corner there were five large open shelters.

In hopes of fooling the bombers from the sky, the Nazis had erected a dummy airfield three miles north-northeast of the Giessen airfield. This mock-up included representations of four hangars plus station buildings at the edge of a woods on the eastern boundary complete with dummy aircraft parked near the buildings. It was also equipped with a lighting system ready to attract RAF night fighters

The 40th Combat Bombardment Wing's A group was comprised of thirty-nine aircraft from the 92nd Bomb Group flying out of Podington. For the 92nd Bomb Group this mission was to be one of the most devastating since the September 1944 raids on the oil refineries at Merseburg. Takeoff began at 1000 hours. While excellent weather was forecast for the targets of the day, deep fog covered the runways of Podington, just sixty miles north of London. Crews had been awakened at 0500 hours and had trouble making their way to the mess hall through the dense fog. Every flyable plane on the field was at the ready, a total of fifty-three B-17s destined for the air bases either at Giessen or Nidda. Soon they were lining the perimeter track, cautiously awaiting their turn to depart in the suboptimal ground visibility.

Years later Pilot Harry Culver described his own experience that morning. His plane, loaded with 6,000 pounds of bombs and 2,780 gallons of high-octane fuel, was in the queue for takeoff ahead of a plane piloted by Lt. Robert A. Seeber. Culver steered off of the hardstand and inched his way forward in the long line toward the runway. Suddenly the plane jolted to a stop, throwing him forward in the pilot's seat. His copilot, Lt. C.R. Christenson, had hit the brakes and snapped, "There is a plane in front of us!" Tucked almost against their nose and barely beyond the whirling prop blades was the amber taillight of a B-17. Normally visible for miles, the definitely dense fog obscured one only feet away.

Within seconds the plane in front of them and its faint taillight were gone, and the control jeep gave Culver a green light for takeoff. Concerned about the narrow runway and the mud deep on either side and fearing a hooked wheel in the mud that could result in a cartwheeling crash, Culver opted for a visual rather than all-instrument takeoff. Suddenly a fine mist completely fogged the windshield. There were no wipers and their view went blind. It was too late to switch to instruments. He instinctively jerked the control column back into his lap for a three-point takeoff position and tried to "feel" the rudder to maintain a straight line. As they left the ground there was a tree just off their left wing. Culver yanked hard right. His copilot Chris Christenson spotted a tree on the right and hit the left aileron and rudder. Seconds later they broke through the overcast and into brilliant sunshine. The crew cheered.

Then someone in the back said, "There's a red glow through the clouds. It looks like a flare. Maybe the mission's been scrubbed." It wasn't until evening that they learned the red glow was the crash of one of their formation's planes on the runway, the plane immediately behind them at the morning's takeoff. Its pilot, 2/Lt Robert A.

Seeber, was recently assigned to the unit. He, like Culver, was unable to see the trees about 200 yards to the left of the runway's end. Lt. Seeber began to turn to get on course before much elevation was attained. He encountered prop wash from the plane in front of him, Culver's plane. Then he quickly lost altitude and crashed into the treetops. Within minutes, the burning aircraft exploded, killing six crew members and leaving three others seriously injured. The crash delayed the remaining aircraft behind Seeber's plane, but the assembly and formation were quickly made. Despite the tragic incident on the runway, the remaining formation was only six minutes late on departure from the buncher. By the time they reached the first control point, they were right on schedule. At the IP the squadrons took interval for visual bombing. The lead and high squadrons bombed individually with the lead's drop occurring at 1442 hours and from 22,200 feet. The low squadron made a second pass, bombing at 1501.5 hours from 21,600 feet. The bombing of all three squadrons was excellent. The lead and high squadrons executed a 360-degree turn at the rally point and then headed directly back to Podington.

The formation had experienced some very accurate flak over the target, flak that claimed four aircraft from the 92nd Bomber Group. Two were from the 327th Squadron, the second to cross the target, and two were from the 407th Squadron, last to bomb. From the 327th Squadron the plane in the number three position of the lead squadron successfully bombed the target but was seriously damaged by flak. There is no Missing Aircraft Report for it because the pilot successfully nursed it back into friendly territory over Belgium. One crewman was injured and treated in a Belgian hospital, while the other eight were safely transported back to their home base in England.

The second downed plane of the lead formation was piloted by 2/Lt Joe B. Spencer, and the story of this plane is documented by MACR 11112. The facts are somewhat unclear, however. The aircraft had been transferred to the 92nd Bomb Group shortly before the mission. After-mission reports by the 92nd state the aircraft took off from Podington at 1047 hours and "did not join our formation and no report has been received since takeoff." It is also referred to as an aircraft of the 303rd Bomb Group. Yet the plane clearly shows on the 327th Squadron's formation at assembly and over target. Bombing by the lead squadron began at 1442 hours. Spencer apparently did not make the rendezvous point. And neither did the low squadron. Spencer's plane was hit by very accurate flak, killing Navigator 2/Lt Roy N. Powell, Ball Turret Gunner Sgt. John L. Krajcik, Waist Gunner S/Sgt Charles M. Garrison, and Radio Operator Sgt. Harland B. Parks. The tail gunner, Sgt. Charles R. Utz, and Top Turret Gunner S/Sgt. Donald L. Sheddy were the first to bail out. Spencer was blown out by an explosion as the plane was going down. Spencer, Sheedy, Utz, Togglier S/Sgt. James J Savage, and the copilot, 2/Lt Philip J. Rock, were all captured, though Sheddy avoided apprehension for three days. These five airmen were POWs until the end of the war.

The downed plane from the 92nd's 407th Squadron was piloted by 1/Lt Joseph B. McConnell flying in the squadron's deputy lead position. With serious flak damage, McConnell coaxed his aircraft back to a crash-landing in the safe territory near Ohey, Belgium, just southwest of Liege. The journey from the target was one of high drama. Intent on reaching Allied-held territory despite the fluid combat line and knowing he could not land the plane safely, McConnell waited to give the bail order until he believed he was beyond the ground combat front. Tail Gunner S/Sgt. John Caravello and Waist Gunner S/Sgt Leo Labonte were the first to jump. P-51 fighter escort protection stuck with them and literally tried to create air currents to put them past the German fighters in the area. Their efforts were successful, but Caravello inadvertently headed in the wrong direction when he hit the ground. He quickly realized what he had done and recovered to the American side of the conflict. Labonte landed in a tree without his flight boots. He spent the night in the woods. Hearing church bells in the morning, he walked in their direction hoping to be sheltered by the local priest. Instead he walked directly into a column of British tanks. They took him to a Belgian home where he received care and a bottle of cognac.

Shortly before McConnell's plane crashed, Copilot 2/Lt Alfred J. Greco, Flight Engineer Terry Sakyo, and 2/Lt Frank J. Purtzer bailed safely. 1/Lt Anthony Piekarz, the navigator, bailed out, but his parachute — possibly damaged in the flak attack — failed to fill out completely and he fell to his death. T/Sgt. John Booth, the radio operator, jumped, but his parachute became entangled in the horizontal stabilizer and the tail dragged him to his death. McConnell jumped and landed on a picket fence, breaking both legs. S/Sgt Harold H. Parke, a waist gunner, was possibly hit in the flak attack and went down with the plane.

Another crew from the 407th Squadron flying in the low echelon was also seriously damaged in the flak barrage. The pilot sought refuge in France and brought the plane down at Lille. One injured airman was hospitalized there. The plane was not flyable, but the remaining eight crewmen safely made their way back to England.

The 40th Combat Bombardment Wing B group came from the 306th Bomb Group flying out of Thurleigh. Takeoff was from 0948 to 1028. All takeoffs were by instruments in heavy fog and snow on the ground. Two aircraft failed to take off due to mechanical problems. Assembly was made over Mt. Farm and was four minutes late. Point N was omitted to make up time, but the formation was still five minutes late when departing the Clacton coast. The route to the target was as ordered, though late at all turning points due to a change in the winds from those forecast.

Bombing at Giessen was visual with good observed results

confirmed by strike photos. During the bomb run the lead bombardier felt that his assigned aiming point had already been well hit and adjusted his target sighting to gain better coverage of the field. The low squadron's bombs fell in the built-up area to the southwest of the field. Friendly fighter support was very good throughout the mission, and the only flak experienced by this group was meager and generally inaccurate. One aircraft of the 306th also dropped ten loads of leaflets, referred to as "nickels," over Giessen.

Giessen bombing reconnaissance photo.

After bombing the group did not turn off the target as planned but went wide and intercepted the briefed course thirty-five minutes later, then returning to England according to the original plan. Entering British airspace, they were diverted to the field at Debach, where they landed without incident at 1816 hours.

The 40th Combat Bombardment Wing C group came from the 305th Bomb Group home based at Chelveston. Thirty-six aircraft were sent, though one returned to base because of mechanical problems before reaching enemy territory. Takeoff for this group occurred at 0950 hours, and Major O.W. Shelton flew lead. The group flew as briefed to point "J" where a dogleg to the right was made in order to let the 40th CBW A group move into its proper position. The crew then flew as briefed all the way to the target, Giessen.

With clear skies at the target area, the group leader was able to see the target, so the squadrons took interval at the IP and each squadron made a visual run on the target with good bombing results. After bombs were released the lead and low squadrons rallied and returned to England along the briefed route. But on the turn away from the target, the high squadron was cut off by a B-24 group from the third attack force that was operating in the area, and it was unable to rejoin the lead and low squadrons. Rather than falling into its position in the formation, it followed along the trail back to England while maintaining visual contact with the lead and low squadrons ahead. No enemy aircraft were encountered by this group and flak was only encountered at the combat lines in eastern Belgium and at Giessen, though it was meager and fairly accurate. One aircraft from the 40th C group turned back because of mechanical problems prior to reaching enemy lines. One other failed to drop over the target, but found a target of opportunity at Siegen, Germany, a town considered to have a critical rail hub. Not known at the time, it was also used as a rendezvous point for transferring Jews to the camps earlier in the war. By December of 1944, Siegen had been repeatedly bombed by the Allies. (Flight documents for Mission 760 mistakenly identify the location bombed as "Herrmarnstein 5035N-0630E." There is no such town, but the coordinates locate a "Hermanstrasse" in Siegen.)

The Giessen attack delivered good coverage to the target by all attacking units. Large concentrations of bursts blanketed the south half of the landing ground, six of the seven hangars and western half of the accommodations. Incendiary bombs covered the northwest side of the landing ground. Three aircraft visible did not appear to be damaged, but the landing strip was cratered and rendered no longer serviceable. The three largest hangars took three direct hits and four near hits. The central hangar was seen burning and the east hangar took two near hits. The two medium and two small hangars on the west took direct hits plus near hits. The east hangar took three direct hits, two near hits, and was seen burning. The western half of the barracks area was blanketed by bursts, and at least five buildings received direct hits. An explosion was seen among the repair shops, and four buildings received direct hits. The control tower also received a direct hit. There was also damage done in the woods and fields north and northeast of the landing strip, as well as in the residential and wooded areas along the road into Giessen. Bursts blanketed the junction of the Giessen-Homberg Railway and the Giessen-Grossen Buseck road.

As the attack force made its way back across the Channel, it found rapidly deteriorating weather conditions and the Podington, Thurleigh, and Chelveston runways closed. Planes from the 305th Bomb Group were diverted to Horham, Westcott, Enstone, and Great Ashfield. Those from the 306th Bomb Group were sent to Framlingham, Debach, and Bury St. Edmunds. Some of the earliest flights from the 92nd Bomb Group were able to get into Podington, but as visibility became impossible, the remaining flights were diverted to Bury St. Edmunds. It was there that the last tragedy of the day occurred. Congestion on the runways, the tracks, and in the sky with all of the diversions that night left some planes with insufficient fuel on board in a precarious position. Such was the case with a plane from the 327th Bomb Squadron of the 92nd Bomb Group. Pilot Donald K. Lathram came in on fumes and was unable to make the runway. His plane fell short near Rougham, just southeast of the landing strip at Bury St. Edmunds. The crash killed the entire crew with the exception of Ike Harder. Those killed were: Don Lathrum, Bob Berry, Will Burrows, Wiltran Stanteen, Jim Bryan, Angelo Greco, Myron Goodman, Jack Isbel.

Kirch-gons 1428 hrs.
Effective 54 Bomb Tonnage 135

The operational airfield at Kirch-Gons was located less than a mile from the center of the small rural village. The village itself was less than ten miles north of Hitler and his bunker Adlerhorst. The grass landing field appears to have limited regular use during the war years and no known permanent fighter unit assigned there in December of 1944. It was an ideal stopping-off point for refueling and replenishment of armament, however. The flight distance to the battlefront was less than 130 miles for this and each of the other targeted aerodromes in the area (Ettinghausen, Giessen, Merzhausen, Nidda). There was no paved runway, but fuel and ammunition were readily available. A branch rail line served both the southwest and northwest boundaries of the property. There were a group of workshop-type buildings on the southwest boundary that were connected by taxi track to the landing area. A small group of barracks were located off the southwest boundary, and there were a few stores buildings in the west corner. There was a dispersal area to the northwest with fifteen hardstands cut into the woods and fronted with a paved apron. These were also connected by taxi tracks to the landing area.

The 1st Combat Bombardment Wing's C group was assigned Kirch-Gons for the day. The lead formation came from the 91st Bomb Group flying out of Bassingbourn and departing at 1031 hours after a delay due to ground fog and the crowd at the air base due to the 303rd Bomb Group's presence due to a diversion after their previous mission. The 381st Bomb Group out of Ridgewell supplied the high squadron, and the 398th Bomb Group flying out of Nuthampstead supplied the low squadron. Assembly was made at the Bassingbourn buncher.at 11,000 feet, dropping to 10,000 feet on the way to the Channel. Since the 1st B group was delayed because of their conditions on the ground, the C group fell in directly behind the A group as they departed the English Coast at Clacton. They were also joined by the C group of the 41st Combat Bombardment Wing that was a composite of available aircraft from Great Ashfield and Grafton Underwood.

Sgt. Marion C. Hoffman, a tail gunner with the 91st Bomb Group, later described how he was amazed at the view from his position. He estimated he could see fifty to seventy-five miles to the rear and saw nothing but B-17s flying in ordered formation. He requested and was granted permission to come up to the front of the plane to see the view. The sight looking forward appeared to be another fifty miles of B-17s and, according to Hoffman, "It was the most awesome one could ever imagine."

Flying an excellent formation and arriving at Ostend at 1228 hours and 17,500 feet, they then continued their climb to a 22,000-feet bombing altitude. Just as they approached the IP, a message from the scouting force reported that the target weather conditions were excellent for visual bombing. Despite cutting the IP a little short, they dropped their bomb load at 1429 hours with excellent results, leaving the landing ground at Kirch-Gons unserviceable.

Follow-up review showed two concentrations totaling at least 200 bursts extending across the center of the landing ground and into the fields to the west. There were several hits on the small group of station buildings at the western edge of the airfields as well as the stores area at the northwest corner. A number of bursts were also seen on the rail siding along the perimeter. There were a number of hits across the Giessen-Butzbach rail line, as well as scattered bursts in fields to the northeast. Later images showed that five of the station buildings were destroyed with minor damage to several buildings in the wooded area nearby. The center of the landing ground was covered with deep craters. There was evidence of an explosion northwest of the main buildings. At least four aircraft were visible on the edge of the woods, though they had no place to go.

No enemy fighters were observed on this attack, and friendly fighter support was good throughout. As they rendezvoused and withdrew, the group flew slightly right of the briefed course. In the area of the front lines they made frequent minor variations in course to avoid the uncharted flak they had seen on the way in and on the horizon on the way out. The flak they experienced was light and inaccurate. They flew at 22,000 feet until about 1530 hours, crossing the continental coast at 1552 hours at 12,500 feet. Notified that Bassingbourn's runways were closed due to extremely poor weather, the 91st Bomb Group lead squadron was diverted to Bury St. Edmunds. The 398th Bomb Group low squadron was diverted to Ridgewell, the home base of the 381st Bomb Group. All three landed at approximately 1700 hours and began their Christmas celebration.

Mike Banta of the 91st Bomb Group, who flew as copilot on *Ma Ideel* piloted by Lt. Raisin on Christmas Eve, was only on his third mission. It was also his first experience of loss of lives and equipment. He recounted later that, though the mission began with take-off under impossible conditions, the crash of two aircraft with the loss of nine young airmen, his actual bombing mission was a "milk run," absent accurate flak or enemy attack fighters. His greatest discomfort of the day came on the return when the weather forced the entire Eighth Air Force to land all its aircraft on only three fields. Banta's plane was diverted to Bury St. Edmunds, the home of the 94th Bomb Group. There his crew found B-17s lined up by the hundreds, wingtip to wingtip. His crew, famished from the full day's mission, found that they had to wait in line for hours as the cook tried to feed nearly 900 airmen they had not expected.

Once fed, the visiting airmen looked for a place to sleep. They were told there was no room and they should try to catch some sleep in their aircraft. Though it was scrubbed the next morning, there had been a repeat mission scheduled for Christmas Day. The crews attempting to sleep in their unheated, uninsulated metal planes were told they could not use their electrically heated flying suits because batteries would be quickly drained without the engines running. The temperature for the night was in the teens. Banta said he had never in his life been so miserable from the cold. He thought he had slept thirty minutes total, if that.

Ready for an early breakfast, Banta and his crew walked past ice-covered aircraft and support equipment. They noted a de-icer truck rationing out pints of de-icing fluid on each wing and wondered how many would crash on takeoff. Fortunately, the "brass" had the same thought. By noon trucks arrived to transport the men back to their home base at Bassingbourn. Most collapsed into their bunks and slept the rest of Christmas day, a Christmas they would never forget.

Merzhausen 1428 hrs.
Effective 198 Bomb Tonnage 495

The largest force attacking a single target for the day was Merzhausen. The scale of this attack—larger than any other of the Christmas Eve mission—makes this a very intriguing target. The village of Merzhausen (Hesse) is of little note and located in a rural area about three miles west of Usingen and about six miles southwest of Ziegenberg Castle, the headquarters of Field Marshal Gerd von Rundstedt. A half mile behind the castle was Adlerhorst, Hitler's underground lair, camouflaged as a quaint village in the woods. In December of 1944, it was commonly believed by the Allies that von Rundstedt was the primary planner and commander of the Ardennes Offensive. Hitler's active role was not fully understood until after the war. The Allies knew that von Rundstedt had been using Ziegenberg as his personal headquarters and it was also understood that many of the Nazis' top leadership utilized the nearby aerodrome at Merzhausen throughout the war, particularly Hermann Goering. No evidence has been found that the attackers on Christmas Eve suspected that they were bombing in such close proximity to the Fuhrer himself.

The field at Merzhausen was the closest aerodrome to Adlerhorst of all the targets assigned for the day. The airfield was built in 1937, shortly before construction commenced on the Adlerhorst complex. The Adlerhorst was constructed according to plans from Martin Bormann and architectural designs by Albert Speer. Hitler is said to have found it too luxurious for his tastes and reputation. During the Battle for Britain Hitler deferred the Adlerhorst to the commander of the Luftwaffe, Hermann Goering, a man who certainly appreciated luxury. The proximity to the aerodrome at Merzhausen is assumed to have been a good fit for Commander Goering and his Luftwaffe cadre of command.

The airfield, like Adlerhorst, was disguised as country farm-houses and barns. Aircraft parked on the edge of the woods

Merzhausen bombing attack strike photo.

surrounding the landing area was covered with camouflaged net-ting. There was also a branch rail line that served the airstrip. The runway was a grass surface. There was ample storage for ammuni-tions and fuel, including an underground fuel storage located in the woods off the northwest boundary. There were a few buildings in the woods off the north and south boundaries. Flak gun emplace-ments were scattered around the property. The airfield had been attacked once before on September 5, 1944 by a low-level attack by VIII Fighter Command's P38 and P-47s. That attack claimed three Bf 110s, one ME 410, two Ju88s, three He 111s destroyed, plus one Fw190, two He 111s, one DO217, and four other unidentified air-craft damaged.

The Nazis had done an excellent job in early December of keep-ing credible intelligence of the planned Ardennes Offensive clear of the Allies' ULTRA intercepts. Certainly, it was clear that they were building manpower, equipment, and materiel on the Western Wall, but Generals Eisenhower and Bradley believed they would have to be crazy to launch a full-scale attack through the Ardennes. They believed that von Rundstedt was in charge and respected him as ca-pable and calculating. They were certain that he lacked the means, particularly in petroleum supplies, to initiate such a bold attack. And they saw nothing to dissuade themselves from this conclu-sion. Little did they suspect that the Fuhrer himself was leading the campaign from Adlerhorst. And from available information it does not appear that they knew he was in residence at the Adlerhorst.

On December 10 an intercept from II Jagdkorps, Jagddivisionen 1,3, and Jafue Mittelrhein indicating that "SS units are maintaining radio silence." Patton, who kept his own troops quiet on the air-waves just prior to a big attack, was immediately suspicious. Yet, Allied leadership remained convinced that it was only defensive strategy intended to block invasion. Then the surprise came on December 16. Despite the poor weather conditions, General Otto

Weyland of the XIX Tactical Air Command sent the 12th Squadron of the 19th Photographic Reconnaissance Group to scan the east Ardennes. Much to their surprise they received a heavy flak reception while flying over Merzhausen and Bad Nauheim. Then they were aggressively pursued by four FW-190s. Apparently, there was something of import going on in the Merzhausen-Ziegenberg-Bad Nauheim corridor. And it looks to have been something important enough to be information sent to the Mission 760 planners, though their focus was aerodromes rather than concealed Fuhrerbunkers.

The lineup for Merzhausen for the Sunday attack included 198 B-17s in a combined formation. (As the C group of the 1st Combat Bombardment Wing proceeded to Kirch-Gons, the D group led the attack on Merzhausen. The lead squadron was from the 91st Bomb Group in Bassingbourn. The high squadron came from the 381st Bomb Group, and the low squadron was made up of planes from the 398th Bomb Group. All three formed at the Bassingbourn buncher. There had been a brief delay at takeoff, which was being done in "zero-zero" visibility conditions. The fifth plane in the lead formation lost control in the fog and crashed seven minutes after takeoff, about eighteen miles away from the airfield, near a town called Shepworth. T/Sgt Vivian R. Chowning suffered a broken leg, the only injury in the crash.

Target conditions were excellent. The IP was reached at 1415 hours, though the formation cut the IP a little short. Bombs were away at 1429 hours. The bombing was all visual and the results were excellent. No enemy fighters were observed, and fighter support was good. There was light and inaccurate flak over the front lines both on penetration and withdrawal. On return the formation found conditions had deteriorated to the point where Bassingbourn was completely closed in. They were diverted to Bury St. Edmunds for the night. By the time they arrived, the best available accommodations were sleeping in their freezing aircraft. Years later S/

Sgt Kent Stafford, a waist gunner with the 401st Squadron in the Lt. Thomas Holmes crew, told his son one Christmas Eve: "I'm sure glad I'm not sleeping in my plane tonight."

Post-Christmas Eve attack analysis showed three concentrations of bursts totaling at least 235 on the landing ground, extending to the south and southwest. At least one and possibly two buildings were hit in the station buildings area, and there were four hits in the perimeter track. There was also a concentration of hits in a wooded dispersal area at the south side of the landing ground. Given the scale and resolution of the high-altitude photographs, no aircraft on the ground were readily identifiable.

There were other concentrations of approximately seventy-five bursts seen a little over a mile south-southwest of the landing ground in open fields and extending east-northeast into the built-up area of the town of Merzhausen. Almost a mile south of the target was a group of thirty hits in a wooded area. Half a mile to the northeast was a visible grouping of nineteen hits northeast of the landing ground with a possible hit on the railway line between Usingen and Wilhelmsdorf, the line that also had been severed at Giessen, a rail connection hub to Berlin.

Over the following six weeks aerial photos were taken regularly to evaluate the initial damage and steps taken to recover the field. By the middle of February there were two runs that were unobstructed by craters. One was about six hundred yards long running from west to east. The other was about the same length but ran from northeast to southwest. Most of the craters in the field appeared to remain despite the lapse of time. There were no aircraft found to be on the field. And by the end of January 1945, there were very few dignitaries visiting either Ziegenberg Castle or the neighboring Adlerhorst. Neither served their previous purpose as command and control centers for either von Rundstedt or Hitler. For his part, Hitler had retreated to Berlin and his last underground concrete bunker. He demanded that his staff join him and remain despite repeated brutal attacks on the capital of the Reich.

In retrospect and separated by more than seventy years, one might wonder if the significant size of the attacking force on this particular target wasn't overkill. Of course, damage to the landing field and the destruction of a major rail connection here and at Giessen eliminated the ease of use of either the Adlerhorst bunker or Ziegenberg Castle as command and control centers.

"Spoof" 1615 hrs.
Effective 26 Bomb Tonnage ?

At 1345 hours twenty-six aircraft took off from the 351st Bomb Group's station at Polebrook. Led by Major Leonard B. Roper, a Texan who was the operations officer for the 351st BG, their mission for the day was unique among the 2,046 planes sent out against the Hun on Christmas Eve. They took to the air as planes from the First Attack Force were completing their bomb runs and heading home, while other groups were still approaching their targets. Roper's squadrons gathered and circled at the buncher at Kings Cliffe, departing from there at 1448 hours. Just as the earlier formations had, they headed to Clacton on the coast. But instead of turning toward Belgium, they proceeded ninety miles northeast over the Channel, vectoring in a direction that would take them—if they stuck with it—to northern Holland and Germany. They headed directly toward one of the densest areas of German radar monitoring on the Continent. The radar grid was protecting the oft attacked cities of Emden, Wilhelmshaven, Bremerhaven, Bremen, Hamburg, and Kiel.

"Spoof" missions had been a regular part of the 8th's countermeasure operations. From December of 1943 to the end of the war, they were assigned to the 36th Bombardment Squadron, a special operations and electronic warfare unit with specially modified B-24s. Initially the 36th BS was assigned to the 482nd Bomb Group in Alconbury and, as part of the Carpetbagger Project, flew agents and supplies to resistance groups in the enemy-occupied countries. As the Eighth Air Force's only electronic warfare squadron specially equipped with B-24s able to jam German VHF communications, it flew both daylight raids and night missions with the RAF. In mid-December the 36th BS had been moved to the RAF Watton Station near Thetford, a rustic station with grass runways and muddy hardstands unable to accommodate the heavy B-24 when the ground was not solidly frozen. Though the 36th BS flew successful missions during the Battle of the Bulge, it does not appear to have flown on Christmas Eve. It flew on December 28 and 31 with jamming equipment which compromised German tank communications at the battlefront. They were able to fly again on January 2nd and 7th, this time interfering with ground communication with German-speaking operators Lt. Morris Burakoff and T/Sgt. Ernest Asseln. In January the 36th BS was returned to Alconbury for more reliable flying conditions.

The afternoon "spoof" flight on Christmas Eve was intended to be a distraction, and apparently using the 351st Bomb Group and not the 36th Bombardment Squadron was part of the spoof. The move was launched as formations from the First Attack Force were just completing their bomb runs and were making their way back to their home bases. The Germans were faced with a new game, and one headed in an unexpected direction. It would have been clear to radar monitors that the approaching bomber stream was devoid of fighter support. While distracting, as the aerodromes supporting the Ardennes Offensive were being brutally attacked, it was also inviting. As we know years later, much of the active and able Luftwaffe fighter strength had been moved to northern fields during the buildup in anticipation of the Ardennes Offensive. The

Germans had to decide whether this new and unescorted addition to the day's spectacular armada was a risk or not. They had to decide if it was worth checking on the distraction while so many bombers were over the Reich.

In the end the spoof formation solved the problem for German Intelligence. About ninety miles from the coast of England, at 1615 hours, twenty minutes after sunset, it dropped its bomb load, whatever that was, into the middle of the Channel. Then it quickly turned and returned to Polebrook with no further ado. Just as all the other formations who had successfully attacked their targets were finding, most of the air stations in England suddenly had zero/zero condition weather. The spoof formation from the 351st Bomb Group was diverted to the already crowded Ridgewell air base, where it remained until December 26.

"The first lesson is that you can't lose a war if you have command of the air, and you can't win a war if you haven't."

—Jimmy Doolittle

Chapter 10

THE TARGETS OF THE THIRD ATTACK FORCE

WHEREAS THE FIRST two attack forces of Mission 760 were comprised of B-17 Flying Fortresses, the third attack force, made up of the units of the Second Combat Wing, was flying B-24 Liberators. The targets for this attack group were primarily rail tracks, bridges, and marshalling yards along with roadways in addition to communications connections and centers. Despite the Allies' aggressive bombing campaign of 1944 and the successful securing of air superiority in the skies over Europe, rail traffic in Germany continued to succeed with monumental movement. POW crews were enslaved masters of rapid track repair. From November to December and under the strictest of secrecy, 3,000 special trains loaded with soldiers, weapons, ammunition, and supplies were sent westward over the Rhine in preparation for the Ardennes Offensive.

Ahrweiler 1506 hrs.
Effective 54 Bomb Tonnage 144.3

Ahrweiler is located in the wine country of the Ahr River valley about nine miles southwest of Bonn. A small town, it has an ancient history, leaving its medieval fortified walls up until World War II. It also had a notable Jewish population with medieval roots, but the synagogue was desecrated on Kristallnacht in 1938 and the last of the Jews were transported to concentration camps in 1942. The town possessed a bridge strong enough to carry heavy military equipment across the Ahr River. This bridge was a key link between the Ludendorff Bridge at Remagen to Euskirchen and on to the battlefront in the Bulge. There were also extensive rail yards.

Ahrweiler had been bombed on 23 December by forty-eight B-26 aircraft of the 391st Bomb Group (M) from the Ninth Air Force. Flying from a base in France, this was one of the few attacks made that day in the below minimum weather. It was a disastrous mission for the 391st. They failed to rendezvous in the poor visibility and were bounced by more than fifty enemy fighters. At the end of that ambush, sixteen aircraft were missing in action and the returning planes were badly battle-damaged. On the 24th Ahrweiler was revisited by fifty-four aircraft of the 20th Combat Bombardment Wing Bomb, dropping 144.3 tons of bombs. They included groups from 93rd and 446th Bomb Groups. The aiming points were rail lines, the canal, and roads.

The 93rd Bomb Group, "The Traveling Circus," formed up as planned over Hardwick and were joined by a formation from the 446th out of Bungay. Difficulties arose as they approached the target. They were bombing visually and missed the Initial Point because of a partially frozen river and crowding by the 96th Wing. The large attacking force was comprised for five formations, two each in an A group and a B group in addition to a C group comprised of 93rd and 444th Bomb Groups aircraft. The A group attacked by squadron, though its high right squadron was interfered with by friendly B-17s apparently returning from the bombing of Giessen and at an altitude close to that of the attacking formation. That high right squadron of the A group also had an early release, and seven other aircraft in the formation dropped on his lead.

This target was at one of the three potential intersection points in the original planning. Seven bombers of the high right squadron were able to bomb, though three found it necessary to divert to avoid collision. Those three aircraft identified a secondary target but found themselves unable to drop because the release wires on the lead craft had been severed by flak and were inoperable. They turned and vectored to their home base because no second runs over target had been authorized for the mission without specific command approval.

Ahrweiler bombing attack strike photo.

The B group's high echelon lead squadron also experienced problems. Led by Lt. Aden with nine aircraft from the 93rd Bomb Group, it was primarily comprised of aircraft from the 446th Bomb Group. The lead dropped on target okay, but the deputy lead had their rudder shot away by flak and jettisoned their bombs in the target area. Following his release seven planes flying with toggliers rather than a bombardier dropped in the area, but not on target. The leader of the high right formation had his bomb release system shot away and was one of three planes that returned to base with load.

The after-mission reviews show that a concentration of at least ninety bursts hit among houses extending east from the eastern side of the town, across the road bridge over the Ahr River, a tributary of the Rhine. They extended into open fields. Hits were visible on the secondary road to the north end of the bridge. Three hits seen to the secondary road bridge were also noted.

Arzfeld 1443 hrs.
Effective 10 Bomb Tonnage 25.5

Arzfeld is a small farming community with a population of less than 1,000 people located about six and a half miles east of the Luxembourg border and a bridge at Dasburg crossing the Our River into Luxembourg. It is roughly twelve and a half miles southwest of Schoenecken and fifteen and a half miles northwest of Bitburg. Today a street identified as "Bahnhofstrasse" marks the location of a long-gone rail line. The main road through town connects Prum, a strategic hub with Dasburg on the frontier with Luxembourg. Bastogne lies twenty-five miles west of Arzfeld, though the terrain is rugged and the roads were marginal for much of that distance. The road through Arzfeld was heavily used by retreating German troops after their defeat in the Battle of the Bulge, and by the middle of January what was left of it was blocked by hundreds of trucks and tanks along with soldiers on foot.

On Christmas Eve of 1944, however, Arzfeld was not an identified target in the 8th Air Force plan. Yet in the heat of the action ten aircraft of the 389th BG accidentally released twenty-five and a half tons of bombs on the village. Aerial observation conducted on 25 December reported an area of approximately fifty bursts in an open area about one mile southeast of the town.

Arzfeld bombing attack strike photo.

Bitburg 1436 hrs.
Effective 35 Bomb Tonnage 87

Bitburg is located about thirteen miles north of Pfalzel and fifteen miles north of Trier. It is fourteen miles west of Wittlich and situated in the Kyll River valley. Since its founding by Romans, Bitburg has been a crossroads, a place to stop while traveling from the southwest of Europe to the northeast. The whole region has been a pawn in European geopolitics and wars for the past 1,000 years. Between the wars, the economy in Bitburg and the region around it had tended to be stagnant, though since the rise of Prussia, it was best known for Bitburger Bier, a widely marketed product in and out of Germany. Hitler recognized the strategic location of the ancient city and its transportation links. He is said to have visited a number of times and even maintained an office in Bitburg.

Just prior to the arrival of Hitler's hoped-for cloud cover, reports of a buildup of German forces were emanating from Bitburg. On December 14, a Luxembourg woman by the name of Elise Dele reported to US First Army headquarters that she had seen "many vehicles, pontoons and boats and other river crossing equipment" coming from there. Though seen by some as an indication of an impending attack through the Ardennes, these reports were generally ignored by General Omar Bradley and his command staff. They were convinced by their own advances that the Hun was only reinforcing his western wall.

Two and a half miles north of Bitburg was a Luftwaffe airfield at Putzhohe. It was used early in the war during the invasion of Luxembourg, Belgium, and France, but was later abandoned and converted to a POW camp for captured French soldiers. Five miles southwest of Bitburg was another base, Wolsfelderberg. It was also used during the invasion to the west, but was rarely used after 1941 other than as an emergency landing field. It was decked out as a mock airfield, complete with plywood dummies of the German bomber Heinkel HE 111. A third air base in the Bitburg area was Wolsfelderberg, the largest air base in the southern Eifel region, complete with a concrete

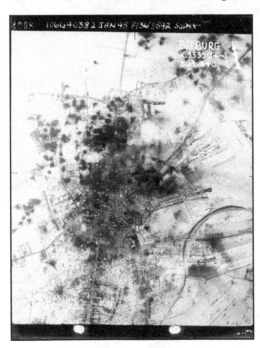

Bitburg bombing attack strike photo.

rather than grass landing field. It was used for transport between Germany and the German forces in Italy. It was also a test site for an experimental micro ramming aircraft being developed in 1944. Wolsfelderberg was bombed in the summer of 1944 and ceased to be of importance to the Luftwaffe after the D-Day invasion put Germany in a defensive mode. During the middle of December, the area around this base had been the site of numerous attacks and dogfights, including one on December 17 between fighters of JG2 and the Allies 474th and 428th Fighter Groups. The Americans had come in to strafe the abundant transport passing through the area. Despite damage to the air base, early in 1945, Wolsfelderberg aerodrome became the command base for the Wehrmacht 7th Army's LXXX Infantry Corps.

The target areas for Christmas Eve were the railways, roads, the airfield, and built-up areas. The B group of the 445th Bomb Group taking off from Tibenham led the attack on Bitburg. Five planes aborted for various reasons along the way, though no combat losses were experienced. One squadron of ten aircraft and one element of three from the 389th Bomb Group were assigned to the composite E group of the 2nd Combat Bombardment Wing. They were joined by four aircraft from the 453rd Bomb Group, others from the 448th Bomb Group, and followed the B group. That second formation was led over the target by Bombardier Lt. Orville F. Burda. Navigator Jack Woolsey of the 564th Squadron of the 389th Bomb Group had mailed a letter to his family in New York on December 23rd saying, "We hope to get a mission to Christmas and if we do we're going to take some chalk out to the planes and address the Christmas presents accordingly."

Returning crews reported a large area of camouflage netting just east of the Kyll river and south of the town of Kyllburg. Presumably this was protecting supplies or equipment for the advancing German ground troops. Fresh tank and truck tracks in the snow were also observed. The bombing results were mixed. Damage to rail and rolling stock was considered excellent. Major damage was done to the built-up area of this ancient city founded by the Romans, but damage to the airstrip was only moderate. Follow-up aerial photo reconnaissance revealed that the main roadway passing from Trier to the north of Bitburg was heavily damaged and blocked with craters and debris. The business and residential center of the city was also seriously damaged, including its medieval palace, though the area of the airfield was generally intact.

Blumenthal 1441 hrs.
Effective 8 Bomb Tonnage 21.75

Blumenthal is located five miles from the Belgium border and just south of Hurtgenwald, the deep and rugged forest where the Americans and Germans had been carrying out a bloody and bitter ground battle through nearly impossible terrain since the 19th of September into the bitter winter. The Americans assumed German defense of the area was merely an effort to defend their western front, unaware of the massive staging going on in the region in preparation for Hitler's surprise offensive on December 16. Though Blumenthal was a small village, it contained rail and road connections that were critical to the Wehrmacht's movement from Euskirchen in the east and the Prum region to the south to a surprise attack across the border and on to Malmedy, just seventeen miles distant.

Despite the fact that the German force had far advanced from this point by Christmas Eve, the attack on Blumenthal as a target of opportunity by 458th Bomb Group temporarily damaged the supply lines to the advancing German troops already in Belgium. This area close to the front lines of the starting point of Hitler's Ardennes Offensive contained reserve troops and supplies.

The 458th Bomb Group of the 96th Combat Bombardment Wing left Horsham St. Faiths at 1016 hours, flying two formation groups designated as A and B, with the lower left and lead boxes of B group attacking the primary target of Prum, while the other squadrons fanned out to a series of secondary targets. These included Blumenthal, Hellenthal, and Wetteldorf. The A group went on to Schoenecken. Due to the congestion in the area, at one point the A group was crowding squads of the B group. Target sighting problems were also encountered due to the snow cover. Though the visibility was clear, from an altitude of 20,000 feet it was difficult to visually target road intersections and rail intersections and overpasses in a cluster of five small villages all in a circle about two and a half miles in diameter and with a defense of flak guns.

Bollendorf 1433 hrs.
Target of Opportunity Effective 1 Bomb Tonnage 3

Located on the Sauer River southwest of Bitburg and northwest of Trier, this tiny village possessed a rail line and a vehicle bridge connecting Germany and Luxembourg across the Sauer River. This link was used on December 16 for the initial attack and it was one of the crossing points for German 7th Army as they secured the southern portion of the "bulge" into Luxembourg and surrounded Bastogne. After the war, Bombardier Lt. Raymond Parshall of the 44th Bomb Group described how his crew assigned to the formation attacking Wittlich broke away to attack this critical secondary target. They bombed visually without interference, debilitating the roadway, bridge, and rail connection with six 1,000-pound bombs. With westward Wehrmacht traffic stopped on the German side of the river, Patton's 3rd Army began to secure the land south of Bastogne on the Luxembourg side. Bollendorf was attacked as a "target of opportunity," but its strategic location made it a high-impact hit.

Bonn 1404 hrs.

Target of Opportunity Effective 43 Bomb Tonnage 107.5

Bonn, located on the Rhine River, was one of the key crossing points of the natural divide created by the river. South of Cologne, an ancient city ravaged and bridgeless by repeated city-busting attacks in the prior twenty-four months, Bonn's Rhine crossing was still intact. It had been an undetected artery for Hitler's secret amassing of the Ardennes Offensive attack force. In the battle plan it was located in the territory where the Wehrmacht's 15th Army was staged and anchored the west end of a graceful bridge across the Rhine. That bridge remained functional until May 8, 1945, when the retreating Wehrmacht destroyed it after they evacuated to the other side of the river. Prior to that Bonn was a crossroads for both rail and autobahn movement of troops, supplies, ammunition, and equipment integral to the Ardennes Offensive buildup. Under Hitler's battle plan, the 15th Army was to be part of a secondary flanking attack on the Allies, an action that never occurred. Yet the cold and hungry Germans continued to fight aggressively on through early January in the extreme cold, ice, and snow to delay the Americans' advance into Germany and on to Berlin.

The Bonn Hangelar aerodrome had been utilized by the Luftwaffe I/NJG 4, NSG 1, and I/SG 4 during the winter of 1944–5, and it was not on the primary target list for Mission 760. But it was hit as a target of opportunity by aircraft of the 398th Bomb Group diverting from Ettinghausen and aircraft of the 94th and 95th Bomb Groups diverting from Koblenz and Daun. The RAF followed up with additional bombing of the Bonn Hangelar aerodrome during the night of December 24/25.

Cochem 1443 hrs.
Effective 11 Bomb Tonnage 28

Cochem is located about twenty-three miles southwest of Koblenz on the Mosel River. It lies on the Koblenz-Trier Rail Line and at the edge of the three-mile-long Kaiser Wilhelm Tunnel, the longest rail tunnel in Germany. This route also connects Trier with Berlin. Cochem is about thirty-three air miles from Pfalzel, but on the same rail system that snaked twice that distance along the Mosel river valley. Like Pfalzel, it was in a position to support the original placement of the Wehrmacht's Seventh Army and keep it supplied as the

Cochem reconnaissance photo showing Rhine bridge destruction.

fighting continued into January and until the Allies conquered the west side of the Rhine in February, crossing the Rhine on March 7, 1945.

There had been active air combat over Cochem on December 17, while Wehrmacht ground troops were moving rapidly into the bulge. In the midst of the intolerable weather and poor visibility, a bevy of P-47s were active in the region, driving Luftwaffe Lt. Heinz Krause spinning to his death in his Fw-109 into Cochem. In one of the few bomber attacks successfully completed on December 23, bombers of the 1st Bomb Division, with a primary target of Ehrang marshalling yard near Trier, sent squadrons to Cochem and

Idar-Oberstein to attack the rail yards in each of those towns.

The Christmas Eve aiming points were a bridge, rail lines, road-ways, and built-up areas. The flight plan for the 2nd Air Division's 2nd Combat Bombardment Wing brought the A group of the 389th Bomb Group, "the Sky Scorpions," to the target area of Cochem at 1443 hours. On the way in they had sighted nine or ten Me109s, but there was no engagement. Ground haze and a frozen bombsight in the lead formation caused targeting problems immediately. The deputy lead was not able to respond quickly enough to pick up the assigned targets. Aircraft were detached to alternate targets of opportunity at Kirn and St. Wendel. After completing their bomb runs, the entire 389th Bomb Group returned to their base at Hethel without incident. There was also an element of the 453rd Bomb Group flying out Old Brackenham that were part of this A group formation.

Success at the targets that were hit ranged from "fair" to "excellent." Two roundhouses suffered structural damage, and five craters were visible in the yard area. The rail embankment immediately north of the north entrance to Cochem rail tunnel showed some displacement of tracks, though at least half of the through lines were intact. The road bridge crossing the Mosel east of the tunnel entrance was collapsed for a distance of 170 feet. There was also damage to businesses and residences adjacent to the rail center.

Daun 1448 hrs
Effective 24 Bomb Tonnage 58.1

Daun also lies in the Vulkaneifel, near Gerolstein and on the Lieser River. It was also a station on the Trans Eifel Railroad at the time of the war. Less than two miles south of Daun is the village of Gemund. In the weeks before the 16 December surprise attack by the Germans, US night fighters had reported a buildup of military equipment visible in that area. Their report was dismissed as nothing out of the ordinary and fitting with the Allied narrative at the time, namely that the Wehrmacht knew they were losing the war and were building a strong defense at the Western Wall to delay the obvious. The hubris of success on the battlefield since D-Day left the intelligence experts blind to the possibility of an offensive move coming from the east as it did. By 24 December it was clear that the original intelligence conclusion was mistaken. The Christmas Eve aiming points for Daun were the roadways, rail lines, and the built-up area.

Twenty-four aircraft from the 467th Bomb Group, "the Rackheath Aggies," mounted the attack as part of the force pounding marshalling yards at nearby Gerolstein and Mayen. Their attack resulted in extensive hits to the roads, rail line, and built-up area.

Eller 1440 hrs.
Effective 32 Bomb Tonnage 89

The quaint and picturesque village of Eller is situated on the Mosel River deep in the wine country of the Mosel Valley. It is the opposite end of the three-mile-long Kaiser Wilhelm railroad tunnel from Cochem and a major link. That tunnel entry and the continuation of the Trier-to-Berlin rail line were the target of this attack. That rail line and tunnel also connected Germany with the rich coal and steel resources of the Saarland. The attack force came from the 491st Bomb Group, led by an aircraft

Eller Rail Tunnel Entrance Prior to 24 December 1944 bombing.

from 44th Bomb Group, and it successfully closed the entrance of the tunnel. A bridge over the Mosel River was also hit as a target of opportunity but had already been damaged by an attack by the 9th Air Force medium bombers on the previous day.

The lead of the attacking squadron, aircraft 42:50668 from the 44th Bomb Group, developed mechanical problems with its number two engine, which failed and had to be feathered. Unable to keep up, the lead aborted and left the formation over Belgium. The deputy lead took command and bombed visually, dropping a concentration of fifty hits on the track leading into the tunnel at Eller. A rake of railway wagons at the entrance to the tunnel likely took a direct hit, interrupting both rail and road transport to the battlefront. After the attack the bridge at Eller appeared to be impassible. There were groups of craters at each end, a hole stretched two-thirds of the way across the width of the bridge, and one track was cut. There may have been damage to the pier foundations at the southern end.

Euskirchen 1447 hrs.
Effective 62 Bomb Tonnage 174.4

The town of Euskirchen was a rail and road hub located in the North Rhine Westphalia region, at the heart of Germany's buildup in anticipation of the Ardennes Offensive. It is west of the Rhine in an area that was the staging area for Hitler's offensive. It was a transit point to Gemund, an area where Allied night fighters had spotted a buildup of equipment prior to December 16 but discounted it as routine. About fifteen miles southwest of Bonn, its roads and rails extended in all directions, providing easy of transport of men, machines, and supplies. Those transportation links provided for the movement of the Wehrmacht's Fifth and Sixth Panzer Armies' supplies, munitions, and replacement equipment after that army had retreated to the Ardennes in response to the Allies' advance after D-Day.

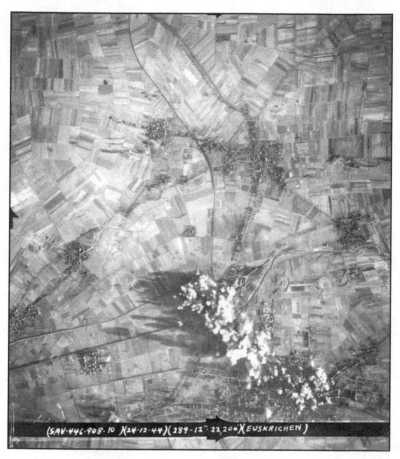

Euskirchen attack strike photo.

Euskirchen was also one of the transportation hubs supporting the Sixth Panzer Army, a newly created unit formed in the autumn of 1944 specifically for the purpose of launching the Ardennes
Offensive. One of its most notorious units was Kampfgruppe Peiper,
the lead attack unit on December 16, 1944 responsible for the atro-
cious massacre of eighty-four captured US soldiers near Malmedy.
Sixty-two aircraft of the 20th Combat Bombardment Wing were assigned to hit road and railway junctions. One squadron of the 446th
Bomb Group began bombing from 22,200 feet at 1447 hours. Four

squadrons of the 448th Bomb Group followed up four minutes later, bombing from altitudes of 20,000 feet to 34,400 feet. The cover of ground snow caused them some difficulty, obscuring the actual targets. Despite the sighting difficulties, at least 1,000 bursts were seen blanketing the pinpoint and within the surrounding town. At least twenty direct hits were made to the railway line leading into the east end of the marshalling yard. Another fifteen hits were made to the road junction. The targeted rail bridge was hit directly at the approaches at each end. The approach to vehicle bridge crossing the Erft River was also hit with three craters. Fourteen bursts were counted on the railway line branch to the north and at least twenty bursts were seen in the targeted marshalling yard. Approximately 200 bursts were seen in open fields one mile northwest of the target. Four of these were direct hits on the road between Euskirchen and the one-time village of Lommersun, which is today a large cemetery.

Gerolstein 1446 hrs.
Effective 59 Bomb Tonnage 174.4

Gerolstein is located on the Kyll River in the Vulcan-Eifel, a mineral-rich volcanic region that has been occupied since the Stone Age. Its location set it up as a critical rail hub in the center of some of the most challenging topography in the area. At the time of the war six different major rail lines converged in Gerolstein connecting to Cologne, Euskirchen, Trier, Daun, Kaiseresch, Andernach, Prum, Mayen, Koblenz, and St. Vith. Much of the rail system is built deep in the river valley with the city on the heights on both sides of it. Gerolstein was bombed so often from the beginning of Hitler's Ardennes Offensive until the end of the war that 80 percent of the city was left in ruins. Repairs to the rail system were hastily made shortly after each attack, typically by POW work crews. According to one such POW soldier, Edward Kilburg of Bellevue,

Iowa, they were instructed to run for shelter if a subsequent attack was made while they were working and threatened that after that attack was over they should immediately return to their work. If anyone tried to escape, every tenth man would be executed until the entire work crew was accounted for.

The aiming points on Christmas Eve were the marshalling yard, rail lines, built-up areas , and roadways. 59 aircraft from the B and C groups of the 96th Combat Bombardment Group included aircraft from the 466th and 467th Bomb Groups. The overall damage to the area was considered good. Approximately fifty craters were visible

Gerolstein attack strike photo.

in the station sidings and at least sixteen wagons were derailed and damaged. Through tracks running south to Paris and northwest to Prum were cut in several places. Damage was also done to commercial and residential areas in the town.

Hillesheim 1436 hrs.
Effective 10 Bomb Tonnage 22.5

Hillesheim was a target of opportunity for the high right element of the B group from the 453rd Bomb Group of the 2nd Combat Bombardment Wing. Located just north of Pelm and Gerolstein, Hillesheim is twenty-four miles west of the 453rd's primary target, Mayen. A small village, Hillesheim was located on the Eifelbahn rail line connecting the ground battle in Belgium with Wehrmacht reinforcements, supplies, and equipment located to the east. The line also provided connection by rail from Cologne to Trier by way of Euskirchen and Gerolstein.

Though the lead and low left squadrons had no trouble picking up the target at Mayen visually, the high right squadron had inadvertently passed it. Squadron lead bombardier, Lt. Robert Ronaldes, continued on to the rail connections at Hillesheim and bombed visually, experiencing only meager flak and without sighting any enemy aircraft. The deputy lead reported that "the target was too small pick up (on H2X)" so he bombed on the leader's drop. Later analysis evaluated to bombing on target as "good" with hits on the road that was a critical choke point and the built-up areas of the town.

Kirn 1455 hrs.
Target of Opportunity Effective 11 Bomb Tonnage 29

Kirn is a small town in the Nahe River valley with the unlucky distinction of having a rail station on the Nahe Valley Railway that connects Bingen on the Rhine with Saarbrucken. It also connects to Bad Kreuznach—eighteen miles to the east—and Mainz. The town itself is a market town that dates back to prehistoric times. Before the war it was internationally known for its tanning of fine leather. It had a modest Jewish population dating from the Middle Ages up until Kristallnacht in 1938. The Holocaust Memorial at Yad Vashem lists fifty prominent residents of Kirn who died in concentration camps.

On Christmas Eve 1944, Kirn became a target of opportunity for the 389th Bomb Group. As three squadrons were approaching their primary target at Cochem, the bombsight of the lead of the lower formation froze up and Bombardier Lt. S. Beno called for the deputy lead to take over. It was too late for the deputy to bomb the primary target. Navigator Lt. Walter G. Klose quickly plotted a route to Kirn and its double-track train station that was supplying the Wehrmacht troops in the Ardennes. The attack damaged the rail and vehicular roadway.

Koblenz 1348 hrs: 1st Force, 1515.5 hrs. 2nd Force, throughout the day for A/C or formations separated from their units.
Effective 42 Bomb Tonnage 1105

Koblenz is a large commercial center at the confluence of the Rhine and Mosel rivers, a focal point of river, rail, and roadway traffic. The Romans gave the city its name in 9 BC, "Castrum ad Confluentas," the Camp at the Confluence. It has been a critical communications center for over 2,000 years and the target of warriors for as long. An ominous fortification, Ehrenbreitstein sits on the towering summit on the east side of the Rhine, just opposite of the juncture of the two great rivers. The summit has held fortifications since prehistoric times. During World War II Koblenz and the Ehrenbreitstein fortress across the river were stations for antiaircraft guns. The rail yards and bridges of the city connected rail transportation to the north, west, and south and was a key juncture in all three directions, especially during the buildup prior to the Ardennes Offensive. Sitting parallel to the Rhine, it provided alternatives to the Germans as the Allies applied pressure in other locations. Boats on the Mosel River could easily transport personnel, supplies, and equipment from the rail yards at Koblenz up to Trier, Ruwer, and the port at Eller. Though Hitler's 7th Army, the southernmost army as well as the most poorly staffed in the Ardennes buildup and attack, Koblenz was critical to positioning and supplying it.

Throughout air war the location of Koblenz made it a popular target and target of opportunity for bombers who for one reason or another had failed to drop on their primary. That was certainly the case for the Christmas Eve mission. Planned targets for the day included the marshalling yards and two power plants serving the area. Before the day was out Koblenz was visited by aircraft from the 91st, 93rd, 94th, 351st, 381st, 389th, 401st, and 457th Bomb Groups. The 457th flying from Glatton began the day with marginal conditions. They also had several aircraft joining their formation from other bases because of weather condition diversions from a previous mission on December 19th when poor visibility had split their squadrons in attacks on Schleiden, Stadtkyll, and Koblenz. Koblenz was again their assigned target on the 24th. Initially, six planes were able to take off before an accident killing one crew member closed the runway. Two others from another field joined them at the buncher, and the formation of eight was directed to join the 401st Bomb Group forming over Deenethorpe.

Ray Armor, a pilot with the 398th Bomb Group who was targeting the rail marshalling yard at Koblenz, recalling the start of the day said, "I can remember lots of times taking off with no forward vision from the cockpit because of the ground fog. It was necessary to keep the plane straight down the runway as it raced past. This was not a very comfortable way to take off, with a plane heavily loaded and carrying a full bomb bay." On his return Christmas Eve, he found thirty-six diverted aircraft all arriving for landing at one

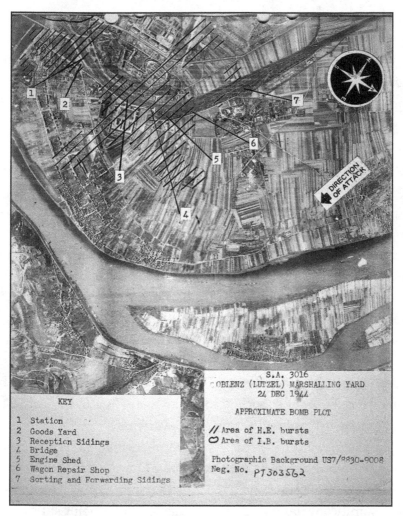

S.A. 3016
COBLENZ (LUTZEL) MARSHALLING YARD
24 DEC 1944

APPROXIMATE BOMB PLOT

// Area of H.E. bursts
⌒ Area of I.B. bursts

Photographic Background US7/?830-9008
Neg. No. P7303562

KEY
1 Station
2 Goods Yard
3 Reception Sidings
4 Bridge
5 Engine Shed
6 Wagon Repair Shop
7 Sorting and Forwarding Sidings

Koblenz marshalling yard bombing reconnaissance photo.

time, an incredible traffic problem. Pilots were all suffering from fatigue and the planes were all running low on gas. He recalled looking out and seeing two other planes on the final approach with his plane, one on each side, each trying to "out-chicken" the others, each concerned about their actual remaining fuel levels. "Then," Armor noted, "we landed right behind someone else and raced to get off the runway before the guy behind ran up our tail."

Copilot Robert H. Dee of the 398th Bomb Group's 601st Squadron wrote in his diary that his target for the day was two power plants in Koblenz. The attack was a "b" plan, taken on after formation delays prevented them from a rendezvous with their first assigned target formation. He was flying with a new crew piloted by 2/Lt. Bornstedt to check them out. They were delayed in the cold and fog on the field by the crash of two planes ahead of them. In one the bombardier had been killed as was a member of the ground crew attempting to help him get free of the wreckage.

Dee's plane was flying low squadron with a composite group from the 381st in Ridgewell and 91st in Bassingbourn. Because of their delayed takeoff they missed the planned rendezvous. Trailing their assigned group and once over the battle lines they found themselves in moderate but accurate flak for nearly forty-five minutes. Though their tail gunner wasn't injured, there were multiple holes all around him. The flak had also punctured the supplemental "Tokyo" gas tanks. After dropping their load of thirty-eight 100-pound bombs, they returned to England without incident, but found their home base socked in. They were diverted to Tattleston and then on to an already crowded Lavenham.

Later in the afternoon forty-two bombers made a second visit to the marshalling yards at Koblenz as a target of opportunity. They included aircraft from the 351st and the 457th Bomb Groups. The most significant damage that day was to choke point sidings and bridges critical to moving freight through the yard, rather than the expansive sorting yard itself.

Mayen 1445 hrs.
Effective 59 Bomb Tonnage 152.5

The city of Mayen is located on the Nette River as it comes out of the Eifel Mountain Range and enters the Koblenz Plain. It is located sixteen miles west of Koblenz. Mayen has long been referred to as "the Gateway to the Eifel," the German range just east of the Ardennes. It was the staging area for Hitler's attack in November and December of 1944. Mayen was a connecting rail junction for traffic from Koblenz to Gerolstein, Bonn, Cologne, and St. Vith to the north. It also connected those cities with Trier and Pfalzel to the west.

Because of its strategic location for the movement of the Wehrmacht, Mayen was bombed multiple times during the war, the previous time on 12 December by the 387th Bomb Group of the 9th Air Force. By the time the war ended, 90 percent of the buildings in the city were leveled.

On December 24th the aiming points were roads, the rail junction, and rolling stock. A total of fifty-nine B-24s from the 2nd Combat Bombardment Wing's B group, comprised of aircraft from the 453rd Bomb Group departing from Old Buckenham, were joined by eleven from the 445th Bomb Group departing from Tibenham. Together they executed the attack on Mayen. The lead and low left squadrons attacked Mayen, and the high right separated out to attack a target of opportunity, Hillesheim. End-of-mission reports indicate no presence of enemy fighters; only meager flak was experienced at Mayen and none at Hillesheim.

The C group followed to the target at Mayen, bombing visually by squadrons. Its low-left component was cut out on the bomb run by another group and had to dogleg. By the time the bombardier picked up the target again, he had a very abbreviated run. His results were fair. The other groups all reported good results at interrogation. The composite group led by a crew from the 389th Bomb Group experienced come confusion in the crowded attack and left some doubt as to whether they had the correct MPI (targeted Mean Point of Impact for optimal formation bombing). The overall results of this group were evaluated as fair, though damage to rail and rolling stock was good.

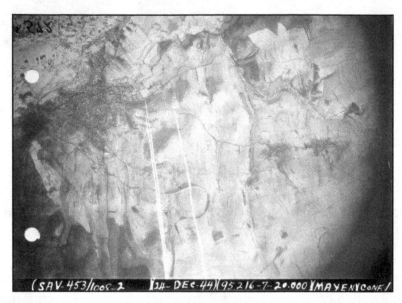

(SAV-453/1008-2   24-DEC-44)(95 216-7-20.000)(MAYENYCONE)

Mayen bombing strike photo.

Nettersheim 1441 hrs.
Target of Opportunity Effective 1 Bomb Tonnage 2.5

Nettersheim was hit as a target of opportunity, just twelve miles in from the Belgian border. The town contained a significant north-south rail line, train station, and marshalling yard for movement of troops, supplies, and equipment to the front. It was also the junction point for improved roads from north to south and northeast to Cologne. There were armed bunkers just outside of the town, part of the Siegfried Line, Germany's West Wall fortification.

Nettersheim was not on the original primary target list, but as the day wore on, bombers from the Third Force's 20th Combat Bombardment Wing were spread out aggressively and visually attacking rail and road connections just behind the advancing German line. Post-mission reports for the 446th Bomb Group, flying with aircraft from the 93rd and the 448th Bomb Groups, indicate that they hit at least seven "unknown targets." The actions of three crews not bombing the primary targets of Ahrweiler and Euskirchen are recorded. One from the 93rd Bomb Group had left the formation and, sighting on rail and roads, experienced engine problems and jettisoned his payload over an "unknown target" short of the intended. Another developed a gas leak, aborted, and returned to Bungay with its bombs. A third made the bomb run with the formation over Rheinbach but experienced a bomb rack malfunction. While flying the sixteen miles southwest, the malfunction was corrected, and the bombardier sighted on the rail and road junctions in the center of Nettersheim. Evaluation reported the damage to the target area to have been "good."

A later reconnaissance photo shows the Rheinbach target marshalling target had generally been missed by all bombing in the area.

Oberettingen ("Ober") 1446 hrs.
Target of Opportunity Effective 9 Bomb Tonnage 18.625

Oberettingen, located just a mile west of Hillesheim, was a small town identified simply as "Ober" on many of the documents of the day. It is located on a railhead connecting cities of the east along the Rhine Valley with the combat on the front. Nine aircraft of the 467th Bomb Group in a one-and-a-half-minute flyover from 21,600 feet at 1446 hours leveled the town with more than eighteen tons of explosives. Given its position as a railhead serving the advancement of German troops and supplies to the rapidly advancing battlefront, it was considered an excellent target of opportunity.

Pelm 1441 hrs.
Target of Last Resort Effective 9 Bomb Tonnage 24

Pelm is a small village located just two miles east of the major rail marshalling yard in Gerolstein and on rails that feed that marshalling yard. The village is an ancient settlement dating back to Roman times and sits beneath the Medieval Kasselburg castle. It was a target of last resort for the 445th Bomb Group. An element of nine aircraft ran into problems when the lower left element was overrunning the lead and had to "s" on the run to maintain order in the formation. In their maneuvering to order the attack, the telescope drive cable broke, limiting their ability to do precision targeting. They were experiencing light but very accurate flak. They picked up the primary target, Bitburg, too late to swing the squadron into position. They dropped smoke markers on the group ahead and then had an accidental release with the entire squadron dropping on that error. One can imagine that with so many things going wrong and the intensity of the flak, some among the crew might have been thinking that they would never be going home alive.

While the rest of their forces were attacking Mayen and Bitburg, the nine aircraft addressed this aiming point at Pelm which contained both road and rail "communications centers" supporting the Wehrmacht advance to the west. Despite all their difficulties, their results were considered excellent. The mission planners might have considered the damage superfluous, but, coupled with the attacks on the same rail line as it progressed westward to Gerolstein and Schoenecken, it became a triple play guaranteeing that there would be no quick resumption of troop, munitions, equipment, or supplies heading to the front if they were not already in place. It was a good day's work for the airmen, and they returned to East Anglia safely.

Pfalzel 1351 hrs.
Effective 28 Bomb Tonnage 25.3

The B group of the 392nd Bomb Group left Wendling on the tails of the A group of the same bomb group. They, too, were led by a crew and aircraft from the 44th Bomb Group equipped with Gee-H radio navigation system and H2X Mickey radar. Cpt. McDonnel of the 44th BG flew lead. The lead bombardier for this crew was 1/Lt J.E. Bennett. This crew successfully led the 392nd formation to the target while avoiding interference from the A group in such a tight bombing location on both sides of the Mosel Valley within a half hour of each other. Two-hundred-and-fifty-pound bombs were dropped on Pfalzel rather than the 500-pounders dropped by the A group across the river. The citizens of Pfalzel experienced a greater volume of less potent bombs than their neighbors across the river. There the aiming points were where the roads, rail lines, a rail bridge, and the built-up area of equipment, warehouses, businesses, shops, stores, and homes all converge. Fair to good results were achieved by the B

Wing. Both the lead plane from the 44th Bomb Group and a plane from the 392nd Bomb Group experienced problems with a rack of bombs hanging up, further complicating their attack.

Pfalzel is located on the northern bank of the Mosel River, directly across from the village of Ruwer and downstream from Trier. Site of an ancient Roman settlement, it is situated on a plain that has long held a relatively large harbor that can accommodate the offloading of equipment, materiel, vehicles, supplies, and manpower delivered by ship through Germany's extensive river system from and to the Rhine, Main, Saar, and Mosel rivers. Behind the harbor is a large railroad marshalling yard with trackage heading north into the Ardennes through tunnels and south across a rail bridge to Trier and the Saar industrial area to the south. A rail line also provided one of the major connections between the Saarland, Trier, and cities on the east side of the great Rhine River. During 1944, Pfalzel would have been a very active supply line in support of both the buildup and the continuing execution of the Ardennes Offensive from the south. It was the access point to the Ardennes region for the Wehrmacht's Seventh Army as well as the access point for its resupply of munitions and equipment. The aiming points were roads, rail lines, a rail bridge, the Mosel port, and the built-up area, all of which served as a critical artery for the buildup and continued execution of the Germans' Ardennes Offensive.

After completing its drop with fair to good results, the 392nd Bomb Group B Wing returned to Wendling as planned. The bombing damaged the roadway, rail lines, the rail bridge, dock loading equipment, and the immediate warehousing structures.

Reconnaissance photo of bridge and other damage at Pfalzal.

Prum 1426 hrs.
Effective 9 Bomb Tonnage 24

Prum, famous for its monastery that dates to Carolingian times, is located on the Prum River at the southeast point of the Schnee-Eifel. It had rail lines that connected it to St. Vith in Belgium less than thirteen miles to the west, though the trains terminated at Prum since Americans had advanced to the border. It was located a mere 7.5 miles to the border between Germany and Belgium that was part of the "West Wall" and the battlefront on December 16, 1944. In the weeks before zero hour, multiple units of the 6th Panzer Army were encamped in and around Prum. The 1st, 2nd, and 12th SS Panzer division were billeted about the city and engaged in training activities in anticipation of orders to move out in attack. Sixty trains for each division had delivered them in November. Morale was said to be high among the troops sensing a monumental attack on the Allied enemy. Their training proceeded, only hampered by the fog, bitter weather conditions, and a serious shortage of fuel caused in part by the US 8th Air Force's relentless attacks on Germany's synthetic fuel refineries in the preceding months. At 5:30 a.m., this mammoth force moved out and began to establish their bulge of control into Belgium and Luxembourg.

On 24 December 1944, nine aircraft of the A group of the 458th Bomb Group bombed the rail yards in the central city of Prum. Thirty-seven other aircraft from the A group attacked secondary targets in the immediate region. Crews from the 458th Bomb Group reported very good hits on the railroad and the town.

Rescheid (50°26N 06°26E) 1425 hrs.
Effective 17 Bomb Tonnage 40.5

Located just three miles from the Belgium border and eighteen miles east of Malmedy, Rescheid was a small village with road junctions leading to the front. Though the record is scant, one can assume the Wehrmacht troops and equipment passed through there on their way to Malmedy while backup munitions and supplies were stored here. Documents of the day don't name the village as a target, but only identify it by its coordinates. Some references mistakenly identify it as Hellenthal, which is located four miles to the north.

Bombing was done visually by nine aircraft from the 458th Bomb Group and eight aircraft from the 466th Bomb Group. Efforts were made to crater the roads and level storage facilities. Narratives from the 458th Bomb Group identify the target of opportunity as "an unidentified road center" from their 21,500-foot perspective of the snow-covered landscape below.

Rheinbach 1455 hrs.
Effective 25 Bomb Tonnage 71

Rheinbach is a small town about nine miles southwest of Bonn. It is located on the road system providing access to Euskirchen and the supply line to the Ardennes Offensive front. The aiming points were rail lines and the built-up area.

The D group of the 446th Bomb Group led the formation, which also included aircraft from the 448th Bomb Group. Congestion along the route had caused considerable weaving along the way and eventual spread to targets of opportunity including Nettersheim and Bitburg.

Post-mission surveys indicated that at least 200 bursts were seen blanketing the pinpoint target as well as the residential community that surrounded it. At least twenty-five hits were counted in the railroad marshalling yard and another five hits on the road adjacent to the marshalling yard.

Ruwer 1425 hrs.
Effective 27 Bomb Tonnage 71.3

The village of Ruwer is located at the mouth of the Ruwer River where it drains into the Mosel River, just north of Trier. It is directly across the Mosel from Pfalzel, another target for the day. The aiming points were roads, rail lines, a rail bridge, and the built-up area. The village itself was in the center of a wine region and insignificant to the immediate battle. But the roadway, rail yard,

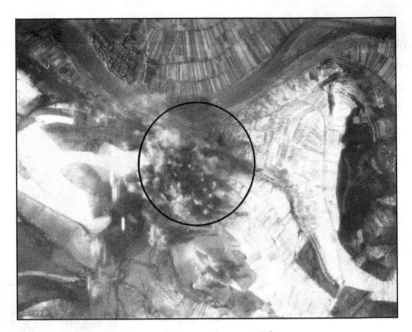

Ruwer Reconnaissance Photo

and bridges over the Ruwer and the Mosel were critical to chok-
ing off the supply and replacement line for the execution of the
Ardennes Offensive. They were arteries supplying Trier to the west
and Hitler's Seventh Army to the north and cutting them was critical to bringing an end to the Wehrmacht's continuing aggressive
strength in the surprise offense.

This first target of the day for the 8th Air Force's 3rd Force was assigned to the 392nd Bomb Group stationed in Wendling. The actual
lead aircraft for the formation, designated as the A formation for
392nd and attacking Ruwer came not from the 392nd but from the 44th
Bomb Group. Pilots Major G. A. Player and Major J. A. McGregor
each led a squadron as air commanders. Their aircraft were among
the number of aircraft in the 44th that were equipped with Gee-H
radio navigation system and H2X "Mickey" radar. With their advanced equipment, particularly in comparison to the many war-
weary planes rallied for this maximum force mission, crews of the

44th Bomb Group, the "Flying Eight Balls," were leading formations throughout the 14th Combat Bombardment Wing.

This A formation was sent to the southernmost target for the 3rd Wing. The massive B-24s had a more rapid flight speed capability than the B-17s that left the coast of England earlier in the day. Their superior speed allowed them to form later, reach their targets at approximately the same time as some of the First and Second Force B-17 formations, and return to England quicker than some of them.

This A Wing for the 392nd left its assigned assembly buncher as scheduled at 1206 hours. It was fourteen minutes late when it finally crossed the Channel and then for some unknown reason it circled Brussels, losing an additional ten minutes. It arrived at its target in the Mosel River Valley at 1425 hours. As they hit the target, they were an hour and seven minutes behind the original plan. Bombing on Lead Bombardier 1/Lt J. E. Bennett's drop, they achieved excellent coverage, quite an accomplishment for visual bombing of a relatively contained target from 23,000 feet above. The bomb load dropped on the Ruwer side of the river was all 500-pound bombs plus some smoke bombs. The high component, the lead, experienced moderate, accurate flak as they approached the IP though suffered no losses. For those on the ground, the terror lasted for less than five minutes, though the power of those heavy bombs for that brief period was very real and most certainly destructive.

The men of the 392nd BG returned to their home base at Wendling safely at 1558 hours, more than nine hours after they had gathered for mission briefing in the morning and five hours since their take-off. It was a relatively routine and successful mission. They had seen no German fighters, though they had flown through flak that they classed as "meager." Nonetheless, this moderate flak had left serious battle scars in the thin skin of eight of their aircraft.

The attack did damage to the rail line, the built-up area of the village, and the main roadway.

Schoenecken 1426 hrs.
Effective 26 Bomb Tonnage 53.5

Schoenecken is located four miles southeast of Prum. The 62nd Volks Grenadier Division of the Fifth Panzer Army had been billeted there and like other units had been completing training in anticipation of an order to move out. A rail spur provided continuing supplies in the shadow of a towering medieval castle ruin that had been destroyed by the French fighting with the Germans in the "Nine Years War" 250 years earlier. The geography, roadways, and rail connections made Schoenecken, which translates as "beautiful corners," a critical juncture for focusing men, equipment, and supplies to the front lines both in the buildup and the execution of Hitler's Ardennes Offense. The rail yards in its southern suburb, Wetteldorf, and the rural road connection in Oberlauch just three miles south of Prum provided for vehicular traffic from the north, east, and south. They also made Wetteldorf and Oberlauch assigned targets along with Schoenecken.

At Horsham St. Faith's the men of the 96th Combat Bombardment Wing's 458th Bomb Group were told at briefing their mission was to "eliminate the troops and supplies at Schoenecken and dislocate and delay enemy transportation by disrupting traffic facilities, demolition of storage facilities, cratering roads, leveling buildings, blocking woods and attack towns where reserve troops and supplies were located." Under the leadership of Lt. Col. W.H. Williamson they took off at 1016 hours for what was to be a six-hour-and-fifteen-minute mission. Fifty-nine aircraft flew carrying 1,099 250-pound "Ground Pounders." Though Schoenecken was the focal point, aftermath accounts read more like a roving fighter/bomber attack than a traditional bombing mission. While twenty-six aircraft are counted as participating in the attack on Schoenecken, another eighteen hit nearby Wetteldorf, all with good to excellent results. Additional aircraft from the unit bombed the railhead at Prum four miles to the northwest, and others bombed a road junction at Oberlauch, where there was some uncertainty because of the snow cover on the narrow roads (official records of the mission refer to it simply as "Ober"). Other aircraft ventured farther from the central target. Two reported hitting an "unidentified road center" and an "unidentified town." In a slip of navigation, nine aircraft thought they were bombing Hellenthal, but they were actually bombing Rescheid, a small rural farming community in Germany, but just eighteen miles east of Malmedy in Belgium and in one of the buildup areas for Hitler's December 16 advance.

Most of the bombing in the Schoenecken region was visual and accurate except for the unidentified targets. No aerial offense was experienced by the 458th, though they did encounter some flak. In one case it was lethal. Shortly after "bombs away" on Schoenecken, aircraft 42-109812, piloted by 1/Lt Charles Giesen was hit just aft of the bomb bay. It was split in half and the tail section containing S/Sgt Edward Racek broke away. The wreckage fell near St. Vith, just twenty miles from the site of the earlier attack on Mission 760's lead formation. Six of the crew on Giesen's plane were killed, including Giesen, whose last act was to call for a check to see if all on board were all right immediately after the hit. Ironically, the tail gunner, Racek, was one of the three crew members to survive. The other two were Copilot

The Charles Giesen crew of the 458th Bomb Group.

2/Lt John Thompson and Waist Gunner S/Sgt Alphonse Wolak. Wolak was immediately captured and sent to Dulag-Luft West at Nuremberg. Racek and Thompson successfully avoided apprehension and made it back to Allied lines. Those dying in the crash in addition to Giesen were Navigator 1/Lt Donald McNeely, Radio Operator T/Sgt Earl Richey, Upper Gunner T/Sgt Marion Funderburk, Nose Gunner S/Sgt James Burke, and Waist Gunner S/Sgt Stephen Molek.

St. Wendel 1455 hrs.
Effective 13 Bomb Tonnage 25

St. Wendel is located about twenty-three miles east of Saarbrucken and south of the Mosel River Valley. During World War II it housed a large German Army fort, one that was used heavily in the manning of the Ardennes Offensive. That fort also housed a POW camp that at times held French and American airmen as prisoners. It was located on rail lines connecting Saarbrucken with Frankfurt Rhein Main airport. As the lead formations of the 389th Bomb Group began their run to attack Cochem, they had a locating problem because of bad haze at the target. Additionally, the lead aircraft bombsight being operated by Lt S. A. Verstraete froze, and bad ground haze obscured the Cochem target area. The deputy lead took over too late to adequately bomb the intended target. Instead squadron formations were diverted to targets of opportunity in St. Wendel and Kirn.

The St. Wendel targeted areas were primarily the rail connections and marshalling yards. They were hit mainly by the A group from the 389th's formation. A squadron of ten aircraft and one element of three aircraft of the composite E group were diverted to target Bitburg.

Wetteldorf 1426 hrs.
Effective 18 Bomb Tonnage 47

Though it no longer shows on maps, Wetteldorf in 1944 was a small village at the juncture of roadways, rail lines, and rail yards located just south of Schoenecken and within sight of the ancient castle ruin that overlooked the town of Schoenecken and the plain south of it. That plain gave the medieval castle and town their name, Schoenecken, which translates to "beautiful corners." On Christmas Eve the B Wing of the 96th Combat Bombardment Wing made up of eighteen aircraft from 458th Bomb Group was assigned to destroy those rail and roadway connections coming from Gerolstein in the east and Bitburg to the south, feeding Prum and the advancing German force into Luxembourg to the west. The bombing was visual and some of the crews believe they dropped nearly twenty miles north of the intended target, though others reported dropping over an "unidentified road center" at the intended coordinates.

Wittlich 1433 hrs.
Effective 62 Bomb Tonnage 168.1

The third bomb group of the 14th Combat Bombardment Wing, the 491st Bomb Group stationed at Metfield and known as "The Ringmasters," was assigned the town of Wittlich as its target for the day. The second of its two formations was led by a ship from the 44th Bomb Group equipped with Gee-H radio navigation system and H2X "Mickey" radar. Unfortunately, that lead aircraft, #42-50668, experienced a mechanical failure on its number two engine, which failed and had to be feathered. It was unable to keep up with the formation and was forced to return home prior to reaching the IP.

Wittlich is located north of the Mosel River valley and west of

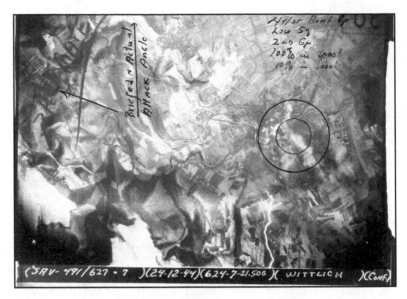

Wittlich reconnaissance photo.

Koblenz. Its relatively benign terrain is a buffer between the Mosel and Rhine valleys and the higher and more diverse lands of the Eifel and Ardennes. It has long been a hub for transportation from Trier and the western frontier of Germany to the bridges on the Rhine and to the cities of the north and the east. It served as a marshalling area for movement of troops, equipment, supplies, and armament to the front in the Ardennes Offensive. In 1944, rail from Koblenz to Trier to Saarbrucken passed through Wittlich, as did trains from Luxembourg to Berlin. Trackage was in place and actively used from Metz in France to Hamburg in the north. There were also regional lines servicing Daun and Bernkastel-Kues. In addition to the ample rail capability, Wittlich was also the center of modern, improved roads from Trier to Koblenz. Tactically, its transportation lines were a key to slowing and stopping the progress on the Ardennes Offensive. The targets hit on Christmas Eve were roads, railways, and the central city which was blanketed.

In formation as the C wing of the 14th Combat Wing, 491st Bomb

Group was charged with destruction of the bridges over the Liesser River, which passes through the town and carries water from the Eifel to the Mosel River. The first formation had experienced meager flak coming into the target area. Though the skies were clear, there was a ground haze. At 1428 they began the bomb run visually, dropping on the signal from the lead bombardier, Lt. Purdy. Each squadron bombing for one minute at a time, they cleared away from the town in three minutes, making way for the next onslaught from the D wing. That wing had experienced light to moderate flak on the way in. They followed through and dropped their load of 205-pound bombs. Lead bombardier on the Foy Shoemate crew remembered years later that the weather was good enough for visual bombing, but he also had a good setup on the Norden bombsight during the run on the bridges. On the way home they ex-

Marshalling yard bombing damage.

perienced unexpected flak near Trier and into Luxembourg. The C wing landed safely back at Metfield at 1601 hours, absent an aircraft flown by Lt. James A. Struthers of the 67th Bomb Squad from the 44th Bomb Group. Early in the mission, Struthers knew they did not have enough fuel on board to complete the mission. He radioed the lead plane and was told to use his own discretion. He decided to continue the mission and successfully made the drop. Then, low on fuel, he landed at Paris, France, to refuel and spend the night. Before leaving the next morning, he took on passengers, including a crew from the 466th Bomb Group.

The D wing landed at Metfield at 1620 hours, nineteen minutes after the C wing on the 24th. Crews returning from Wittlich reported heavy rail activity in a marshalling yard to the northeast of the town, though it was not attacked. East of Wittlich twelve large rectangular buildings were observed in a wooded area, including a barracks building with a red cross on the roof.

The urban mythology of the old city of Wittlich, for centuries a crossroads in human conflict, tells of the city fathers locking the city gates with a turnip because of the lack of a suitable lock. During the night a local pig found his way to the turnip/lock and ate it, allowing the attacking enemy to enter the walls and conquer the city. On 24 December, the crews from the 491st were not quite as lucky to receive an assist from a pig. The sixty-two planes attacking did damage, but their results were found to be only "fair" at this city with multiple bridges, rail yards, and roadways.

I have a simple philosophy: worry about those things you can fix. If you can't fix it, don't worry about it; accept it and do the best you can.

— **General Jimmy Doolittle**

Chapter 11

FIGHTERS
"LITTLE FRIENDS"

THE TOTAL EFFORT ORDERS for the Christmas Eve mission included every flyable P-47 and P-51 fighter in the 8th Air Force from the fifteen fighter groups scattered across England, a total of 858 fighters dispatched. Of that number, two units—the 78th and 339th Fighter Groups—were fogged in and unable to join in the mission. All the fighter units were operating under "Doolittle Rules," operating guidelines that had been enacted earlier in the year and had resulted in significantly improved and safer missions for fliers in the 8th than had been experienced in the first two years of the war when the protocol directed that fighter escorts remain "tethered" to their bomber formations to the target and back.

In January 1944, Lt. General Jimmy Doolittle, famous for his daring raid leading sixteen B-25s on a Tokyo raid in 1942, took command of the 8th Air Force, replacing General Ira Eaker. He quickly instituted one of the most significant changes in policy during the air war, one that resulted in a major shift in the results of aerial attacks of Germany. Though small in stature (5'4"), Doolittle was a giant of a man, a daring pilot, a skilled strategist, an inventive, insightful leader. He was also a well-respected leader. Under his new directive, fighter escorts continued to accompany bomber formations, but their role shifted from a defensive one to a combined defense and aggressive offense toward encountered Luftwaffe fighters. To accomplish this, fighter formations would fan out to police the area around the bomber formation boxes, engaging any incoming enemy attackers. Pilots with sufficient fuel and ammunition were also encouraged to engage appropriate ground targets as they returned from the mission objective. These changes not only increased bomber protection but improved the morale of fighter units.

While Doolittle has been generally credited with implementing this major procedural change, he did not do it unilaterally or in a vacuum. As Doolittle was assuming command of the 8th in January of 1944, Col. Hubert "Hub" Zemke was returning to his command of the 56th Fighter Group after two months in Washington as part of a team led by Brig. Gen. Curtis E. LeMay to brief Pentagon superiors and Congress.

Zemke and Doolittle were kindred spirits, both dynamic leaders and creative strategists. Zemke was the son of immigrant parents and fluent in German. He had attended Montana State University on football and boxing scholarships. Before the war broke out, he had enlisted as an aviation cadet. In 1940 he was sent to England as a combat observer. A year later he was reassigned to the Soviet Union to instruct Russian pilots in flying lend-lease P-40 Tomahawks. Returning to the States, he was involved in the P-47

Thunderbolt development. He was assigned as commander of the 56th Fighter Group and led it to England in January of 1943. There, he quickly achieved the status of "ace" with five kills. As his citation in the National Aviation Hall of Fame states in part, "Zemke's philosophy, forged in the boxing ring, and refined by the military, would help mold his successful fighter group, Zemke's Wolfpack. He advised his men to 'use your wits, size up the opposition, keep hitting him where it hurts…and always keep the initiative.'"

While other commanders and pilots were criticizing the deficiencies of the P-47, Zemke was bragging about its excellent dive performance and superior rate of roll. Before leaving for his brief assignment in Washington, he had made his own fifth kill and established himself as an ace. Additionally, his 56th Fighter Group's efficiency had established "Zemke's Wolfpack" as the leading air superiority group of VIII Fighter Command. He was transferred to command of the 479th Fighter Group in August and P-51 Mustangs in August of 1944. There he is credited with one of the first probable shoot downs of a German jet fighter. Zemke found himself in unexpected turbulence during a mission on October 30, 1944 and was forced to bail out as he lost a wing. He was captured after several days of evasion. After extensive periods of interrogation, he was sent to Stalag Luft I at Barth on December 16, 1944. As ranking officer, he assumed command of the POWs there and remained there until liberation by the advancing Russian army.

The changes instituted by General Doolittle in January 1944 were a modification of the approach that had already been tried and proven by Zemke in October of 1943 when the 56th FG shot down thirty-nine German aircraft, while only losing one of their own. The technique was known as "the Zemke Fan" with elements of fighters scattering and fanning out by flights in a 180-degree arc.

After the Battle of France, the Luftwaffe had achieved air supremacy over Western Europe, though it never achieved the superiority over Britain it desired and had over Russia. In February 1944, Doolittle's change in orders permitted P-51 Mustangs to fly far ahead of the bomber formations instead of closely escorting them. By March this had become standard operating procedure. This massive "fighter sweep" tactic was part of a plan to clear German skies of Luftwaffe fighters. By D-Day, June 6, the Allies had successfully achieved supremacy over Europe. During the D-Day attack there were 11,590 Allied aircraft—all allied nations and service—of one sort or another in the air as compared to 391 for the Luftwaffe. The 8th Air Force alone had 1,805 bombers dispatched and another 466 fighters. Two of the P-38 Lightnings that took off that morning were piloted by Lt. Gen Jimmy Doolittle and Maj. General Earle Partridge, the commander and deputy commander of the 8th.

Doolittle, also a skilled and experienced pilot, recognized that the fighters just enlarged the enemy's aerial target resulting in heavy losses of bombers, fighters, and crews. In Doolittle's approach, fighters were still assigned to specific bomber units, but their "leash" was cut. They scanned and surveyed the planned route, engaging the enemy where they found them. In a sense, the bomber formation became bait. Once the enemy focused on them, the enemy became the surprise victims of the roving fighters. As the capabilities, including range, of the P-51 Mustangs and their pilots improved, the Allies gained air superiority over the Luftwaffe. They were able to maintain it through an oil strategy that produced serious fuel shortages for the Germans and by aggressive attacks that left the Luftwaffe with a shortage of skilled and experienced pilots. By the end of 1944, fourteen of the 8th's fifteen fighter groups had replaced their P-38 and P-47s with superior Mustangs.

In later life Doolittle frequently was quoted as saying: "Adolf Galland said that the day we took our fighters off the bombers and put them against the German fighters, that is, went from defensive to offensive, Germany lost the air war. I made that decision and it was my most important decision during World War II. As you can imagine, the bomber crews were upset. The fighter pilots were ecstatic." Doolittle was also frequently quoted as saying, "Colonel Hubert A. 'Hub' Zemke was my greatest fighter group commander."

The Germans quickly picked up on this change in Allied procedure and responded to these new and very effective tactics with a new approach of their own, a full company front formation in mass attack on the bomber stream. They timed their massive attack to hits on an unprotected bomber formation and then dispersal before the P-51s showed up. This was exactly the scenario on December 24, 1944, when the lead formation of the largest bombing mission in history was attacked south of Liege, Belgium.

Takeoff times for each fighter group had been meticulously planned to choreograph with the bombing group schedules, yet as the day unfolded not all plans were executed as originally planned. Though it should be noted that archived records of the day contain a number of inconsistencies in specific times reported and it is assumed that real-time radio reports to MEW Control are probably more reliable than recollections captured in after-mission reports from combat-shocked memories.

Support for the 1st Attack Force

Escort for the lead formation of the 1st Attack Force (3rd Bomb Division) headed for Babenhausen was assigned to the A and B groups of the 357th Fighter Group, 55th Fighter Group, and 479th Fighter Group for the first three bomb groups. They were scheduled to meet the bomber stream over Belgium at Control Point #3 5053N-0500E at seventy-three minutes after zero hour. That Control Point #3 is approximately 7.5 miles west of Andenne, Belgium, and the Meuse River. It is ten miles northwest of Namur and twenty-five miles southwest of Liege. It is also 175 miles southwest of Gutersloh, Germany, the origin air base of the surprise attack Luftwaffe force. Two P-51s from each fighter group were to arrive at their respective targets twenty minutes prior to the bombers.

As it turned out, General Castle's lead formation passed the control point approximately eight minutes behind schedule and no escort fighters were within sight. The 55th Fighter Group was over Brussels and nearly seventy-two miles away from the location where the lead formation was being subjected to brutal attack and destruction. The 479th Fighter Group did not even arrive at Brussels until 1200 hours. At 1229 hours Castle's plane sent its first abort message from south of Liege and near the enemy front.

The B group of the 357th Fighter Group, based at Leiston, had been instructed during their morning mission briefing that they were to accompany the first three boxes of the attack force but were not planning to meet up with them until the rendezvous point. General Castle's lead attack formation arrived late to that point, and their assigned escort of 37 P-51s was even later. The B group reported meeting fifteen Me109s and 190s in singles and pairs at 1212 hours in the area of Namur, about forty-one miles from the location where a formation of an estimated eighty Luftwaffe FW0190s and Me109s ravaged Castle's lead formation beginning at 1229 hours. Regarding the late rendezvous, the Mission Control ("NUTHOUSE") Oakland Summary report for the day states, "This left coverage of front of 1-ATF pretty thin early in mission due to (fighter) groups coming from behind bombers and not planning to catch up until R/V." After-mission reports state that both the 55th FG and the 357th FG were "pulled up forward by MEW control" to intercept the incoming attack in strength against Vinegrove 1-1 and 1-2, the two lead boxes in the formation. The reports also state, "It is believed that the enemy executed 2 passes before these two groups reached the head of the column. Engagement ensued to our advantage." The 55th FG claimed sixteen kills and seven enemy aircraft damaged in this first combat. Of course, the 357th FG had a mission assignment to escort these lead formations from the original rendezvous point through to the target Babenhausen. They failed to rendezvous until the battered remains of the lead formation had crossed the front into Germany. The 55th FG had been assigned to escort the 4th through 6th boxes of the formation destined for Gross Ostheim.

After the Germans had departed and the remains of the bomber formation regrouped under the leadership of Captain Mayfield Shilling in Captain John Edwards' plane, the 357th Fighter Group B Squadron began to police the area around the lead box. Shortly after crossing into German-held territory and considerable ground flak, an accident occurred just north of Daun, Germany. Fighters of the 357th were in pursuit of "bogies" sighted to the south of the bomber stream. As they approached, they encountered two flights of "unidentified" P-51s. These planes were later identified as fighters of the 55th Fighter Group, who were responding to a call from "NUTHOUSE" of "rats—Heine rats—approaching the front box of Big Friends from the northeast." In the noise and panicked excitement of the high-speed pursuit, there was apparently no communication between the two fighter units. A dogfight ensued with four Me109s, which were preparing a hit on the remnant of the lead bomber formation. Lt. Vincent Gordon of the 55th FG reported on what occurred next: "...I kept my element about the same height relative to the group and was maneuvering to the left when P-51s were called in flying through our formation. I observed one low ship which appeared to be making a pass to the left. I identified it as a P-51 and turned up end to the left to prevent a chance of collision, and as I did so, I noticed this P-51 break down, then up and down all executed very suddenly. It was at this moment I identified the color and first two numbers of the ship as red and yellow checkered nose with red tail and the letters B-6. I immediately looked behind to my right to see if Lt. Mix cleared him. The two ships collided mashing the engine of Lt. Mix's ship into the fuselage, tearing off the right wing, part of the tail assembly and part of the left wing." There were no parachutes. Both 21-year-old Lt. Kenneth Mix of the 55th FG flying *Miss Marilyn* and 19-year-old Lt. Wendell Helwig of the 357th FG flying *Big Beautiful Doll* were killed in action.

Later in the day as the bomber groups were returning to their bases, 2/Lt. Walter C. Klank of the 55th FG flying *Miss Jane I* was on a scouting mission in the region of Frankfurt. He was intercepted at approximately 1450 hours and bailed out. Coming down near Florsheim am Main, he was quickly apprehended and spent the remainder of the war as a POW.

The 35 P-51s of the A group of the 357th FG reported their rendezvous with the bomber stream over Knocke on the Belgium coast at 1240 hours, long after the initial fatal action was over. They were actually thirty minutes late at Control Point 3 and were vectored forward by MEW control. From the details of the group's mission report it appears that, though Fighter Command's Field Order 1446A for the day called for them to escort the first three boxes of the mission to the target at Babenhausen and out, instead Major Richard Peterson's A Squadron headed north in pursuit of the retreating attackers and in response to a report that there were another fifty or sixty FW-190s at 26,000 feet over Fulda. The A Squadron engaged that Luftwaffe formation and found itself involved in wild high-speed dogfights. During this action two flyers from the 357th FG were casualties of the battle. Lt. William Gilbert was shot down during the skirmish and was killed. A second pilot, Cpt. William H. Mooney Jr, flying *Libby B*, also entered the fight and was shot down. He was seen to have bailed out. Once on the ground, Mooney was captured by a German soldier by the name of Hoffman who was also an official in the local Nazi party. Hoffman and a fourteen-year-old boy by the name of

Hans-Peter Keller marched Mooney toward the town of Jubach. On the way Hoffman pulled his revolver and killed the pilot, burying him in an unmarked grave in a local cemetery. At the end of the war Keller testified against Hoffman, who was then hanged at Landsberg War Crimes Prison in August 1946. The 375th FG claimed thirty kills in the fight over Fulda that day. One aircraft of the 357th landed with battle damage safely in Belgium.

The 479th FG based in Wattisham was vectored forward to help the 1st box at 1225 hours and had been originally assigned to escort the 7th through 9th boxes targeting Zellhausen. They arrived at the lead bomber formation while there were still enemy aircraft active and successfully bounced four FW109s, one of which crashed and burned in the area of the attack.

The second contingent of three bomber groups from the 387th, 446th, and 486th Bomb Groups headed for Gross Ostheim were to be met by the 55th FG A and B groups at Control Point #3 ten minutes ahead of schedule at eighty minutes after zero hour. They had been vectored forward by MEW control after reports of the initial attack. The area was full of smoking debris, but the aerial action had moved to the east and across the ground combat front. Fighters of the 55th FG escorted the formation through to the target at Babenhausen. On the return they broke off near Heidelberg and continued to police the area. Though not engaging any aircraft, they did strafe rail tracks and equipment, destroying several engines and supply cars.

Similarly, the next three groups of the First Force (3rd Division), the 447th, 390th, and 100th Bomb Groups targeting Zellhausen were to be met by the 479th Fighter Group A and B groups also arriving ten minutes early at zero plus eighty-six minutes. With the mission having regained supremacy of the sky, fighters of the 479th diverted to the area around Fulda in response to the earlier attack there.

The 355th FG had been assigned to escort the 10th-13th boxes formed by the 95th and 100th Bomb Groups supplemented by additional aircraft from the 1st Bomb Division. These units were targeting Biblis. Weather conditions at the 355th's home base in Steeple Morden caused the fighters of the 355th to be grounded during the planned takeoff time. Later in the day conditions cleared sufficiently for them to take off as the bomber units were completing their attacks and withdrawing back to their bases in England. Both the A and B groups of the 355th FG finally took off at 1428 hours. Under MEW control, they were vectored to Amsterdam, then to Aach, and then down to the northern section of the Duchy of Luxembourg, before returning across the Channel from north of Dunkirk to their home base at 1630 hours.

The 353rd FG stationed at Lashenden escorted the 14th to the 19th boxes to Darmstadt. These were comprised of aircraft from the 388th, 96th, 452nd, 456th, and 493rd Bomb Groups as well as aircraft from the 1st Division in box 1-19. They took off at 1118 hours, rendezvoused with the bomber stream at 1226 hours, and returned to their home base at 1630 hours. After leaving the target area, fighters from the 353rd FG checked results at Babenhausen and Gross Ostheim. They then vectored to the vicinity of Fulda, where other Allied elements were engaging the large formations of German fighters.

The 339th FG stationed in Fowlmere had been assigned to escort the 1-20 to 1-23 boxes to their targets in Frankfurt and Darmstadt. This force included the 34th, 490th, and 493rd Bomb Groups. The 339th FG was held on the ground because of weather conditions at their home base.

Fighter support for the 1st Attack Force certainly had significant impact, both positive and negative, on the events of the day. Weather hampered execution of the original mission as planned and caused the absence of a total of 141 P-51 Mustangs in the critical first hours of the mission, though later in the day sixty-three of them from the 355th FG were able to join in the fight during a critical dispersal of a second major attempt by the Germans to amass a hit on the bomber stream, albeit the stream in withdrawal from its targets of the day. The initial tragic attack of the day claimed on of the five general officers killed in the European war, eight aircraft of the 487th BG, and thirty-four crew members. Notable also is the number of unit post-mission reports which include sightings of German jet aircraft, though none of them report contact or interaction. For the day, the fighters supporting the 1st Attack Force downed fifty-three enemy aircraft and seriously damaged six others. They suffered seven fighters lost and one damaged beyond repair. The general success of the individual unit bombing strikes in the absence of a traditional close escort is testimony to the success that the 8th Air Force had progressively achieved throughout 1944 as it secured superiority and finally supremacy in the skies over Hitler's homeland.

Support for the 2nd Attack Force

Escort for the 2nd Attack Force (1st Bomb Division) was assigned to the 359th, 364th, 4th, 356th, and 20th Fighter Groups. Both A and B groups of each Group were scheduled to meet the bomber stream over Belgium at 5053 – 500 at Control Point #3 at the following times: 359th FG – ZERO plus 119; 364th FG – ZERO plus 123; 4th FG – ZERO plus 127; 356th FG – ZERO plus 141. Eight P-51s from each group were also scheduled to arrive at their respective targets twenty minutes prior to their assigned bombers.

The A Squadron of the 359th FG originating from Wormingford arrived at Control Point #3 fourteen minutes early and was soon joined by first box of the 381st Bomb Group. Designated as

Lt. Arthur Wong

the Vinegrove 2-1 formation of the bomber stream, they proceeded together to their assigned target area. The B group followed closely, making its rendezvous with the 398th Bomb Group as Vinegrove 2-2 with a target of Ettinghausen, flying at 26,000 feet. Several jets were seen from Brussels to the target area, though they were generally at 35,000 feet and not engaging. Bombing went as planned, but the return trip did not. At 1320 hours a P-51 piloted by 1/Lt. Ray A. Boyd Jr of the 368th Squadron was in combat with three FW190s and crashed near Cologne. Boyd bailed out and was captured. He spent the rest of the war as a prisoner at Stalag Luft III. At 1335 an unidentified B-17 was seen spinning down and crashing twenty miles southwest of Bonn. This was likely a plane of the 390th Bomb Group piloted by 2/Lt. Paul L. Herring that had been hit by flak near Gerolstein about this time. Three of the crew members were killed and the remaining six, including Herring, were captured and held as POWs. At 1420 hours an Me109 being chased by two P-51s safely escaped southwest of Koblenz. At 1430 hours, crews of the 359th FG received communication from 2/Lt. Arthur Wong, a pilot with the 356th Fighter Group. Wong reported smoke in his cockpit and losing altitude. Wong was last seen in the Laacher See area. He bailed out and was captured and held as a POW until the end of the war. At 1450 hours, south of Bonn, one Me262 jet made a half-hearted pass at the B-17s, but it broke off when a single P-51 turned into him. Shortly after the sighting of Herring's plane, an RAF bomber exploded in the area near Cologne and two or three chutes were spotted. Pilots of the 359th FG also reported heavy rail traffic on the Giessen-Limburg-Koblenz and Bonn-Koblenz RR and along the Rhine River moving north and south.

One of the luckiest pilots of the 359th Fighter Group was Lt. Bryce Thomson of the 369th Fighter Squadron. The 22-year-old Thomson, from Flint, Michigan, was flying escort for the 381st Bomb Group attacking Kirch-Gons. Flying with Lts. John Kelly and John Keur of his squad, they encountered and engaged an Me109.

During the chase, Keur got the first strikes, then Thomson scored and destroyed. Kelly spotted an enemy aircraft going after a bomber at the same time and entered into a successful combat. As the three pulled away, Thomson became aware that he had a fire on board and turned to withdraw from enemy territory. He got as far as Belgium, just east of the Meuse River and the city of Dinant. At 10,000 feet he bailed from his burning plane. He worked his chute to fall as far to the west as he could, successfully landing on the west bank of the river. It was only after landing safely that he learned the fluid combat front of the Germans' offensive had brought German ground units to the eastern side of the Meuse, close to where he had jumped from his plane, his parachute journey had started over German-held territory, and he was shocked at what a close call he had.

Lt. Bryce Thomson was transported to a field hospital in Dave castle near Namur. There he met two members of the crew of a B-17 from the 92nd Bomb Group that had just gone down in the area where Thomson had ditched his fighter. The bomber flown by 1/Lt. Joseph McConnell had been severely damaged by flak. Two of the crew members had been killed and a fourth, the radio operator, bailed out, but his chute was snagged by the tail of the plane, which then dragged him down. The waist gunner, S/Sgt Leo Labonte, and Tail Gunner S/Sgt John Cavello bailed out and found themselves being carried into enemy territory until two American fighters came in close pursuit and intentionally generated air currents to safely draw them into friendly land. Their efforts worked and the two happily exchanged stories of their safe landings in Belgium with Lt. Bryce Thomson with his own tale of safe deliverance.

The 364th Fighter Group originating from Honington met the Vingrove 2-3 and 2-4 combat boxes seventeen minutes early at Control Point #3. The A group accompanied the first box, a composite of the 381st and 398th Bomb Groups, to their target in Giessen.

The B group accompanied the second box, a composite of the 384th and 379th Bomb Groups, to their target at Kirch-Gons. As the groups were approaching their targets, a forward observer, Lt. Charles T. Stinson of the 383rd Squadron, was hit by flak, but safely made it back to base. Approaching Brussels on the way in and again on the way out, missiles identified either as a "V-2" rocket or a "a silver white object at 20,000 feet." Another V-2 rocket was sighted at 1410 hours near Kassel. Their report also notes there were all sorts of friendly aircraft in the region. Additionally, there is a report of strange "glass balls, 2-3 inches in diameter seen at 30,000 feet in the target area." The A group went to the Cologne-Koblenz region from 1445-1550, a crowded sky for returning attackers. They chased a Me 262 jet at 1540 hours ten miles west of Koblenz but couldn't catch it. Other than that, they didn't encounter any other enemy aircraft.

Fliers of the 364th FG reported seeing a B-17 go down in the target area at 1500 hours with three parachutes visible. Another B-17 was seen at 1515 hours in the vicinity of Koblenz. There only one parachute was seen. They also witnessed a P-51 spin in and below up at 1400 hours ten miles southwest of Koblenz.

The absence of German defenders was a surprise to many. 1/ Lt. James L. McCubbin, flying in the 385th Fighter Squadron of the 364th FG, was meandering as a wingman for his operations officer, Cpt. Bill Crombie. With their escort duties complete by 2:00 p.m. and no sign of hostiles, Crombie suggested they visit a French P-47 field where he had a friend. So, they stopped in for a drink on their way back to England. About 4:00 p.m. they took off, now lubricated for the rest of their trip across the Channel. Too late they realized that the French ground crews had not refueled their two P-51s, and weather conditions were rapidly deteriorating in England. They circled back to France, lost their way, and ended up landing on an airstrip that had become a junkyard for damaged planes. Crombie landed safely, but McCubbin ended in a bomb crater concealed by the fog and did serious damage to his plane. Though he was never reprimanded when he finally got back to England, he did end up being shot down on February 19, 1945 just east of Bonn and spent the remainder of the war as a POW in Mossberg, Bavaria. The mammoth Mossberg camp identified as Stalag 7-a held some 80,000 prisoners, both officers and enlisted, before it was liberated on April 29, 1946.

The 4th Fighter Group, originating from Debden, escorted the Vinegrove 2-5, 2-6, 2-7, and 2-8 combat boxes. Vinegrove 2-5 was made up of the 92nd Bomb Group attacking Giessen. Vinegrove 2-6 was the 306th Bomb Group attacking Nidda. Vinegrove 2-7 was comprised of 305th Bomb Group aircraft attacking both Nidda and Giessen. Rendezvous with this group was twenty-five minutes ahead of schedule. Vinegrove 2-8 was a composite of aircraft from the 305th, 306th, and 92nd Bomb Groups. The rendezvous with

this group was approximately forty minutes behind schedule, the delay being caused by the tardy bombers.

Bombing went well at each of the targets, with inaccurate, but heavy flak at each. Two Me262 jets were seen "stooging" west of Cologne, but there was no interaction. During the run on Giessen a lone Me109 traveling on the deck just west of Giessen was destroyed and another engaged at 20,000 feet was

Giessen bombing strike photo.

probably destroyed. No other enemy aircraft was seen. Flyers with the 4th Fighter Group witnessed a P-51 with no markings hit another west of Wiesbaden near Oberwesel. The ship that was hit caught fire and the pilot bailed out.

As the weather deteriorated just as planes were returning from the day's missions, incoming 4th Fighter Group planes were diverted from Debden to landing strips at Raydon, Wattisham, and Wormingford. One P-51 — attached to the 65th Fighter Group and piloted by Lt. Dick W. Thompson — attempted to set down at Debden and crashed on landing. Thompson survived, but serious damage was done to his aircraft.

The 356th Fighter Group based in Martlesham Heath escorted Vinegrove 2-9, 2-10, and 2-11. The first of these B-17 formations was manned by the 457th Bomb Group and targeted Koblenz. The 357th Fighter Group was assigned to sweep the areas around Koblenz and Daun. The second was comprised of crews and aircraft from both the 401st and the 351st Bomb Groups, targeting Koblenz and Darmstadt. The third was a 351st Bomb Group formation heading for Biblis. The thirty-five P-51s of the A Squadron made rendezvous with the bomber stream at 1247 hours, north of Ostend and at 24,000 feet. The fighters swept north of the bomber track and patrolled the Koblenz-Frankfurt-Marburg area from 1330 to 1500 hours. During that action they picked up nine combat support wings of B-24s that were without friendly escort and were being trailed by an enemy jet. The fighters escorted them back to the Liege area and began the journey back to England at 1510 hours.

The thirty-four P-51s of the B group of the 356th Fighter Group's rendezvous with the bomber stream was more difficult because of the convening B-17s being anywhere from ten to forty minutes late to the control point.

They were picked up by units of the B group between Liege and Namur from 1326 to 1300 hours. The fighter cover was necessarily

thin and escorted the returning bombers through the ta
the coast.

The 20th Fighter Group, based in Kingscliff, escorted ⟩
2-12, 2-13, and 2-14. They were formations of the 303rd, ⟍⟋⟍, and
91st Bomb Groups respectively. All three formations were aiming at
Merzhausen, the aerodrome located closest to Gerd von Rundstedt's
Ziegenberg Castle and Hitler's Adlerhorst underground bunker.
Eighty-two P-51 Mustang fighters were escorting 198 B-17 heavy
bombers with a collective payload of 495 tons of explosives to the
Fuhrer's airport. This was the largest tonnage dropped on any
single target during the Christmas Eve mission. The A Squadron
broke off from the bombers shortly after rendezvous and swept
ahead. They were vectored to Bonn by NUTHOUSE command, but
without any encounter of enemy aircraft. They then patrolled the
Rhine area between Bonn and Koblenz from 28,000 feet to the deck
without incident. Three Me109s were sighted near Cologne at 1445
hours. They were pursued but could not be caught. Crews of the
20th FG observed one B-24 go down in the target area at 1500 hours.
No parachutes were sighted. Near Koblenz at 1515 hours they saw
a B-17 straggler downed by flak. This was a plane of the 92nd Bomb
Group piloted by 2/Lt. Joe Spencer. It was hit by flak immediately
after completing the bomb run at Giessen, left the formation, and
tried to make its way back on its own. Near Koblenz it took another
flak hit and caught fire. The pilot gave the order to bail out and
the plane blew up at approximately 2,000 feet. Four of the crew
were killed, and five were captured either as they hit the ground or
within a few days. They were taken to Dulag Luft Wetzlar.

At 1540, members of the 20th FG reported seeing another B-17 crash
at Ohey, Belgium, near Malmedy. Piloted by 1/Lt. Joseph McConnell,
it was the deputy lead ship of the 92nd Bomb Group's attack on
Giessen, and it, too, had taken a serious flak hit as it left the target.
Six parachutes were counted. A seventh was tangled in the horizontal

stabilizer with the radio operator, T/Sgt John Booth. In addition to Booth, S/Sgt Harold Paske also went down with the ship. The navigator, 1/Lt. Anthony Piekarz, bailed out, but his parachute failed to fill completely, and he fell to his death. All the other crew members survived, though not without some drama. The pilot, McConnell, hit a fence as he neared the ground and broke both his legs. The tail gunner, S/Sgt John Caravello, and the waist gunner, Leo Labonte, realized as they were coming down that they were literally at the front and there were German soldiers beneath them. As previously noted, two American fighter covering the area also recognized their predicament and took action. They took repeated approaches to the chutes of the airmen, driving them westward and to safe territory with their propeller wash. Their efforts were successful as Caravello and Labonte descended into friendly territory. Labonte had one more hurdle, however; he landed in a tree and without boots. He spent the night in the woods, but when he heard church bells in the morning, he decided to look for the priest. On his way he ran into a column of British tanks and was taken to a Belgian house for care and first aid. The "first aid" included a bottle of Cognac, Labonte reported.

A B-24 belonging to the 448th Bomb Group was also identified as crashing. Spotted at 1502 hours, *Lady Lora*, piloted by 1/Lt. L.C. Barneycastle, was part of the 3rd Attack Force, the 2nd Combat Wing, stationed in Seething. After bombs away, the plane was on the planned return route to England when it was struck by ground flak near St. Vith, Belgium, not far from the combat front. There was a large hole and fire behind the number four engine. As crew members began to bail out, the right wing broke off and the plane went into a spin. Ball Turret Gunner Sgt. John Birkhead, Nose Turret Gunner Linn Garrison, and Tail Turret Gunner Eathen Newcomb all successfully bailed out, but were captured immediately. The rest of the crew — 1/Lt. Barneycastle, his copilot Edward Hanson, Bombardier Bernard Ferrari, Right Waist Gunner Russell Alivis, Top Turret

Gunner Patrick George, Left Waist Gunner Roland Grubbs, and Radio Operator James Lunt—were all killed in the crash.

Support for the 3rd Attack Force

Escort for the 3rd Attack Force (2rd Bomb Division) was assigned to the 56th FG, 78th B, 352nd A, 361st A, and 361st B Fighter Groups, all equipped with P-47 Thunderbolts. Whereas the 1st and 2nd attack forces were primarily attacking German air bases likely to be supporting the Ardennes Offensive, the 3rd Attack Force concentrated on targets in the south and west of the Rhine River. These targets included communications centers, roadways, and bridges located in the area as major support to the Nazi fighters' advance and resupply as they moved Hitler's Ardennes Offensive westward. The bombers involved were primarily B-24s, and their aircraft fighter support was a combination of P-51 Mustangs and P-47 Thunderbolts. The target area was defined as a triangle just behind the enemy's front lines with the objective of neutralizing multiple transportation and communication sites and arteries vital to the continuance of Hitler's original planned advancement to the west. Tactically, it was designed to cripple the German troop, equipment, and supply movement and drive them back to the east side of the Rhine River. Each of the five formations of the 3rd Force were identified as Vinegrove 3-1 through 3-5 and proceeded from initial formation over England and across the Channel to Control Point 3 near Namur, Belgium, as the first two attack forces had. At that point they were instructed to dissipate to the region of their assigned target.

Four fighter units were assigned to geographical reconnaissance rather than specific bomb group escort. The P-47s of the 356th Fighter Group were to provide freelance support and arrive at Koblenz as the first force crossed the enemy coast, following MEW vector directives from that point on. Similarly, the P-47s of the B squad of the

78th Fighter Group were to arrive at Bad Kreuznach as the First Force crossed the enemy coast, providing freelance support and following MEW vector directives. The 352nd Fighter Group was to arrive at Trier at 22,000 feet at zero plus 148 and freelance patrols from that point and under MEW Control. At the same time the 361st Fighter Group B group was to be 22,000 feet over Bonn and provide freelance patrols there under MEW Control. Unfortunately, the aircraft of the 78th Fighter Group were grounded by weather back in Duxford, England, leaving the Bad Kreuznach area with limited protection.

The fighters of the 56th Fighter Group flying from Halesworth (Holton) escorted Vingrove 3-1 to the southernmost targets. The 56th FG was and is legendary. It was the only fighter unit in the 8th Air Force to retain P-47 Thunderbolts for the duration of the European campaign while all other fighter units were moving to the P-51 Mustang for its superior range and agility. Despite favoring the older equipment, the 56th FG finished the war with 674.5 aerial victories, the second highest among USAAF fighter groups in the European Theater of Operations, second only to the 354th FG with its 701 German aircraft destroyed in air-to-air combat. Of the 56th FG totals, 4.5 were Me262 jets. The 56th produced thirty-nine aces (five aerial kills), second only to the 354th Fighter Group of the 9th Air Force and the 357th Fighter Group, both flying P-51s and each with forty-two. The 56th was one of the few units that had successfully flown on December 23rd despite the extremely poor visibility and extreme weather conditions. A total of 403 bombers and 592 fighters had braved the weather that day and attacked three marshalling yards, three communications centers, and one rail junction. Forty Luftwaffe fighters attempted to attack the US bombers that day. The 56th shot down thirty-two of them. Their group commander, Col. David C. Shilling, was responsible for five of those kills and became one of the thirty-eight "Ace-in-a-Day" pilots in the Army Airforce. Shilling, from Kansas, had a degree in geology from Dartmouth College. Shortly after graduation in 1939, he enlisted as an aviation cadet. He became one of the original members of the 56th Fighter Group and its commander in August of 1944. He was promoted to full colonel in October 1944 at age twenty-five.

On Christmas Eve, Shilling was flying his personal P-47 *Hairless Joe* and leading the fifty planes of the 56th Fighter Group. Their departure from Halesworth had been delayed almost an hour and a half by MEW control. Once over the Continent they were vectored to southwest of Koblenz but failed to locate any bandits there. They were then vectored to north of Koblenz with the same results. They patrolled the Koblenz-Frankfurt-Hanau area "uneventfully" and noticed that both rail and road traffic in the Rhine Valley was light. There was also a smoke screen south of Koblenz and west of the Rhine. Barge traffic on the Rhine was seen to be very heavy. But after the excitement of December 23rd, the 56th found their Christmas Eve assignment "uneventful." They found flak at Aachen and Koblenz to be heavy and accurate but aimed only at the bombers. The dogfights with the Luftwaffe of the previous day were missing in the 56th FG's area of operation. They returned to Halesworth (Holton) at 1534 hours, except for four aircraft that had left the formation earlier in the day because of mechanical problems.

Despite the absence of the 78th Fighters of the A group, attacks were successfully completed without Luftwaffe resistance in the southern target region for the 3rd Force. There was, however, moderate and accurate ground flak throughout the target areas. The same was true for the eastern section of the target area where the B group of the 78th—also grounded by fog at Duxford—had been scheduled to escort Vinegrove 3-2 to its targets and provide area support. In both of these areas the bombers successfully made it to their targets without fighter support. This is additional evidence that the 8th had secured air supremacy over Germany, and the Luftwaffe attacks earlier in the day were the remnant of a declining air capability suffering from attrition of equipment, skilled pilots, and able leadership.

Vinegrove 3-3 was escorted by the A group of the 352nd Fighter Group into that same eastern target region and over targets shared with Vinegrove 3-2 (Wettledorf, Gerolstein).

The 352nd FG had a very different start to the mission than the other fighter groups. Dubbed the "Blue-Nosed Bastards of Bodney," they had been abruptly transferred from their long-term "permanent" base in England to Asch Aerodrome north of Liege in Belgium on December 23rd, relocating under the cover of clouds to assist the 9th Air Force providing protection for the ground troops fighting to hold back the German advance. Though the 352nd FG had relocated to the Continent, and were assigned sweep responsibilities, the 52 P-51s of the A Squadron were not in the air until 1255 hours, after the brutal battle just south of Liege that began nearly thirty minutes earlier. Leading that relocation force was Maj. George E. Preddy, commander of the 328th Squadron of the 352 Fighter Group. He was flying his personal P-51 Mustang, *Cripes A' Mighty*. Preddy, who served a tour in the Pacific theater prior to coming to England, was the top ace in the Army Air Forces, credited with 26.83 enemy air-to-air kills. His daring and the proximity of targeted rail, roadway, and communications sites allowed the 352nd to cover for the absent 78th Fighter Group as they protected the 455th and 467th Bomb Groups. Vinegrove 3-4 with the A group of 361st Fighter Group escorting the 458th and 466th Bomb Groups filling much of the same air space provided additional reconnaissance and protection (Schoenecken, Prum, Hellenthal, Gerolstein). They were back at their base in Asch by 1610 hours. Preddy was up again on Christmas Day

Major George Preddy

when the 352nd Fighter Group took down eleven enemy aircraft. Sadly, three fighters were killed by friendly fire at the combat front. Two of them were aces, Major George Preedy and Capt. Donald R. Emerson.

To the north of the region, the 361 Fighter Group was escorting Vinegrove 3-5 made up of bombers from the 93rd, 446th, and 448th Bomb Groups to their targets at Arhweiler, Euskirchen, Rheinbach, Bitburg, and Netterheim. The 361st Fighter Group posted at Little Walden had also been repositioned on December 23. Their sixty P-51s had been dispatched to St. Dizier in France and supplied support to the 9th Air Force also, where they were under control of the XIX Tactical Air Command. The thirty-five Mustangs of the 361st Fighter Group were up at 1215 hours and rendezvoused with the Third Force B-24 bombers. Responding to MEW Control they swept the target area. At 1400 hours they bounced seven aggressive Me109s in the area around Koblenz. The absence of the 78th FG was adequately covered with the location of all these targets being within a fifty-mile proximity of each other. It was beneficial that two units were available on the Continent and with plenty of fuel when they entered the target zone.

Fighter Protection
9th Air Force

The 9th Air Force was not officially part of Mission 760 of the 8th Air Force on Christmas Eve. The reality of the day was that Mission 760 was a turnabout for the 8th Air Force. For the first time it suspended its two-year program of attacking primarily strategic bombing of targets that sustained Germany's ability to stay in the war. Those were the supplies and services behind the front lines that made war possible, things such as synthetic fuel refineries, aircraft and military equipment components, and the rail yards, tracks, and bridges necessary to move them. On Christmas Eve they joined in the tactical mission of combat troop support that had occupied the 9th Air Force since the bloody, but successful landings on the Normandy beaches six months earlier. The change in plans necessitated by the Battle of the Bulge was both essential and at the same time very sensible. The 8th had made their first strike at the oil industry on May 13, 1944. By the end of 1944, only three of the original ninety-one refineries in the land controlled by the German Reich were still fully functioning. Twenty-nine were partially functioning and the remainder had been completely destroyed. That success was in part possible because of the introduction of long-range P-51D escorts and the success of the 15th Air Force over Yugoslavia, Romania, and northeastern Italy.

The 9th Air Force had participated in the Normandy invasion and took as its mission the support of ground troops as they drove the Wehrmacht back across France, Belgium, Holland, and Luxembourg to the West Wall of Germany from bases they had established in France, Belgium, and Holland.

General Hoyt S. Vandenberg, veteran of successful air campaigns with the 12th Air Force in North Africa, was assigned to European Command in early 1944 as deputy air commander in chief of the Allied Expeditionary Forces and commanding general of the American air component. Subsequently he was assigned commanding general of the Ninth Air Force and was involved in planning for the Normandy invasion. Though he understood the importance of strategic bombing, Vandenberg, an experienced pilot in his own right, never forgot the necessity of tactical air support for the ground forces. His 9th Air Force Bomber Command flew B-26 Marauder Medium Bombers, and his Fighter Command flew P-47 Thunderbolts. The IXth TAC, Vandenberg's command, had a great reputation of working hand in hand with Army commanders on the ground as the Allies drove the Germans eastward with unexpected speed. His fighters and medium bombers helped protect the ground troops and they made a hasty advance to the German boarder and the ancient capital of Charlemagne's empire, Aachen.

When the accurately forecast unflyable weather appeared on December 16 as predicted by Hitler's weatherman, Vandenberg's aircraft in Belgium and France bases also found it extremely difficult to fly and were grounded. By coincidence, Brigadier General Frederick L. Anderson, representing the Eighth Air Force, Colonel Robert M. Lee, Solly Zuckerman, and other staff members met with General "Pete" Quesada regarding the bombing plan for the following day at a chateau he was using as a command center near Spa, Belgium. Unable to get out safely because of the weather, they stayed for the night. In the morning they were roused to information about the Germans' sudden and unexpected advance. By the morning light on the 17th, they found themselves within eight miles of the advancing forces of the Nazi surprise offensive. General Courtney Hodges, commander of the 1st Army, had attended their bombing plan meeting on the 16th. Much to the surprise of the air commanders and indicative of the immediate panic, Hodges's headquarters had packed up and retreated to Liege during the night without informing Quesada and his guests.

The officers of the IXth TAC received reports of German paratroopers disguised as Americans infiltrating the area. They also received news of the cold-blooded slaughter of eighty-six GI prisoners by SS troops of SS-LtCol Joachim Peiper's Task Force a scant eight miles to the east. Unable to fly because of the 100-foot ceiling and dense fog, Vandenberg safely drove his vehicle back to headquarters in Luxembourg City by way of Paris. There he briefed General Spaatz at SCHAEF headquarters regarding the state of the invasion and the immediate efforts to contain it. Spaatz placed additional air units at Vandenburg's disposal, and the two agreed that the Ninth Air Force would be shifted and shuffled like a fire brigade to whichever sector it was needed the most to assist the ground troops in regaining control of the "bulge."

Late in the day on the 17th the fast-moving German advance was approaching Stavelot under the "pea soup" cover. In an effort to pinpoint the location of the advancing enemy columns, Quesada found two volunteers to fly a reconnaissance mission in their F-5s (P-38s armed with cameras rather than cannons) at tree-top level. They revealed the Germans' advance toward Stavelot, a mere twenty-two miles from the Allies' critical supply depot in Liege. Immediately P-47 Thunderbolts were launched below the clouds to hit the advancing German armored columns of Peiper's 1st Panzer division. In an unprecedented attack, the air power halted the advance by destroying 126 armored vehicles and trucks and damaging thirty-four more. The remnant of the German force abandoned the advance on Stavelot and diverted to the south and then west to LaGleize, where a bitter ground battle continued until the 24th when the Germans went into retreat.

Though weather conditions continued to be generally dismal over England, the "Russian High" pressure began to clear the skies over Belgium and Luxembourg on the 23rd of December. At Vandenberg's request, the Eighth Air Force was able to dispatch 423 bombers and 536 fighters to assist the Ninth in cutting off the German advance. The 92nd, 303rd, 305th, and 384th Bomb Groups of the 1st Bomb Division successfully dropped 392 tons of bombs on the marshalling yard at Ehrang. Their fifty-four P-51 Mustang escorts claimed twenty enemy aircraft downed and three damaged. The 2nd Bomb Division dispatched 132 planes from 2nd CBW, 14th CBW, and 466th Bomb Groups successfully dropped 268 tons of bombs on roads, rails, and bridges at the "communications centers" of Junkerath, Ahrweiler, and Dahlem just behind the advancing German troops. From the 3rd Bomb Division, 152 bombers attacked the marshalling yard at Kaiserslautern, rail junction and marshalling yard at Homburg, plus a target of opportunity for a total bomb load of 469.6 tons; 636 fighters from all but three fighter units (the 20th, 78th, 339th Fighter Groups) participated in escort and sweep. They claimed sixty-nine enemy fighters killed, one likely, and eighteen damaged for the day. The 352nd Fighter group, "The Blue-Nosed Bastards of Bodney," was moved from Bodney in England to Asch, Belgium, to be in proximity and provide additional support to the ground troops during the Battle of the Bulge.

As the weather continued to clear to the west, the men of the 9th Air Force continued their support of the troops on the ground. From December 23rd to the 27th, the Ninth flew 5,291 sorties, with the enemy force around Bastogne singled out for special attention. There were unfortunate events of "friendly fire" at Malmedy, however. As is typical of older European cities and towns, the main roads pass through the town center. This was true of Malmedy and the neighboring towns, which date back to the twelfth century. American soldiers held Malmedy throughout the German

An image of Malmedy, a victim of a friendly-fire bombing early in the confusion of the Ardennes Offensive.

advance. Peiper's 1st SS Panzer Division changed course and avoided it after the execution of US POWs at Baugnez. On December 21st Skorzeny's 150th Brigade returned to attack the city and roadways. They were turned back by American artillery on the 23rd and 24th. In the midst of all of this, aircraft of the 9th Air Force were providing support and targeting vehicles on roadways. On the 25th, unaware of Skorzeny's 150th Panzer Division retreat, the Americans bombed the center of town, including the Hotel Nicolet, which was housing civilians and approximately 100 GIs. The hotel collapsed, and nearby buildings burned, killing at least sixty-nine of the American soldiers and as many civilians in the rubble.

On December 24, as the Heavy Bombers of the 8th Air Force were busy far into German territory attacking Luftwaffe air bases, marshalling yard, rail lines, bridges, roadway junctions, and other communications centers that were actively being used to support the Ardennes Offensive, the fighter bombers of the 9th Air Force were providing immediate tactical support for the beleaguered allied ground troops frantically fighting their way out of Hitler's surprise attack on their positions. It has been noted that the ground troops not only appreciated the support from above, but they appreciated the tremendous lift to their morale. The plethora of friendly contrails that

finally appeared in the skies above them had also been active on December 23 and 24. Some of this on-the-spot action came with a cost. One of those campaigns occurred at Eller on the 23rd, where the 9th's 397th Bomb Group (M) attacked the key bridge across the Mosel without fighter support and suffered major losses. As they were turning off of the target, they lost eight B-26s to enemy aircraft and two more to heavy flack.

The Royal Airforce (RAF)

The British Royal Airforce also participated in the Christmas Eve mission, sending 338 aircraft to attack airfields at Lohausen and Mulheim an der Ruhr, both in the Ruhr Valley and to the north of the activity and paths of the 8th Air Force attacks. A total of 248 Halifax and seventy-nine Lancaster four-engine heavy bombers, and eleven de Havilland Mosquito fighter-bombers from the 4th, 6th, and 8th groups of the RAF took part in these attacks and were over the two targets between 1430 and 1450 hours. It is assumed that missions on both targeted airfields, located ten miles apart, were to prevent their use in movement of supplies by transport aircraft to the Ardennes battle area. Destruction of the two airfields also prevented their use by Luftwaffe aircraft from any of the aerodromes destroyed or severely damaged in the 8th Air Force attacks of the day. Gutersloh, the home of the attack force that surprised the lead formation of the 8th's armada for the day, is located approximately seventy-five miles northeast of these two landing strips. In the mammoth mission of the day, no effort was made to attack Gutersloh or follow the attackers back to it. The RAF lost six aircraft in their attacks: two Lancasters and one Halifax from the Lohausen raid and three Halifaxes from the Mulheim raid.

The RAF had been maintaining a steady schedule of both day and night bombing missions in coordination with Bomber Command in early December. On December 23rd they had been actively attacking rail centers on the outer line of interdiction and the rail workshops at Trier.

*"It was the largest single bomber strike of
the entire Second World War!
the greatest display of strength since the
beginning of combat operation."*

—Danny S. Parker

*"By rushing out from his fixed defense the enemy may give us the
chance to turn his great gamble into his worst defeat."*

—Dwight David Eisenhower

Chapter 12

RESULTS OF MISSION 760

THE MAGNITUDE OF the 8th Air Force Mission 760 on Christmas Eve 1944 is undeniable, when 2,046 heavy bombers and 852 fighters were sent into battle at a very critical moment in World War II. Collectively they dropped 5,052.1 tons of explosive bombs on a variety of targets. They took out ninety-two enemy aircraft, possibly ninety-eight, and seriously damaged another twenty-one in air combat, plus an additional number in facilities on the ground. They gained time for the Allied combat troops in the fierce Battle of the Bulge by limiting, for a few days, the usefulness of nearby landing strips for Luftwaffe aircraft in addition to destroying their refueling supplies and maintenance/repair facilities and equipment. Bombing results on the enemy's runways were generally excellent, though those at Darmstadt, the largest attack on a single target for the day, were poor and those on Gross Ostheim were only fair. Attacks on those aerodromes' facilities were found to be "excellent," even at Darmstadt, but rated "good" at Merzhausen and Nidda. They were found to be only "fair" at Gross Ostheim.

Attacks on rail bridges, marshalling yards, and trackage were found to be generally successful in temporarily restricting the flow of reinforcements, supplies, and equipment that had been energizing the rapid and aggressive movement of Wehrmacht forces across Luxembourg and Belgium since December 16. The same was true with regard to the heavy bombing of roads and intersections of major arteries headed toward the front.

The aerial evaluation of mission results was an inexact science. Though there were strike photos taken from the bombers showing the distribution of hits, there was not always an immediate reconnaissance of the situation before the attack or even immediately after the attack. Some strike photos were not able to be made until days after the Christmas Eve attacks, days where the events of 24 December had been followed by additional attacks, repairs to tracks, roads, or bridges by emergency ground crews, and in some cases, new fallen snow obscuring the original bombing damage. Targets like Arhweiler had almost continuous bombing of its trackage before and after the 24th and pinpointing the date of the damage was often difficult given the challenge of documenting the scenario from day to day in the challenging weather that Hitler had predicted and counted on. Additionally, throughout the war the Nazis used scores of prisoner labor crews to begin track and runway repairs and restoration immediately after the bombers departed the

Giessen Bombing Reconnaissance Photo

target and while the ground was still smoldering.

While the destruction of targets was a tangible result, the intangible, but significant results were major. The first was the effect on morale and determination of the hard-pressed ground troops. The second was the impact on the leadership in Germany. The Germans had followed their Fuhrer into his personal plan for a massive offensive, and they were watching it unravel after the initial week of surprising and impressive advance. They were witnessing their officers and young men die in the field or being captured by their enemy. They had seen their strategic resources diminished and were experiencing the futility of their continued efforts to sustain the Reich. The reality that their days were numbered was closing in. Those closest to Hitler were conscious that he was ill and playing an "end game" as he retreated from the Adlerhorst to the concrete bunker under Berlin.

After the war had ended, captured general of the Panzertruppen Erich Brandenberger blamed the failure of the Ardennes Offensive on the absence of seven prerequisites: adequate forces, air superiority or at least equality, sufficient supplies of ammunition, POL (petroleum, oil, and lubricants), adequate motor transportation, sufficient engineering equipment, and supplies of spare parts for tanks and armored vehicles. Despite the distinct advantage of surprise and the planned attack during adverse weather for flying, by Christmas Eve the rapidly attacking Wehrmacht found itself mired down by the mud, determined Allied ground counterattacks, and shortage of all of the prerequisites identified by Brandenberger. The Allied air forces had achieved air superiority over Germany in the months since D-Day with their relentless attacks and the attrition of equipment and skilled, trained pilots in the Luftwaffe. The strategic bombing by the 8th Air Force at synthetic petroleum and military supply facilities, as well as rail, bridges, and roadways had choked off the flow of Brandenberger's "prerequisites." The move of the 9th Air Force to France and Belgium had provided ready support for the Allied ground defenses even at minimal flying conditions.

The issues stated by Brandenberger were reinforced by other captured generals. Von Rundstedt testified, "There were no adequate reinforcements, no supplies of ammunition, and although the number of armored divisions was high, their strength in tanks was low — it was largely paper strength." General Hasso von Manteuffel, commander of the 5th Panzer Army, pointed to the worst deficiency of all as petrol. He stated, "Once the foggy weather cleared, and the Allied air forces came into action, its forwarding was badly interrupted."

By Christmas Day, the German salient that had shockingly advanced nearly fifty miles into Allied-held Luxembourg and Belgium in only ten days had begun to retreat. As the Allies were advancing to the east on the ground, the last great attack in the war by the Luftwaffe took place. It was early on New Year's Day on January 1st, 1945, so early that some of the attacking Luftwaffe pilots were still attired in their formal uniforms from the previous evening's New Year's Eve party. The Americans had liberated Bastogne, which had been circled and isolated by the Germans on the 19th, though German ground troops on the defensive still controlled much of the area to the west, north, and east of it. In the wee hours of the New Year the Luftwaffe launched Operation "Bodenplatte" (Ground Slam), sending 1,035 planes from eleven different aerodromes in the north and east. Their targets were twenty-seven different Allied bases in France, Belgium, and southern Holland. Caught off guard, approximately 280 Allied aircraft on the ground were destroyed and another 100 were damaged. Eighty were shot down in aerial combat. About 70 percent of the aircraft were destroyed on the ground in the first bomber wave. A quick success for the Luftwaffe speedily turned into a disaster, however. The surprised Allies scrambled and over 300 of the attacking aircraft were shot down, mainly by Allied antiaircraft guns. In total the Luftwaffe lost over 12 percent (one in eight) of its pilots: eighty-one were killed and another twenty-one were wounded. With the war machine back in the States fully operating at full capacity, the Allied losses were replaced within weeks and the Germans' hoped-for air superiority was never regained.

For the Air Force, the day that began with a shocking attack by the Luftwaffe ended with sound evidence of their mastery of the air over Germany. As the day progressed, there were sightings of Luftwaffe aircraft, occasionally an Me262, but there was limited exchange except briefly in the area of Fulda. Ground flak resistance was a different matter. German air support of the Ardennes Offensive was clearly disrupted, and the dwindling resources of the Luftwaffe were in disarray.

From January 12th to the 28th the line of combat moved steadily back to the original front line held at the beginning of the Battle of the Bulge, Germany's "West Wall."

"The crushing air attacks on transport installations and crossings aimed especially at the middle Rhine Zone, Koblenz-Mainz-Frankfurt, against the valleys of the Moselle, Lahn and Nahe, and against traffic hubs like Giessen, Hanau and Limburg had grave consequences. The difficult transportation situation which had already been in existence for a long time, could not be improved, in spite of every kind of auxiliary service and repair and restoration work. The Rhine was the end of any through railroad movements on a large scale. West of the Rhine islands of communication functioned on individual rail sectors, so that all movements, especially of supplies, had essentially to be made across country."
—questionnaire given by captured Generalfeldmarschall Wilhelm Keitel and Generaloberst Alfred Jodl

Chapter 13

THE AFTERMATH

THE SALIENT OF the Germans' advance in Hitler's Ardennes Offensive was not totally erased by the Allies until January 28th, 1945, when the line of battle was finally returned to its status on the prior December 16. In terms of casualties on the western front, the Battle of the Bulge is second only to the Battle for France in 1940, when nearly 470,000 casualties were recorded. Though neither approach the horrendous casualties of battles on the Russian front at Stalingrad (more than 1.7 million casualties), Operation Bagration (1.2 million casualties, including thirty-one German generals), Moscow (more than one million casualties), Kursk (approximately 388,000 casualties), Kharkov (approximately 300,000 casualties), or Narva (more than 550,000 casualties). During the Battle of the Bulge, 20,876 Allied soldiers and

A not so merry Christmas for the Fuhrer.

airmen were killed, and total casualties were in excess of 90,000. German losses totaled more than 85,000.

Hitler had returned to Berlin and his underground bunker from Adlerhorst on January 16th in advance of the final end to his Ardennes Offensive on January 28th. As Albert Speer described after the war in his memoirs, Hitler had made it clear that regardless of rank or prestige, "anyone who tells anyone else that the war is lost will be treated as a traitor, with all the consequences for him and his family." The bombers of the 8th Air Force continued to provide tactical support to the advancing Allied ground troops throughout the month of January 1945, attacking rail bridges, marshalling yards, and roadway communication centers. They also destroyed German tanks and equipment in retreat.

On February 3, 1945, they made a major shift away from continued support of ground troops, sending 1,437 bombers and 948 fighters to the airfield at Magdeburg and marshalling yards and rail stations in the heart of Germany's capital city, Berlin. Contrary to prior US bombing procedure, orders were given to "carpet bomb" from the edge of the once great city to rail facilities at its heart. Hitler was safely ensconced in the concrete caverns of his bunker when the bombers attacked, though the bomb pattern was extensive in the government district directly above him. While the Fuhrer was safe, the mission did extensive damage to the already heavily damaged capital, setting off fires that would burn for days and killing thousands of citizens plus throngs of refugees from the east fleeing by rail from the rapidly advancing Russian army. Not only was the morale of the civilian population shaken, but the confidence of many in the Command Bunker was wavering as they surveyed the damage.

The relentless tactical bombing by 8th Air Force in conjunction with the 9th and RAF had squeezed supplies for the retreating Wehrmacht and made bridges and roads impassable for their tanks and heavy equipment. The twenty-two road and twenty-five railroad bridges crossing the massive Rhine River were down. They had been essential for the German buildup for their Ardennes Offensive. They were also the primary escape route for retreating trips and equipment as the Allies took the offense and reclaimed Belgium and Luxembourg on their way to capture Berlin. The Allied air forces had made bridge busting a key objective, one that helped to turn the battle during that last week of December and first week of January.

Hitler had ordered his commanders to hold the West Wall Siegfried Line at all costs, but that action trapped approximately 400,000 of his troops west of the Rhine with no way to escape. By the first week of March those bridges that had not been destroyed by the bombers of the 8th Air Force and the RAF were in the process of being blown up by the Germans, intent on keeping the Allies on the west side of the Rhine. Nearly 280,000 of those trapped German troops were captured and another 120,000 were killed, wounded, or missing in action. As the American forces advanced to the river, they were prepared to build a series of pontoon bridges to enable the crossing of advancing troops, supplies, and combat equipment. Eisenhower had given his commanders latitude in selecting their own crossing point.

Late in the day on March 7, an American reconnaissance patrol reached the hills overlooking the river town of Remagen. They were shocked to see that the Ludendorff

Allied pontoon bridge crossing of the Rhine.

railroad bridge spanning the Rhine was still standing and usable. It had previously been targeted by seventy-one bombers from the 8th's 1st Bomb Division dropping 209.5 tons of bombs. Apparently, the attack had not done structural damage of any significance and the Germans were able to restore it to functioning condition in the intervening weeks. As the Americans launched a full-scale assault on the defending Germans on the bridge, the Germans were attempting to detonate explosive charges to destroy it. The Americans successfully reached the east side of the river and secured the bridge. They began moving all available equipment and units across it, while the Germans were busy trying to put an effective counterattack together. Hitler was furious. He ordered an immediate inquiry and called for the death penalty for anyone responsible for failing to blow up the bridge. He ordered heavy weaponry to the area to destroy the invading Americans. After repeated unsuccessful aerial attacks, Hitler ordered the unprecedented use of V-2 rockets to destroy the bridge. On March 17th eleven rockets were fired from

Hellendoorn in the Netherlands. The inaccurate missiles hit every-where but on the bridge. Some landed as much as forty miles away. Finally, Hitler called special operations commander Otto Skorzeny to make an underwater attack with seven SS frogmen. They floated downstream with empty oil drums for support. They were spotted. Two died of hypothermia in the forty-five-degree river. Two were killed and three were captured.

On March 17th the structure of the Ludendorff bridge began to shift and sag after ten days of heavy shelling by the Germans and the excessive load of the American tanks. Finally, it fell into the water. Before it failed the Americans' 25,000 Allied troops had crossed to the eastern bank, and the American bridgehead at Remagen was eight miles deep and twenty-five miles wide. Eisenhower had nine First Army divi-sions already across the

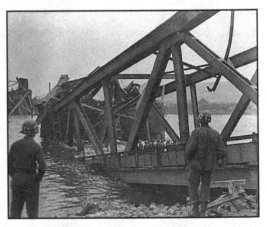

The Ludendorff Bridge at Remagen after being destroyed by the Germans.

river. Patton's Third Army was on the way and crossed quietly across the Rhine without air, artillery, or airborne troops. By March 31, all four American armies were across the Rhine and moving with deliberate speed in the direction of Berlin. Eisenhower called the capture of the bridge at Remagen "one of those rare and fleet-ing opportunities which occasionally arise in war and which, if grasped, have incalculable effects on determining future success."

Things moved quickly for the next month as the Americans, British, and Russians each tried to be the first to take Berlin. Their journeys were slowed by holdout defenses by the Wehrmacht, sometimes staffed with old men and young boys. Thousands of "disarmed combatants" had to be processed along the way. The horrors of the Nazi concentration camps were discovered. There the living required medical care and sustenance. Local citizens were conscripted to bury the dead. US soldiers were shown the atrocities they had been fighting to eliminate.

Fast work by the Army Corps of Engineers begins the drive to Berlin.

The Eighth Air Force continued to fly combat missions, focusing on marshalling yards, airfields particularly in the west and northwest, ports, submarine facilities, and remaining pockets of German strength. Night flights of leaflet dropping to convince the civilian population that the end was near became a regularly scheduled activity for the bombers. Though there was never a "maximum effort" mission again, occasional missions were mounted by the 8th dispatching a thousand or more heavy bombers. The largest after Mission 760 on Christmas Eve was an attack on March 24, 1945. Called "Operation Varsity" and numbered Mission 911, it sent 1,749 bombers and 1,375 fighters out in support of the American and British forces crossing the Rhine in the move that had begun on March 17. Most of the missions at the end of the war were tactical, though two significant strategic bombings took place after the clear outcome of the war was certain to both sides. On March 19, 197 Heavy Bombers from the 3rd Air Division bombed the huge military optics manufacturer Zeiss Optics located in Jena, Germany. Then, on March 25, 8th Air Force Bomber Command attempted to reinstate the strategic targeting of petroleum refineries and synthetic petroleum plants; 1,009 bombers from all three Air Divisions took off for attacks on seven oil plants and a tank factory, but adverse weather caused all of them to be turned back.

Airfields were primary targets in the final month of the war and were indicators of the success that the Allies had achieved in securing mastery of the skies over Germany. In 1945, the Luftwaffe had an acute shortage of experienced pilots. From December 1944 and going forward, the people involved as pilots tended to be inexperienced and were learning by attempting to fly. On many of the bombing missions, there was limited defensive action. In several major attacks, critical German bases were leveled without resistance. On March 21st the target of the day was jet airfields. The 1,400 bombers found most of the fresh German fighters on the ground with limited ground-to-air activity or aerial defense. Nine German fighters were shot down with another forty-six jet fighters destroyed on the ground. This pattern was repeated on April 13th when 256 1st Air Division P-51s flying escort to the Neumunster marshalling yard engaged the defending Luftwaffe and destroyed 137 in the air and a probable eighty-three more. Then ninety-seven P-47s flying freelance bomber support strafed German airfields and claimed 147 aircraft on the ground with a possible additional 137. On April 16, 724 German fighters were destroyed on the ground with a possible 373 being claimed. Again, on April 17th US fighters escorting 1,054 bombers in attacks on rail yards and junctions around Dresden, Aussig, Roudnice nad Labem, Fischern, Kladno, Falkenau, and Beroun shot down thirteen fighters, but destroyed another 286 on the ground. During the month of March, the 8th Air Force destroyed 128 German aircraft. In April it destroyed 1,557. The Luftwaffe was short of skilled, trained pilots since its Operation Bodenplatte attack on New Year's Day. By the month of April, it was also short of both fuel and morale. There was no doubt that the 8th Air Force had achieved supremacy in the skies over Germany.

On April 16, news was received from Washington that President Franklin Roosevelt had died. The three-term president who brought the United States into war on December 7, 1941 and shepherded it and its allies through the ups and downs of the global conflict for four gripping years was not to see the end but had provided the leadership and determination to enable its success. At the time of his death, the air war over Europe was also trailing off. Crews and equipment were deploying to the Pacific or returning to the States after the completion of their missions. The final heavy bomber mission of the war took place on April 25th and targeted airfields and rail targets in Czechoslovakia and southeast Germany. A total of 554 bombers from the 1st and 2nd Air Divisions and 539 fighters participated. From that day until the end of the war, all that was dropped on Europe were leaflets and food supplies.

On April 30th as the Russian forces were closing in from the east, Adolf Hitler in his Fuhrerbunker beneath the Reichs Chancellery committed suicide with a single shot from a gun. On May 8, after a confusing series of regional capitulations, the Germans officially signed an unconditional surrender, and the war was over. Among the architects of the ill-fated Ardennes Offensive, Alfred Jodl and Wilhelm Keitel were arrested and extensively debriefed. They were imprisoned and brought up for trial and convicted. To underscore the criminal rather than military nature of their crimes, both were denied death by firing squad. They were both killed by hanging at the prison in Nuremberg on October 16, 1946. General Wilhelm Burgdorf, who had been involved in the planning of the Ardennes attack from the beginning, committed suicide in the Fuhrerbunker with Hitler, Goebbels, and Krebs. Hermann Goering had also been convicted and condemned to death by hanging, but he took his own life on October 15th using a potassium cyanide capsule that had been smuggled into his cell.

Field Marshal Gerd von Rundstedt had been relieved of his

command of the Ardennes Offensive by Hitler on March 9, 1945. He declined a proposal to move to the Italian theater and submitted a resignation, ending his 52-year military career. He was not charged by the Nuremberg tribunal, but requested that he be allowed to testify for the defense. He presented convincing testimony that he and other field military officers were following military law and serving at the direction of Hitler's political followers in the dock. In response to his exhortation the entire military component of the German High Command was acquitted.

At the end of the war Werner Schwerdtfeger, the meteorologist who successfully identified the date for the initiation of the Ardennes Offensive, left Germany with his wife and two children for a new life in Argentina. Beginning his South American career in Buenos Aires, he became prominent in Antarctic research. In 1963, his reputation and global renown brought him an invitation to join the University of Wisconsin Meteorology Department. At the University in Madison, Wisconsin, he was reunited with an old colleague from prewar Germany, Dr. Heinz H. Lettau. The two collaborated on a number of studies of wind turbulence in different environments. Before the first voyage to the moon, their work convinced NASA scientists that the moon's surface would have only a few inches of dust rather than the ominous and problematic estimates of others that the proposed lander would come down in a foot or more of fine dust.

As for the Americans who executed the massive mission on Christmas Eve 1944, the shock, then success of the German invaders in the days after the initial surprise attack had tremendous impact. For those brave young fliers who lost their lives, most quickly found rest in hastily made military cemeteries in Belgium, Luxembourg, and Holland. General Frederick Castle and his pilot, 1/Lt. Robert Harriman, are buried in the American Military Cemetery of Hombourg (Henri-Chapelle), province of Liège, Belgium.

Those airmen wounded in the initial attack of that mission were in close proximity to needed aid and quick evacuation. Eighteen-year-old Sgt. Robert C. Yowan was a good example of that. He was the ball turret gunner on Lt. Kenneth Lang's crew, and they flew their first mission on November 24, 1944. Christmas Eve was their tenth mission. Lang was flying the dread "Tail End Charlie" position in the formation. Yowan, one of the six survivors of Kenneth Lang's crew, landed in a Belgian community and was quickly found and tended to as well as they were able. The glass of cognac they gave him was the extent of their available medications. Military help came quickly from the 298th Field Hospital in nearby Liege. Yowan was there by late in the night on Christmas Eve. He was stabilized, presented with a Purple Heart, and then transferred to the hospital at Orly Field in Paris. A cargo plane took him from Paris back to Mitchell Field on Long Island. By early January he was back at Deshon, Pennsylvania, and close to his family. He received numerous surgeries to restore use of his leg and celebrated his nineteenth birthday (and the continuation of his life). Deshon was his home until he overcame his wounds as well as osteomyelitis and hepatitis. He was still at Deshon in May when Germany surrendered. Once discharged from the hospital, he secured a degree in mechanical engineering and a career in instrumentation and control in the steel power generation industries. He has also spent a lifetime sharing the story of his military adventure and praising the heroes of "the Great War."

Most of the 8th Air Force crews that survived the attacks on Christmas Eve were close to completing thirty missions at the time and rotated back to the States and civilian life before the end of the war in Europe, though many opted for a promotion and reassignment in the Pacific. Cpt. John Edwards, the pilot of the deputy lead plane that took over when General Castle's plane went down, went on with his crew to participate in thirteen more missions, two of them to Berlin. The thirtieth and final mission of their tour of duty was the destruction of a marshalling yard in Marburg on March 12. After drinking a toast to the occasion, they packed up, said good-bye to their base in Lavenham, and resumed civilian life. Kilburg was processing out of the service on April 12th, the day the commander in chief, President Franklin Roosevelt, died. Captain John Edwards, who was awarded the Distinguished Flying Cross for his part in the Christmas Eve mission, completed one additional "last" mission when he returned Stateside. He was assigned to ferry the legendary *Memphis Belle* to the Air Force "bone yard" in Kingman, Arizona. Edwards already had a BS degree from Erskine College before entering the service, but he returned to his native South Carolina to earn a degree in pharmacology and launched a lifelong career with his own drugstore.

Donald Kilburg Sr., bombardier on Edward's plane, was also awarded the Distinguished Flying Cross for his role in the success of the Christmas Eve mission. Kilburg was reunited with his wife in Chicago and entered Northwestern University. He completed a lifelong career at Armour and Company, specializing in finance and accounting and computers at the beginning of the digital age.

The third Distinguished Flying Cross awarded for the mission went to Aubrey Carlton "A.C." Wilkinson, pilotage navigator assigned to Edwards' crew for this mission. Wilkerson was an experienced lead navigator of exceptional skill assigned to the crew of Charles Kulp. This was his first assignment with the Edwards crew, augmenting the navigation crew of dead reckoning Navigator Lt. Dawes Lott and Radar Operator Lt. Saul Goldberg. The Christmas Eve mission was the sixteenth and most memorable flight of their war for Edwards' crew. They went on to finish their thirtieth mission on March 12th in an attack on Marburg and then promptly packed up for their return trip to the States. Those who flew on that lead crew also included Gerard Gauthier, the crew copilot; William Renner, the engineer; Sherwin Bosse, the tail gunner; and

Grover McDuff, the radio operator. Gauthier moved back to waist gunner to accommodate Captain Mayfield Shilling, the deputy air leader who took command of the mission when General Castle was shot down. After the war, Gauthier remained in the Air Force reserve in Michigan, eventually retiring as a lieutenant colonel. Dawes Lott returned to his family ranch in Twin Bridges, Montana. Sherwin Bosse returned to his family's industrial supply business in Steubenville, Ohio, eventually becoming president of the company. William Renner, the flight engineer, returned to his job as a machinist in Baltimore.

The Christmas Eve mission—with its dispatch of 2,034 heavy bombers and 853 fighters carrying more than 21,000 determined young airmen committed to a cause—was a shock to Hitler and his top leaders, even though they were able to anticipate its arrival through their own surveillance systems and draw first blood. The broad scope of the mission was beyond their comprehension and certainly beyond the defensive capabilities of the declining Luftwaffe. The aggressive action of the 8th Air Force was not a conclusion, but rather a turning point. It was the beginning of the end for Hitler's Ardennes advance. The pounding of the Allied ground troops and the continuous tactical bombing that followed the Christmas present from the sky helped to turn the tide.

After the war had ended, prisoner Generaloberst Alfred Jodl told his interrogators that he and Hitler firmly believed that by a successful offensive "a decisive turning point in the Campaign in the West, and possibly the entire war could be achieved." In listing the reasons for the eventual failure of the Ardennes Offensive, Jodl included, "The enemy superiority in the air which made itself felt in particular in the major fighting of 24 December." Clearly the 8th Air Force Mission 760 on Christmas Eve 1944 had a major impact on turning the advantage in the Battle of the Bulge to the Allies and the advancing combat ground troops.

GLOSSARY

AFCE – Automatic Flight Control Equipment installed with the Norden bombsight that enabled it to link to the autopilot and enabled the bombardier to control lateral movement of the bomber through his adjustments of the sight.

Ball Turret – A ball turret was a spherical-shaped, altazimuth mount gun turret, fitted to the underside of B-17 and B-24 Bombers.

Box Formation

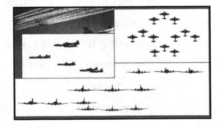

Combat box of a 12-plane <u>B-17</u> squadron developed in October 1943. Three such boxes completed a 36-plane group box.

1. Lead Element
2. High Element
3. Low Element
4. Low Low Element (added for Lead Formation of Mission 760)

The **Combat Box** was a tactical formation used by heavy (strategic) bombers of the US Army Air Forces during World War II. The combat box was also referred to as a "staggered formation." Its defensive purpose was in massing the firepower of the bombers' guns, while offensively it concentrated the release of bombs on a target. Each of the three squadrons would be assigned to a certain altitude. The lead squadron or lead box might fly over the target at 26,100 feet. The high box would fly 600 feet above them and slightly behind at 26,700 feet, and the low box 600 feet below and slightly behind at 25,500 feet. The boxes were also staggered laterally so that none would be directly below another.

Briefing – The early morning reveal of targets, routings, and special instructions for flight crews before each mission. They opened dramatically with a pull of a cord opening a large curtain at the end of the room and revealing a huge map of Europe strung with red yarn stretching from point to point, marking the flight path to the target and back to England.

Buncher Beacon – Fixed location and frequency radio signal near the individual Bomb Group air bases used for gathering and organizing unit formation. After takeoff each bomber would fly in a large rectangular pattern around their assigned radio signal buncher, gradually gaining altitude and forming combat boxes until they followed the lead formation over their assigned **Splasher Beacon** in their designated order and moving to Control Point 1 and then crossing the English Channel at the assigned location and back to England with precise geometry utilizing the newly developed and highly sophisticated Gee-H radar system.

Control Point – A marked checkpoint used for orienting and coordinating the path of a bomber formation. On Christmas Eve 1944, the planned route for the formation included three initial control points after individual bomber formations were achieved at each Bomb Group's assigned Buncher. The first Control Point was the location at the coast where they began their Channel crossing. The second was the point where they entered Belgian airspace at the coast. The third was south of Liege, Belgium, and near the Meuse River and Namur. The third Control Point was identified as the location where fighter escorts were intended to rendezvous with their assigned bomber units in the bomber stream.

Enigma Machine - A complex encryption device used by the German Wehrmacht during World War II to encode secret transmissions. Their code was first cracked in June 1941 by British Intelligence.

Flak – Non-English terms for air defense include the German *Flak* (**Flieger**a**bwehrK**anone, "aircraft defense cannon"), commonly referred to in English as *flak*. Flak antiaircraft guns on the ground fired exploding metal shells up to the bomber stream that spread a barrage of destructive metal fragments into the thin aluminum skin of the bombers.

Gee-H – A beam radar navigation system for navigation or blind bombing utilizing an airborne transmitter interrogating two ground beacons to obtain a fix. It had a range of approximately 300 miles at 20,000 feet, but it was susceptible to jamming.

H2X – An airborne ground-scanning "x" band (3cm) radar, H2X was a US development of the earlier British H2S ARI 5119. Popularly known as "Mickey" in the 8th Air Force, it was the major blind bombing and navigational device used during the final eighteen months of hostilities.

IP (Initial Point) – This is the point on the flight plan of the bombers where they begin the "bomb run" toward the target and the bombardier takes over lateral control of the plane.

MACR – Missing Air Craft Report for planes down in enemy territory (not filed for aircraft down in friendly territory).

MEW – Microwave Early Warning Radar, one of the most important developments during the second world war, proved to be invaluable for the US Army Air Forces. Rather than for early warning, it served as an entire control system for both fighters and bombers over friendly and hostile territory. In October of 1944, the control of all missions of the 8th Air Force was governed by the MEW radar that had been moved from England to Eys in the Dutch province of Limburg near the borders of Germany and Belgium.

"Mickey" – Code name for H2X radar system.

MPI – Targeted Mean Point of Impact for optimal results in formation bombing.

Norden bombsight – A revolutionary mechanical analog computer bombsight with revolutionary precision and high-altitude bombing capability. The device computed information bomb ballistics, ground speed, drift, and trail, fed in by the bombardier. With a telescopic attachment on the sight, the bombardier established and compensated for deflection to synchronize the instrument. The bombs then were released automatically when the bomber reached the point computed by the sight. The base unit incorporated the Automatic Flight Control Equipment (AFCE), which was linked to the autopilot that enabled the bombardier to control lateral movement of the bomber through his adjustments of the sight.

PPF – Abbreviation of Pathfinder Force, a radar unit that facilitated targeting bombing through overcast weather.

SHAEF – Supreme Headquarters Allied Expeditionary Force

ULTRA - The designation adopted by British military intelligence in June 1941 for top secret wartime signals intelligence obtained by breaking high-level encrypted enemy radio and teleprinter communications at the Government Code and Cypher School (GC&CS) at Bletchley Park.

Vickers's Unit – Top turret gun emplacement on the B-17.

Zero hour – The time that a military operation is scheduled to start.

Appendix A

AIRCRAFT OF MISSION 760

Boeing B-17G Flying Fortress

Power Plant: Four 1,200-hp Wright Cyclone radial engines.
Wing Span: 103 ft. 9 in.
Length: 74 ft. 9 in.
Gross weight: 65,000 lbs.
Range: 1,850 miles with a 4,000 lb. bombload
Maximum speed: 302 mph at 25,000 ft.
Armament: Thirteen .50-caliber Browning machine guns; standard bombload 6,000 lbs; maximum 12,800 lbs
Crew: 10

*B 17 Training diagram indicating crew
stations and escape routes.*

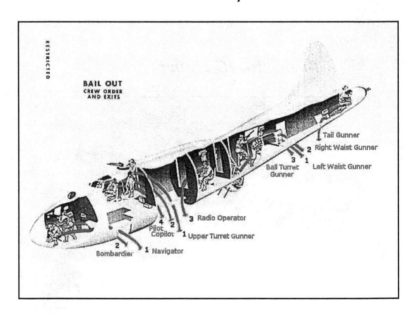

Consolidated B-24 Liberator

Power Plant: Four 1,200-hp Pratt & Whitney radial engines.
Wing Span: 110 ft.
Length: 67 ft. 8 in.
Gross weight: 56,500 lbs.
Range: 2,100 miles with a 4,000 lb. bombload
Maximum speed: 290 mph at 25,000 ft.
Armament: Thirteen .50-caliber Browning machine guns; standard bombload 5,000 lbs; maximum 12,800 lbs
Crew: 10

Martin B-26-C Marauder

Power Plant: Two 2,000-hp Pratt & Whitney engines
Wing Span: 71 ft.
Length: 58 ft. 3 in.
Gross weight: 37,000 lbs.
Range: 1,150 miles with a 4,000 lb. bombload
Maximum speed: 317 mph at 14,500 ft.
Armament: Twelve .50-caliber Browning machine guns; maximum bombload 4,000 lbs.
Crew: 9

De Havilland Mosquito B. Mark XVI

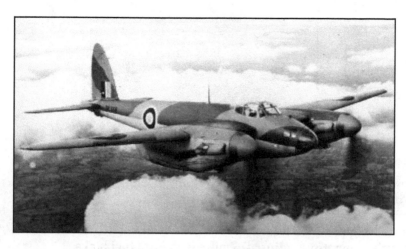

Power Plant: Two 1,290-hp Rolls-Royce Merlin engines
Wing Span: 54 ft. 2 in.
Length: 40 ft. 6 in.
Gross weight: 25,917 lbs.
Range: 1,370 miles with a 4,000 lb. bombload
Maximum speed: 408 mph at 26,000 ft.
Armament: Four 500 lb. bombs internally , plus two 500-lb bombs underwing: or one 3,000-lb; maximum bombload 4,000 lbs.
Crew: 2

Republic P47-D Thunderbolt

Power Plant: One 2,000-hp Pratt & Whitney Double Wasp engine.
Wing Span: 40 ft. 9 5/16 in.
Length: 36 ft. 1 3/16 in.
Gross weight: 17,600 lbs.
Effective operating radius: 475 miles with extra fuel tanks
Maximum speed: 429 mph at 30,000 ft.
Armament: Eight .50-caliber Browning machine guns: bombs could be carried under fuselage or wings: maximum, 2,500 lbs.
Crew: 1

North American P51D Mustang

Power Plant: One 1,490-hp Rolls -Royce/Packard Merlin engine
Wing Span: 37 ft.
Length: 36 ft. 1 3/16 in.
Gross weight: 11,600 lbs.
Effective operating radius: 950 miles with extra fuel tanks
Maximum speed: 437 mph at 25,000 ft.
Armament: Six .50-caliber Browning machine guns: could carry two 1,000-lb. bombs or six 5-in rockets on underwing racks.
Crew: 1

Focke-Wulf 190

Power Plant: One 1,790-hp BMW radial engine
Wing Span: 34 ft. 5 1/2in.
Length: 29 ft. 4 3/4 in.
Gross weight: 10,800 lbs.
Effective operating radius: 942 miles with extra fuel tanks
Maximum speed: 408 mph at 20,670 ft.
Armament: Two 13mm MG 131 machine guns and up to four 20mm MG 151 cannon .50-caliber Browning machine guns: could carry two 1,000-lb. bombs or six 5-in rockets on underwing racks.
Crew: 1

Wednesday
MAY
17

S	M	T	W	T	F	S
	1	2	3	4	5	6
7	8	9	10	11	12	13
14	15	16	17	18	19	20
21	22	23	24	25	26	27
28	29	30	31			

PHOTO © 2022 BILL CRUMP

Hawker Sea Fury

The Sea Fury is not a huge airplane, with its 38 foot 4.75 inch wingspan and maximum gross weight of 12,500 pounds, but the huge prop spinner and closely cowled engine give it the appearance of being much larger than it is. The original Sea Furys had 2,550 horsepower Bristol Centaurus engines.

Messerschmitt Bf 109E

Power Plant: One 1,455-hp Daimler-Benz engine
Wing Span: 32 ft. 6 in.
Length: 29 ft. 7 in.
Gross weight: 7,495 lbs.
Effective operating radius: 621 miles with extra fuel tanks
Maximum speed: 398 mph at 20,669 ft.
Armament: Two 20mm MG 151 cannons, one 30mm MK108 cannon, and two 13mm MG 131 machine guns.
Crew: 1

ME 262

Numerous after-mission reports from Christmas eve 1944 include sightings of Me262 jets flying by, though none detail engagement with these extraordinary aircraft. The revolutionary Messerschmitt 262 jet was ahead of its time but introduced too late to stem the flow of Allied bombers over Germany. Nearly 1,430 of these novel high-speed jets, capable of 540 miles per hour, were built by the Germans prior to the end of the war, though many were reported as destroyed on the ground by the Allies in late 1944 through 1945. The one pictured here was being flown by a defecting Luftwaffe pilot. It was shipped back to the United States and thoroughly studied.

The concept of jet aircraft was under development by the Nazis in 1936, prior to their invasion of Poland, yet they did not become operational until April of 1944. The delay had a number of causes, from design, testing, and materials to reluctance on the part of leaders, including Hermann Goering, of introducing them as a substitute for conventional fighters. Additionally, Hitler preferred the idea of a revolutionary jet-powered fighter/bomber. Many have speculated that the air war might have resulted in a different outcome, had the final development of the Me262 and the necessary training not been delayed.

ME 262

Power Plant: Two Junkers Jumo 004B-1 Turbojet Engines
Wing Span: 40 ft. 11 in.
Length: 34 ft. 9 in.
Gross weight: 8,378 lbs.
Effective operating radius: 652 miles with extra fuel tanks
Maximum speed: 541 mph at 37,565 ft.
Armament: Four 30-mm MK 108 cannons in nose.
Crew: 1

Appendix B

MAPS

Mission 760 Pre-Mission Map of Known Flak Batteries

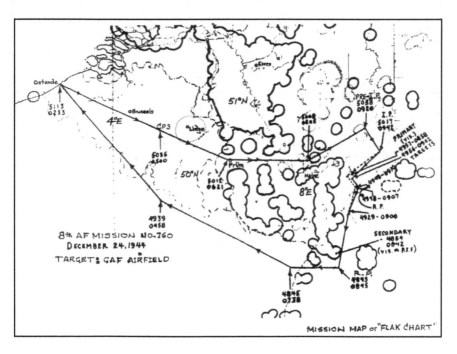

Original Route Map for Mission 760

24 Dec 1944

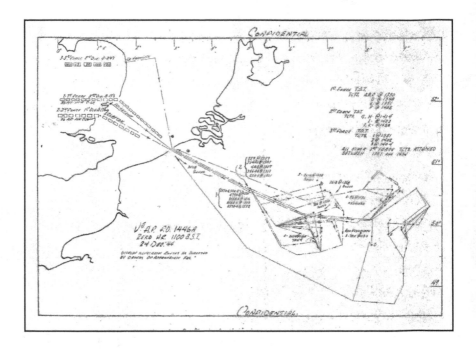

Routes to targets of the 8ᵗʰ AF First Attack Force

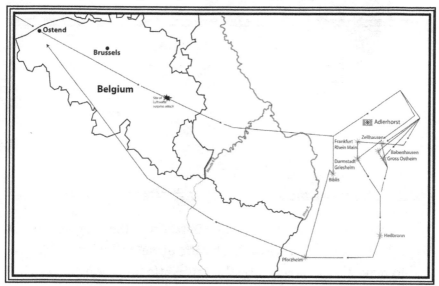

The bombers of the First Attack Force were all B-17s and directed to "posthole" runways and destroy grounded equipment and stationary facilities at German aerodromes on the east side of the Rhine River. They led the entire formation of the day and in their advance to their targets they unknowingly passed over Adolf Hitler's bunker and within observation by the Fuhrer and two of his secretaries. Presumably, he had already received news of the Luftwaffe attack on the first squadrons of this mammoth formation as it passed south of Liege, Belgium.

The assigned targets for this first force (Babenhausen, Biblis, Gross Ostheim, Darmstadt, Griesheim, Frankfurt) were all Luftwaffe airfields that were known to have been active in support of the ground war rapidly advancing to the west as part of Hitler's Ardennes Offensive, and the objective was to immobilize them. The plan was carefully choreographed to have the attacks to be simultaneously or new simultaneously.

Pforzheim and Heilbronn were added in flight as "targets of opportunity." There the selected targets were a rail bridge and marshalling yard in Heilbronn and a marshalling yard at Pforzheim.

Routes to targets of the 8th AF Second Attack Force

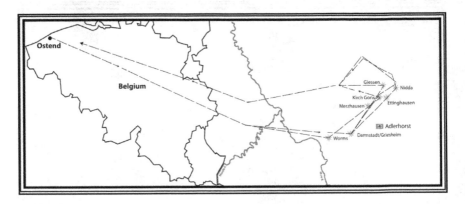

Similar to the attacks of the First Force, the targets for the Second Attack Force were all Luftwaffe airfields, and the objective was to make them unusable by the Luftwaffe for as long as possible in order to protect the Allied ground advancement in the Battle of the Bulge. A communications center in Worms was added during the mission as a target of opportunity. The attacking force was all comprised of B-17-equipped groups.

The northernmost airfield attacked by this force was Giessen, a full ninety-three miles south of Gutersloh, the base of the Luftwaffe unit that made the surprise attack on the 8th Air Force lead formation earlier in the day. Gutersloh was located in a cluster of thirty Luftwaffe bases protecting the border with Holland and the North Sea, bases instrumental in Operation Bodenplatte, the last great air attack of the war by the Luftwaffe on New Year's Day.

Routes to targets of the 8ᵗʰ AF Third Attack Force

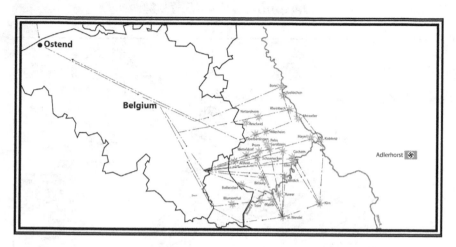

The Third Attack Force was comprised of B-24 equipped groups focused on numerous targets in a congested area between the Rhine River and German border with Belgium and Luxembourg, the region supplying the Battle of the Bulge with advancing Wehrmacht troops, equipment, and supplies. The specific targets were rail centers, marshalling yards, and rail bridges, but also included "communications centers" or roadways connecting resources with the ongoing ground battle. In the area along the Mosel River, transport facilities for supplies brought west by barge and boat were also attacked.

The Ardennes Offensive/ Battle of the Bulge
December 16 – 25, 1944

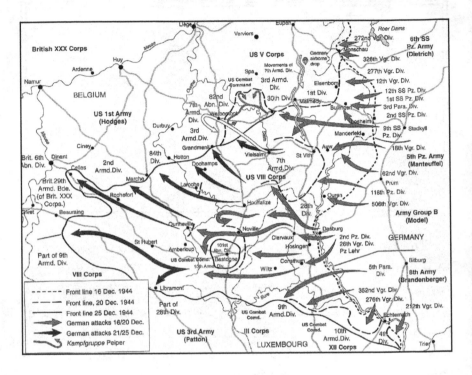

Appendix C

8th Air Force Structure
December 1944

1st Bombardment Division	2nd Bombardment Division	3rd Bombardment Division
1st Combat Bombardment Wing	2nd Combat Bombardment Wing	4th Combat Bombardment Wing
91st Bomb Group	389th Bomb Group	94th Bomb Group
381st Bomb Group	445th Bomb Group	385th Bomb Group
398th Bomb Group	453rd Bomb Group	447th Bomb Group
40th Combat Bombardment Wing	14th Combat Bombardment Wing	13th Combat Bombardment Wing
92nd Bomb Group	44th Bomb Group	95th Bomb Group
305th Bomb Group	392nd Bomb Group	100th Bomb Group
306th Bomb Group	491st Bomb Group	390th Bomb Group
492nd Bomb Group		
41st Combat Bombardment Wing	20th Combat Bombardment Wing	45th Combat Bombardment Wing
303rd Bomb Group	93rd Bomb Group	96th Bomb Group
379th Bomb Group	446th Bomb Group	388th Bomb Group
384th Bomb Group	448th Bomb Group	452nd Bomb Group
489th Bomb Group		
94th Combat Bombardment Wing	96th Combat Bombardment Wing	4th Combat Bombardment Wing
351st Bomb Group	458th Bomb Group	486th Bomb Group
401st Bomb Group	466th Bomb Group	487th Bomb Group
457th Bomb Group	467th Bomb Group	
		93rd Combat Bombardment
		34th Bomb Group
		490th Bomb Group
		493rd Bomb Group

Eighth Air Force Bases in England - 1944

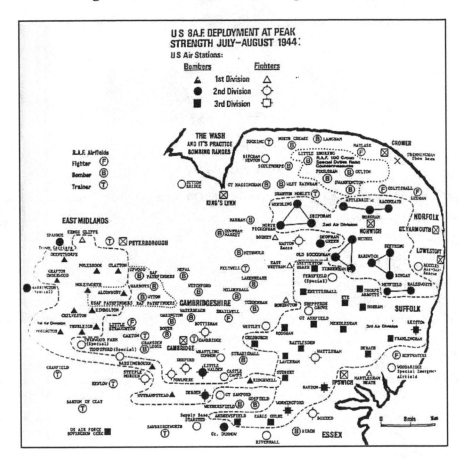

8th Air Force Bomber Bases & Identification
December 1944

Bomb Group	Station	Bomber Type	Unit ID	Missions Flown	Losses
34th	Mendelsham	B-24 to B-17	Black B on White with Red	170	34
44th	Shipdham	B-24	White E on Black Horizontal Stripe on White	343	153
91st	Bassingbourn	B-17	Black Triangle White A on Red	340	**197**
92nd	Podington	B-17	Black Triangle White B On Red	308	154
93rd	Hardwick	B-24	Yellow Z on Black Vertical on Yellow	396	100
94th	Bury St. Edmonds	B-17	Black Square White A On Yellow	324	153
95th	Horham	B-17	Black Square White B on Red	320	157
96th	Snetterton Health	B-17	Black Square White C On Red	321	189
100th	Thorpe Abbots	B-17	White Square Black D On Black	306	177
303rd	Molesworth	B-17	Red Triangle Black C on White Triangle	364	165
305th	Chelveston	B-17	Black Triangle White G On Green	337	154
306th	Thurleigh	B-17	Black Triangle White H On Yellow	342	171
351st	Polebrook	B-17	Black Triangle White J On Red	311	124
379th	Kimbolton	B-17	Black Triangle White K on Yellow	330	141
381st	Ridgewell	B-17	Black Triangle White L on Red	296	131
384th	Grafton Underwood	B-17	Black Triangle Black P on White Triangle	314	159
385th	Great Ashfield	B-17	White Square Black G On Camo	296	129

388th	Knettishall	B-17	Black Square White H On Black	306	142
389th	Hethel	B-24	Black H on Vertical White Stripe on Black	312	116
390th	Framlingham	B-17	Black Square White J on Yellow	300	144
392nd	Wendling	B-24	White N+ on Horizontal Stripe on White	285	127
398th	Nuthampstead	B-17	Black Triangle White W On Red	195	58
401st	Deenethorpe	B-17	Black Triangle White S On Yellow	256	95
445th	Tibenham	B-24	Black C on Horizontal White Stripe on Black	282	95
446th	Bungay	B-24	Yellow N on Black Horizontal in Black Circle on Yellow	273	58
447th	Rattlesden	B-17	Black Square White K On Yellow	257	97
448th	Seething	B-24	Yellow P in Yellow Circle on Black Diagonal on Yellow	262	101
452nd	Deopham Green	B-17	Black Square White L On Yellow	250	110
453rd	Old Buckenham	B-24	Black O on White Diagonal Stripe on Black	259	58
457th	Glatton	B-17	Black Triangle White U On Blue	237	83
458th	Horsham St. Faith	B-24	Red S on White Vertical Stripe on Red	240	47
466th	Attlebridge	B-24	Red K on White Horizontal Stripe on Red Circle L	232	47
467th	Rackheath	B-24	Red U on White Diagonal on Red	212	29
486th	Sudbury	B-24 to B-17	Black Square White W on Yellow	188	33
487th	Lavenham	B24 to B-17	Black Square White P On Yellow	185	48

489th	Halesworth	B-24	Black C on White Vertical on Green	106	29
490th	Eye	B-24 to B-17	848 Sq Black K 851st Sq Black +L 849th Sq Black L B-17 +U on White under Red	158	40
491st	Metfield	B-24	Black O on White Vertical on Green T	187	47
492nd	North Pickenham	B-24	White -H on Black Diagonal	64	12
493rd	Deebach	B-24 to B-17	Black M on White above Red	158	41
Total				**10,631**	**4,145**

Appendix D

TARGETS 24DEC1944

Ahrweiler Rail Bridge "Communications Center" 50°32′24″ N - 07°05′26″ E

Babenhausen Air Field 49°57′20 N - 08°58′15 E

Biblis Air Field 49°42′0 N - 08°28′0 E

Bitburg Air Field "Communications Center" 49°56′43 N – 06°33′54″ E

Blumenthal Target of Opportunity "Communications Center" 50°25′90″N – 06°25′90″ E

Cochem "Communications Center" 40°08′49″N – 07°10′E

Darmstadt/Griesheim Air Field 49°52′N – 08°39E

Daun "Communications Center" 50°11′55″ N – 06°49′55″E

Eller Railroad Bridges and Tunnel Entrance 50°05′53″N - 07°09′03″

Ettinghausen Air Field 50°31′04N - 07°52′24″E

Euskirchen "Communications Center" 50°39′35″N – 06°47′30″E

Frankfurt/Rhein Main Air Field 50°02′N - 08°34′14″E

Gerolstein Marshalling Yard and Road Junction 50°13'26"N – 06°39'41"E

Giessen Air Field 50°32'24"N – 07°05'26"E

Gross Ostheim Air Field 49°55'N – 09°05'E

Heilbronn Target of Opportunity Rail Bridge Marshalling Yard 49°08'36.91N 09°12'37.78"E

Hillesheim "Communications Center" 50°17'33"N – 06°40'30"E

Kaiserslautern Marshalling Yard 49°26'41"N – 07°46'08E

Kirch Gons Air Field 50°28'46"N – 08°38'42"E

Koblenz (S) Marshalling Yard, Power Station 50°21'35"N – 07°35'52"E

Mayen M/Y & Supply Lines "Communications Center" 50°19' N - 7°13'E

Merzhausen Air Field/Depot 47°58'N – 7°49'E

Nidda Air Field 50°24'N-9°00'E

Pfalzel Road Junction "Communications Center" 49°47'33.57N – 06°41'16.3E

Pforzheim Marshalling Yard 48°53'N- 8°34'E

Prum "Communications Center" Rail and supply center 50°11'N – 6°22'E

Rheinbach "Communications Center" 50°38'N – 06°57'E

Ruwer M/Y & Road Junction "Communications Center" 49°47'N – 6°42'E

Schleiden Target of Opportunity 50°31'59" – 06°28'00" E

Schonecken "Communications Center" 50°09'13.3"N

Trier "Communications Center," Bridges, Rail 49°44'N – 6°38'E

Wetteldorf "Communications Center" 50°09'07.59"N – 06°27'52.32"E

Wittlich Rail & supply center "Communications Center"

Worms Target of Opportunity 49°36′N – 8°59′E

Zellhausen Air Field 50°N – 8°59′E

BIBLIOGRAPHY

Source Material

The key details of Mission 760 of the Eighth Air Force come from the mission files stored in the archives of the Air Force Historical Research Agency (AFHRA) at Maxwell Air Force Base in Montgomery, Alabama. That has been supplemented by material found in the many fine histories of World War II that have been written over the past seventy-five years and are listed in the Bibliography. In most cases specific information provided was found in multiple source materials. Specific details from members of the 487th Bomb Group are taken from interviews and articles written by the men who flew the mission on 24 December 1944. The same is true of individuals who flew with other units or were members of the many ground crews anxiously awaiting the return of those brave young fliers who had said good-bye to them hours earlier that Christmas Eve.

Manuscript and Photo Collections

Air Force Historical Research Agency, Maxwell Air Force Base, Alabama

Mission Reports for 8th Air Force Missions 759 and 760

Eight Air Force Fighter Command Reports

Interrogations of combat crews

Unit histories and records of the Eighth Air Force Bomb Groups

Miscellaneous records of the United States Strategic Bombing Survey

**National Archives and Records Administration,
College Park, Maryland**

Combat mission reports, field orders, Division, Wing, and Squadron reports

Mighty Eighth Air Force Heritage Museum, Pooler, Georgia

Unpublished memoirs, diaries, and letters of Eighth Air Force personnel

487ᵗʰ Bomb Group Association Records and Photo Collection

U.S. Air Force Official History

Craven, Wesley Frank, and James Lea Cate, eds. *The Army Air Forces in World War II.*

Vol. 3: Europe: Argument to V-E Day, January 1944 to May 1945. Chicago: University of Chicago Press, 1958.

Frisbee, John L., ed. *Makers of the United States Air Force.* US Government Printing Office, 1996.

Books

Alling, Charles. *A Mighty Fortress: Lead Bomber Over Europe.* Drexel Hill, PA: Casemate, 2006.

Ambrose, Steven E. *Citizen Soldiers: The U.S. Army from the Normandy Beaches to the Bulge to the Surrender of Germany, June 7, 1944 to May 7, 1945*. New York: Simon & Schuster, 1997.

— —, *The Wild Blue, The Men and Boys who Flew the B-24s over Germany 1944–45*. New York: Simon & Schuster, 1997.

Astor, Gerald. *The Mighty Eighth*. New York: Dell, 1997.

Atkinson, Rick. *The Guns at Last Light: The War in Western Europe, 1944–45*. New York: Henry Holt & Co., 2013.

Ayres, Travis L. *The Bomber Boys: Heroes Who Flew the B-17s in World War II*. New York: NAL Caliber, 2006.

Bailey, Ronald H. and the Editors of Time-Life Books. *The Air War in Europe: 1940–1945*. Richmond, VA: Time Life Books, 1998.

Barker, Ralph. *The Thousand Plane Raid: The Story of the First Massive Air Raid – 1000 Bombers Against the City of Cologne*. New York: Ballantine Books, 1966.

Barron, Lee & Cygan, Don. *No Silent Night: The Christmas Battle for Bastogne*. New York: NAL Caliper, 2012.

Baumbach, Werner. *Luftwaffe* New York: Dorset Press, 1960.

— —, *The Life and Death of the Luftwaffe*. New York: Ballantine War Books, 1967.

Bowman, Martin. *1st Air Division, 8th Air Force USAAF 1942–45: Flying Fortress & Liberator Squadrons in Norfolk & Suffolk Barnsley*. South Yorkshire: Pen & Sword Aviation, 2007.

—-, *3rd Air Division, 8th Air Force USAAF 1942–45; Flying Fortress & Liberator in Norfolk & Suffolk*. Barnsley, South Yorkshire: Pen & Sword Aviation, 2009.

—-. *B-17 Flying Fortress Units of the Eighth Air Force (Part 1)*. Oxford: Osprey Publishing, 2000.

— -. *B-17 Flying Fortress Units of the Eighth Air Force (Part 2)*. Oxford: Osprey Publishing, 2002.

— -, *Castles in the Air: The Story of the B-17 Flying Fortress Crews of the 8th Air Force*. Wellingborough: Patrick Stephens, 1984.

— -, *Clash of Eagles: USAAF 8th Air Force Bombers Versus the Luftwaffe in World War 2*. Barnsley, South Yorkshire: Pen & Sword Books, Ltd., 2010.

— -, *Fields of Little America: An Illustrated History of the 8th Air Force, 2nd Air Division 1942–45*. Norwich: Wensum Books, 1977.

— - *Great American Air Battles of World War II*. Shrewsbury: Airlife Publishing, 1994.

— - *The Mighty 8th At War Yorkshire*: Pen & Sword Books, 2010.

Bowyer, Chaz. *Air War Over Europe 1939–1945*. Barnsley: Leo Cooper, 2003.

Butcher, Harry C. *My Three Years with Eisenhower*. New York: Simon and Schuster, 1946.

Caldwell, Donald. *Day Fighters of the Reich: A War Diary, 1942–45*. Yorkshire: Frontline Books, 2011.

Caldwell, Donald & Muller, Richard. *The Luftwaffe Over Germany*. Yorkshire: Frontline Books, 2014.

Craven, Wesley Frank & Cate, James Lea. *The Army Air Forces in World War II Volume 3: Europe – Argument to V-E Day January 1944 to May 1945*. Washington DC: Office of Air Force History, 1983.

Carter, Kit C. & Mueller, Robert. *Chronology 1941–1945*. Washington, DC: Research Center Air University and Office of Air Force History Headquarters USAF, 1973.

Caddick-Adams, Peter. *Snow & Steel: The Battle of the Bulge 1944–1945*. New York: Oxford University Press, 2015.

Copp, Dewitt S. *A Few Great Captains: The Men and Events that Shaped the Development of U.S. Air Power*. McLean, VA: EPM, 1980.

Cross, Robin. *The Battle of the Bulge: Hitler's Last Hope December 1944*. London: Amber Books, 2014.

Crosby, Harry H. *A Wing and A Prayer: The "Bloody 100th" Bomb Group of the U.S. Eighth Air Force in Action Over Europe in World War II*. New York: Harper Paperbacks, 1993.

Davis, Richard G. *Carl A. Spaatz and the Air War in Europe*. Washington, DC: Center for Air Force History, 1993.

Deichmann, Paul. *Spearhead For Blitzkrieg: Luftwaffe Operations in Support of the Army 1939–1945*. New York: Ivy Books, 1996.

DeJong, Ivo. *The History of the 487th Bomb Group*. Nashville, TN: Turner Publishing Co., 2004.

Duffer, Jost. *Nazi Germany 1933–1945: Faith & Annihilation*. London: Arnold, 1996.

Dupuy, Trevor N. et al. *Hitler's Last Gamble: The Battle of the Bulge, December 1944–January 1945*. New York: Harper Collins, 1994.

Eberle, Henrik and Uhl, Matthias eds. *Interrogations of Hitler's Personal Aides*. New York: Public Affairs, 2005.

Eisenhower, Dwight D. *Crusade in Europe*. Garden City, New York: Doubleday, 1948.

Elstob, Peter. *Hitler's Last Offensive: The Surprise German Assault that Triggered the Battle of the Bulge*. New York: Macmillan Company, 1971.

Essame, H. *The Battle for Germany: The true story of the greatest battle in history*. New York: Ace Books, 1969.

Ethell, Jeffrey L. & Price, Alfred. *Target Berlin: Mission 250 1944*. London: Arms & Armor Press, 1989.

Forty, George. *Ardennes Offensive, December 1944*. London: Cassell & Co., 2000.

Freeman, Michael. *Atlas of Nazi Germany*. New York: Macmillan, 1987.

Freeman, Roger A. *B-17 Fortress At War*. London: Ian Allan Ltd, 1977.

––, *Mighty Eighth War Diary*. London: Jane's Publishing, 1981.

––, *Raiding the Reich: The Allied Strategic Bombing Offensive in Europe*. London: Arms and Armour, 1997.

––, *The Mighty Eighth: A History of Units, Men and Machines of the US 8th Air Force*. London: Cassell & Co., 1997.

––, *US Strategic Air Power: Europe 1942–45*. London: Cassell & Co., 2000.

Frisbee, John L. *Makers of the United States Air Force*. Washington, DC: The Air Force History & Museum Program.

Gilbert, Martin. *The Second World War: A Complete History*. New York: Henry Holt & Co., 1989.

Goolrick, William & Tanner, Ogden. *The Battle of the Bulge*. Alexandria, VA: Time Life Books, 1979.

Gregoire, Gerard. *Decembre 44: Feu-Fire-Feuer-Vuur*. La Glieze, 1996.

Groom, Winston. *The Aviators: Eddie Rickenbacker, Jimmy Doolittle, Charles Lindbergh, and the Epic Age of Flight*. Washington: National Geographic, 2013.

Halpert, Sam. *A Real Good War*. St. Petersburg: Southern Heritage Press, 1967.

Hansen, Randall. *Fire and Fury: The Allied Bombing of Germany 1942–1945*. New York: NAL Caliper, 2008.

Hart, B.H. Liddell. *The German General's Talk*. New York: William Morrow & Co, 1948.

Hastings, Max. *Armageddon: The Battle for Germany 1944–1945*. New York: Random House, 2004.

Herbert, Elizabeth Woolsey, ed. *Jack's War: Letters to Home From an American WWII Navigator*. Lexington, KY: Self-Published, 2015.

Hutchinson, James Lee T/Sgt. *The Boys in the B-17*. Indiana: Authorhouse, 2011.

Kaplin, Philip and Smith, Rex. *One Last Look*. New York: Artabras Publishers, 1983.

Kennedy, David M. ed. *Library of Congress World War II Companion*. New York: Simon & Schuster, 2007.

Killen, John. *A History of the Luftwaffe 1915–1945*. New York: 1967.

Koger, Fred. *Countdown! 35 Daylight Missions Against Nazi Germany*. Chapel Hill: Algonquin, 1990.

Linge, Heinz. *With Hitler to the End*. New York: Skyhorse Publishing, 2009.

Lucas, James. *The Last Year of the German Army*. London: Arms & Armour, 1994.

Lucas, Laddie. *Voices in the Air 1939–1945: Incredible Stories of the World War II Airmen in Their Own Voices*. London: 2003.

Maddox, Joey. *The Great Rat Race for Europe*. Bloomington, IN: Xlibris, 2011.

McDonald, Charles. *A time for Trumpets: The Untold Story of the Battle of the Bulge*. New York: William Morrow & Co., 1985.

McNab, Chris. *Hitler's Eagles: The Luftwaffe 1933–45*. Oxford: Osprey Publishing, 2012.

—-, *Hitler's Master Plan, The Essential Facts and Figures for Hitler's Third Reich*. London: Amber Books, 2009.

McPherson, John B. et al. *"Confidential" Picture History of WWII (Vol 1)*. Harrisburg, PA: Historical Times, 1982.

Meurs, John. *Not Home for Christmas: A Day in the Life of the Mighty Eighth*. Branden, MS: Quail Ridge Press, 2009.

Miller, Donald L. *Masters of the Air: America's Bomber Boys who Fought the Air War Against Nazi Germany*. New York: Simon & Schuster, 2006.

—-, *The Story of World War II*. New York: Simon & Schuster, 2001.

Miser, Hugh J. ed. *Operations Analysis in the Eighth Air Force, 1942–1945: Four Contemporary Accounts*. Linthicum, MD: Informs, 1997.

Morris, Rob. *Untold Valor: Forgotten Stories of American Bomber Crews Over Europe in World War II*. Washington, DC: Potomac Books, 2006.

Neal, C.C. *Gentlemen from Hell: Men of the 487th Bomb Group*. Nashville, TN: Turner Publishing Co., 2005.

Neillands, Robin. *The Bomber War: The Allied Air Offensive Against Nazi Germany*. Woodstock, NY: The Overlook Press, 2001.

Newcomer, James. *The Grand Duchy of Luxembourg: The Evolution of Nationhood*. Luxembourg: Le Bon Livre, 1995.

Overy, R.J. *The Air War 1939–1945*. New York: Stein & Day, 1981.

—-, *The Bombing War; Europe 1939–1945*. London: Allen Lane, 2013.

—-. *The Bombers and the Bombed: Allied Air War Over Europe, 1940–1945*. New York: Viking, 2013.

Parker, Danny S. *To Win The Winter Sky: Air War Over the Ardennes, 1944–1945*. Conshohocken, PA: Combined Books, Inc., 1994.

—-, *Hitler's Ardennes Offensive: The German View of the Battle of the Bulge*. London: Greenhill Books, 1997.

—-, *Battle of the Bulge: Hitler's Ardennes Offensive, 1944–1945*. Philadelphia: Combined Books, 1991.

Parton, James. *Eaker & the Command of the Air.* Bethesda, MD: Adler & Adler, 1986.

Pavelec, S. Mike. *World War II Data Book; The Luftwaffe 1933–1945.* London: Amber Books.

Piekalkiewicz, Janusz. *The German National Railway in World War II.* Atglen, PA: Schiffer Military History, 2008.

Pons, Gregory. *Bomber Groups in England 1942-45.* Paris: Histoire & Collections, 2006.

Price, Alfred. *Luftwaffe.* New York: Ballantine Books, 1971.

—-, *The Last Year of the Luftwaffe: May 1944 to May 1945.* London: Arms and Armour, 1991.

Province, Charles M. *Patton's Third Army: A Chronology of the Third Army Advance, August 1944 to May 1945.* New York: Hippocrene Books, 1992.

Schroeder, Christa. *He Was My Chief.* London: Frontline Books, 2009.

Scutts, Jerry. *Lion in the Sky: US 8th Air Force Fighter Operations 1942–45* Wellingborough: Patrick Stevens, 1987.

Slater, Harry E. *Lingering Contrails of the Big Square A: A History of the 94th Bomb Group (H) 1942–1945.* Nashville, TN: Garrett Graphics, 1980.

Spires, David N. *Air Power for Patton's Army: the XIX Tactical Air Command in the Second World War.* Washington DC: Air Force History & Museums Program.

Stevens, Charles N. *An Innocent At Polebrook: A Memoir of an 8th Air Force Bombardier.* Bloomington, IN: 1st Books Library, 2004.

Swanston, Alexander & Swanston, Malcolm. *The Historical Atlas of World War II.* London: Chartwell Books, 2008.

Toland, John. *Battle: The Story of the Bulge*. New York: Random House, 1959.

Tourtelliot, et al. ed. *Life's Picture History of World War II*. New York: Time Inc., 1950.

Visant, Wayne. *Bombing Nazi Germany*. Minneapolis: Zenith Press, 2013.

Ward, Geoffrey C. and Burns, Ken. *The War: An Intimate History 1941–1945*. New York: Alfred A. Knopf, 2007.

Weal, John. *Luftwaffe Sturmgruppen*. Wellingborough: Osprey Publishing, 2005.

Weintraub, Stanley. *11 Days in December: Christmas at the Bulge, 1944*. New York: New American Library, 2007.

Wissolic et al. ed. *They Say There Was a War*. Latrobe, PA: St. Vincent College, 2005.

Unpublished Compilation

A Documentary Compilation of Facts on Crew Members and Aircraft Lost in Europe during World War II completed in 1993.

Website

A website located at http://24december1944.com developed and maintained by Joost de Raaf containing facts, details, and copies of original documents of 8th Air Force Mission 760.

INDEX

Aach................214

Aachen...23, 79, 225, 229

Aden, Lt. Glen E. 168

Adlerhorst....6, 12, 17, 91, 94, 95, 97, 98, 104, 109, 139, 142, 143, 154, 157, 158, 159, 161, 162, 221, 237, 241

Ahr River...166, 168

Ahrweiler...30, 40, 166, 189, 230, 278

Air Force Historical Research Agency.. ...iii, 281

Air Command..22, 26, 28, 159, 227, 289

Alamogordo, NM..101

Alburgh........30

Alconbury...163

Alivis, Lt. Russell...222

Alsace...8

Alvine, FO Samuel..69, 70

Amsterdam...214

Andernach...180

Anderson, General Frederick L...229

Anding, James E. ...92

Andrews, SSgt Benedict ..63

Antwerp..8, 14

Ardennes Offensive.. i, 5, 8, 15, 18, 19, 25, 36, 39, 49, 62, 66, 72, 78, 79, 93, 94, 95, 97, 98, 99, 103, 104, 112, 117, 119, 127, 128, 134, 141, 142, 157, 159, 163, 165, 172, 174, 179, 178, 180, 183, 192, 195, 196, 200, 202, 223, 231, 232, 237, 239, 240, 241, 242, 247, 248, 251, 269, 272, 286, 288

Armor, Lt. Ray... 184

Arnold, General Henry "Hap" II,21, 26, 53, 54, 61, 88

Arzfeld....168, 169

Asch...226, 227, 231

Aschaffenburg.....104, 108, 109

Asseln, T/Sgt. Ernest...163

Associated Press...18
Attack Forces...165, 223
    1st Force...47, 49, 183
    2nd Force... 47, 183
    3rd Force...91, 196, 223, 225
Auer, Cpt. Edmund ...58
Aussig.....246
Aywaille...65, 72
Babenhausen...39, 54, 77, 100,
    102, 103, 104, 104, 106,107,
    109, 111, 209, 211, 212, 213
Bad Kreuznach...183, 224
Bad Nauheim...12, 91, 94, 142,
    160
Ball, Lt. Ira L. 63, 64
Banta, Lt. Michael ...156, 157
Baraque de Fraiture ...68
Barbaras, Lt. Gordon F. ...136
Barajas, Sgt. Ralph R. ...73, 74,
    75
Beroun ...246
Barneycastle, 1/Lt. ...223
Bassingbourn... 35, 48, 154, 156,
    157,160, 186, 275
Bastogne...31, 33, 81, 114, 168,
    173, 231, 238, 283
Battle of the Bulge...II, 5, 37, 59,
    79, 102, 163,168, 228, 231,
    239, 240, 241, 251, 270,271,
    272, 284, 285, 286, 287, 288
Baugnez...26, 232
Baganz, S/Sgt Reuben...63

Becker, Lt. Cuno V....64, 65
Beggs, T/Sgt. Eugene...106
Belgium...III, 5, 8, 12, 24, 31,
    40,47, 48, 49, 53, 54, 55, 57, 60,
    61, 62, 63, 66, 67, 74, 75, 77,
    78, 79, 81, 82, 84, 94, 95, 98,
    100,105, 109, 114, 130, 133,
    135, 136,141, 142, 148, 149,
    152, 162, 170, 172, 178, 182,
    193, 194, 199, 209, 212, 213,
    215, 217, 221, 222, 223, 226,
    228,229, 231, 235, 237, 238,
    242, 248, 254, 255, 269, 271
Bellevue, Iowa...181
Bennett, 1/Lt. J.E. ...191, 197
Beno, Lt. S. ...183
Berlin.... 6, 9, 12, 23, 97, 144,
    161, 174, 175, 178, 202, 237,
    241, 242, 244, 245, 249, 285
Bernkastel-Keus...202
Berry, Robert...153
Bevan, Miss Win...133
Biblis...39, 108, 114, 115, 116,
    117, 119, 120, 214, 220, 269,
    278, 292
Bietingheim... 24
Bingen...7, 182
Birkhead, Sgt. John....222
Biri, Lt. Paul...56, 57, 58, 59
Bitburg...40, 168, 169, 170, 171,
    172, 173, 190, 191, 195, 200,
    201, 227, 278

Blackwell, S/Sgt Robert C. 74, 75

Blumenthal....172, 173, 178

Bollendorf 173

Bonn 9, 29, 31, 81, 139, 166, 174, 178, 187, 195, 216, 219, 221, 224

Bonn-Koblenz RR 216

Booth, TSgt. John 150, 222

Bormann, Martin 158

2/Lt. Bornstedt, 2/Lt. ...186

Borth, Uffz. Paul ...80

Bosse, S/Sgt Sherwin 87, 100, 102, 250

Bradford, Lt. James ...61, 65, 66

Bradley, General Omar ...9, 20, 22, 23, 159, 170

Bremen ...162

Bremerhaven ...162

British 7, 8, 9, 14, 47, 78, 82, 107, 111, 139, 150, 151, 222, 233, 244, 245, 254, 256

British #2 Group ...78

Brockmeyer, Sgt. William J. 48

Broom, Lt. John C. 63, 64, 65

Brown, Lt. Gerald 119

Bruges 51, 84, 85

Brussels ...51, 54, 56, 75, 84, 85, 116, 197, 210, 216, 218

Brandenberger, Erich 237

Bryan, James 153

Bull, Harold R. 22

Bungay....166, 189, 276

Burda, Lt. Orville F. ...171

Burke, S/Sgt James ...200

Burningham, Lt. Haven ...134

Burgdorf, Wilhelm ...8, 247

Burakoff, Lt. Morris ...163

Burrows, William ...153

Bury St. Edmunds ...42, 44, 106, 107, 145, 153, 156, 160

Callaghan, T/Sgt Frank 74, 75

Canterbury, Clifford J. 92

Capraro, Sgt. Joseph 131

Caravello, S/Sgt. John ...149, 222

"Carpetbagger Project" 163

Carter, Colonel William R. ...37

Casablanca, Morocco ...37

Castle, Brigadier General Frederick W. ... *II, 42, 43, 44, 45, 47, 50, 51, 52, 53, 54, 55, 56, 57, 58, 59, 60, 61, 62, 64, 65, 67, 68, 69, 84, 85, 86, 100, 102, 106*

Chaplin, Miss Joy 133

Capwell, Roy V. 92

Chateau d'Englebermont ...59, 68

Chateau de Warnmont 63

Chatterton, Lt. Thomas...76, 77

Chelveston ...144, 151, 153, 275

Christian, Eckhard ...8

Christian, Gerda "Dara"... 94, 95

Christenson, Lt. C.R. ...147

Christmas Day...72, 104, 105, 156, 157, 227, 238

Chowing, T/Sgt Vivian R....48

Churchill, Prime Minister Winston ...37

Clacton...47, 140, 141, 150, 155, 162

Clark, Lt. John....91

Cochem..40, 175, 176, 177, 183, 200, 278

Collins, Father Joe....107

Collins, Lt. Thomas....74, 75

Cologne...29, 124, 125, 139, 174, 180, 182, 187, 188, 216, 218, 219, 221

Comblain-au-Pont...66, 74

Control Point 1...47, 250

Control Point 2...47

Control Point 3...51, 55, 60, 85

Copier, Willem ...138, 139

Crombie, Cpt. Bill...218, 219

Crowell, Col. 51

Culver, Lt. Harry 147, 148

Curtiss, Lt. Willard J. 73, 74, 75

Czechoslovakia....247

Dahlem....30, 230

Darmstadt....39, 79, 117, 121, 123, 124, 125, 126, 127, 128, 130, 133, 134, 136, 214, 220, 235, 269, 278

Darmstadt Greisheim Air Base 121

Dasburg...168

Daun...40, 87, 129, 174, 176, 177, 180, 202, 211, 220, 278

Dave Castle...217

D-Day...23, 37, 49, 52, 94, 99, 101, 171, 177, 178, 208, 237

Debach....121,125, 151, 153

Debden....219, 220

Dee, Lt. Robert H. 186

Deenethorpe...105, 121, 124, 133, 184, 276

Dele, Elise....170

Delmenhorst...79

Deshon, PA....249

Densmore, Lt. Robert....3, 52, 65, 67, 68, 73

Deopham Green....121, 124, 276

Didsbury....44

Dietrich, Sepp....12, 13

Dinant...217

Doherty, Captain William A. ...127, 138

Doolittle, General Jimmy....31, 36, 88, 89, 165, 205, 206, 208, 209, 286

Dortmund....79, 81, 127

Dregne, Lt. Col. Irwin H. 51, 55

Dresden...79, 246

Duisburg/Essen....28, 79, 127

Dulag-Luft West....200

Dulag Luft Wetzlar....92

Dumler, LT Fred....66

Dunkirk....14, 214

Dusseldorf....128

Duxford...30, 49, 224, 225

Eaker, General Ira....53, 88, 106, 206, 289

"Eaker's Amateurs"....53, 106

East Anglia....30, 41, 42, 45, 47, 105, 123, 127, 133, 191

Eberbach.....108

Ecternach....17, 24

Edwards, Lt. John "Pappy"....4, 44, 45, 56, 57, 69, 86, 87, 100, 101, 102, 104, 105, 249, 250

Erft River....180

Ehrang....30, 117, 175, 230

Eifel Mountains....15, 24, 29, 40, 170, 176, 180, 186, 187 193, 202, 203

Eifelbahn....182

Eighth Army Air Corps...*I, II, III, IV,* 5, 6, 37, 40, 42, 43, 45, 46, 47, 50, 53, 55, 56, 83, 107, 130, 133, 141, 169, 194, 196, 205, 206, 215, 224, 227, 232, 233, 234, 237, 241, 169, 194, 196, 205, 206, 215, 224, 227, 232, 233, 234, 241, 242, 245,

246, 247, 251, 254, 255, 270, 273, 275, 281, 283, 284, 289, 290

Air Divisions

1st Air Division...246, 283

2nd Air Division...29, 176, 247, 284

3rd Air Division....245, 283

Combat Wings

2nd Combat Wing....222

4th Combat Wing....42, 43, 106, 202

14th Combat Wing....202

Bomb Groups

34th Bomb Group...134, 136, 137, 139, 274, 275

44th Bomb Group....173, 178, 191, 192, 196, 197, 201, 203, 273, 275

91st Bomb Group....48, 154, 155, 156, 160, 275

92nd Bomb Group....35, 48, 107, 144, 145, 146, 149, 153, 217, 219, 221, 273, 275

93rd Bomb Group...30, 166, 168, 189, 275

94th Bomb Group....31,42, 53,

100, 105, 106, 129,
139, 156, 273, 275,
289

95th Bomb Group.....115,
116, 117, 174, 273, 275

96th Bomb Group....123,
125, 131, 273, 275

100th Bomb Group....91,
112, 115, 119, 120,
213, 214, 273, 275

303rd Bomb Group....35,
149, 154, 273, 275

305th Bomb
Group....144, 151,
153, 219, 273, 275

306th Bomb
Group....143, 144,
150, 151, 153, 219,
273, 275

351st Bomb Group....115,
162, 164, 184, 186, 220,
273, 275

379th Bomb
Group....218, 213

381st Bomb Group....138,
140, 142, 143, 154, 156,
160, 184, 185, 214, 276,
273, 275

384th Bomb
Group....115, 117,
230, 237, 275

385th Bomb Group....77,

92, 100, 108, 109, 218,
273, 275

388th Bomb
Group....121, 122,
123, 125, 126, 131,
133, 214, 273, 276

389th Bomb
Group....169, 171,
176, 183, 187, 200,
273, 276

390th Bomb Group....91,
112, 113, 114, 213,
216, 273, 276

392nd Bomb
Group....191, 192,
196, 197, 273, 276

398th Bomb Group....48,
155, 156, 160, 174,
184, 186, 216, 218,
273, 276

401st Bomb
Group....138, 139,
140, 161, 184, 220,
273, 275

445th Bomb
Group....171, 187,
190, 273, 276

446th Bomb Group....30,
166, 168, 179, 188,
195, 213, 227, 273, 276

447th Bomb
Group....108, 112,

113, 273, 276

448th Bomb
  Group....171, 180,
  188, 195, 222, 227,
  273, 276

452nd Bomb
  Group....121, 124,
  125, 130, 214, 273, 276

453rd Bomb
  Group....171, 176,
  182, 187, 273, 276

457th Bomb Group....48,
  138, 140, 184, 186,
  220, 273

458th Bomb
  Group....172, 173,
  194, 198, 199, 201, 226,
  273, 276

486th Bomb
  Group....108, 109,
  110, 111, 213, 273, 276

487th Bomb Group....3,
  44, 45, 52, 56, 64, 66,
  68, 69, 77, 80, 85, 100,
  101, 102, 103, 104, 105,
  106, 108, 215, 273, 276,
  281, 282, 285, 288

489th Bomb
  Group....273, 277

491st Bomb
  Group.....177, 201,
  202, 204, 273, 277

493rd Bomb Group....
  121, 125, 137, 273, 277

Fighter Groups
  4th FG....215
  20th FG....221
  55th FG....51, 87, 210,
    211, 212, 213
  78th FG....49, 227
  339th FG....49, 214
  353rd FG....85, 214
  355th FG....213, 214
  357th FG....51, 87, 88,
    211, 212
  359th FG....215, 216
  361st FG....22, 226, 227
  364th FG.... 215, 218
  479th FG....51, 213

Reconnaissance
  10th PRG

Eisenhower, General Dwight
  David....III, 4, 9, 20, 21, 22,
  23, 24, 25, 26, 33, 34, 36, 98,
  159, 234, 243, 244, 284, 285

Eller....40, 177, 178, 184, 213,
  233, 278

Emden....162

Emerson, Capt. Donald R. 227

Enigma 9, 26, 254

Enstone....153

Eshleman, Lt. Oscar....63

Ettinghausen....141, 142, 143,
  154, 174, 216, 278

Ettelbrick, Lt. Charles H. 136

Euskirchen....40, 166, 172, 178, 179, 180, 182, 189, 195, 227, 278

Eye....129, 136, 277

Eys....51, 54, 255

Fackelman, Lt. Robert....91, 112

Falkenau....246

Fegelein, Hermann....8

Felixstowe....47, 50, 77, 84, 115, 123, 140, 141

Ferenchak, S/Sgt George....63

Ferrari, Lt. Bernard....223

Fischern....246

Flint, Owen.....1, 2, 3, 4, 5

Florsheim am Main.....212

Fowlmere....49, 214

Fraiture.....59, 66, 67, 74

Framlingham.....113, 153, 367

France....4, 8, 12, 30, 32, 40, 68, 82, 96, 99, 101, 119, 130, 133, 143, 150, 166, 170, 202, 203, 207, 218, 227, 228, 229, 237, 238, 240

Frankfurt-Rheine.....39, 69, 79, 103, 104, 117, 124, 125, 127, 131, 132, 133, 134, 136, 139, 212, 214, 215, 217, 131, 132, 133, 134, 136, 139, 212, 222, 225, 240, 269, 278

Freitas, Sgt. Daniel....132, 133

Fulda....212, 213, 214, 239

Fuhrerbunker.....160, 247

Fullick, Major...143

Funderburk, T/Sgt Marion....200

Galland, Adolf...208

Garrison, S/Sgt Charles M. 149

Garrison. Sgt. Linn...222

Gauthier, Lt. Gerard....87, 100, 102, 251, 222, 250

Gemund....127, 176, 178

George, Sgt. Patrick....223

Gerber, Lt. John D. 132

German Intelligence....164

Gerolstein....40, 91, 176, 177, 180, 181, 182, 187, 190, 191, 201, 216, 226, 227, 279

Ghezzi, Lt. Edward....74, 75

Giesen, Lt. Charles....199, 200, 299

Giessen....12, 39, 141, 145, 146, 150, 151, 152, 153, 154, 155, 161, 162, 167, 216, 218, 219, 220, 221, 256, 240, 270, 279

Giessen-Limburg-Koblenz RR....216

Gilbert, Lt. William....212

Glatton....138, 139, 148, 184, 276

Goebbels, Joseph....96, 247

Goldberg, Saul "Rube" 87, 100, 101, 250

Gordon, Lt. Vincent....211

Goering, Hermann....10, 16, 17, 28, 158, 247, 266

Grafton Underwood....117, 140, 155, 275

Gregory, S/Sgt Jefferson....76, 77

Great Ashfield....108, 153, 275

Great Massingham....133

Greco, Angelo....150, 153

Greenberg, Sgt. Al....131, 132

Griesheim....121, 122, 126, 269, 278

Grinter, Lt. Donald D. 49

Goodman, Myron....153

Gross Ostheim....39, 92, 108, 109, 110, 111, 213, 214, 235, 265, 279

Großenhain....79

Grossman, Max....138

Grubbs, Sgt. Roland....223

Guderian, Heinz....8, 93

Gutersloh....79, 81, 99, 104, 141, 210, 233, 270

Gunsche, Otto....8

H2X system....29, 45, 111, 182, 191, 196, 201, 254

Haildraum....40, 121, 128

Hallendorf....28

Halesworth (Holton) 224, 225, 277

Hamburg....162, 202

Hammonds, Victor R. ...92

Hanau....134, 225, 240

Hanson, Lt. Edward....223

Harder, Ike....153

Hargrave, Sgt. Pearlie....21

Harriman, Lt. Robert....44, 45, 47, 53, 56, 57, 58, 62, 67, 102, 248

Harris, Lt. Theodore....119

Hartsoe, Lt. Hubert....110

Haskett, Sgt Charles "Chuck" 69, 70, 72

Hatfield, Lt. Roger C.....66

Hauck, FahnenjunkerFeldwebel Heinz...137, 138, 139

Heinkel He111....44, 170

Heilbronn....119, 121, 128, 129, 269, 279

Heidelberg...213.

Hellendoorn....244

Hellenthal...173, 194, 199, 227

Helwig, Lt. Wendell....88, 89, 90, 212

Henri-Chapelle American Cemetery...75, 77, 248

Herrin, Lt. Dick....49

Herring, Lt. Paul....91, 112, 216

Hethel....176, 276

High Wycombe....36, 37, 38, 40

Hillesheim....182, 187, 190, 279

Hitler, Adolf....11, 13, 95, 97, 104, 208, 247, 269

Hitler Youth....7, 16

Hirschfelder, Obgefr.
    Hubert....80
Hodges, General Courtney....229
Hodges, Major Robert H. 60
Hoffman, Sgt. Marion C. 155
Hoffman (Nazi Official) 212,
    213
Holland....8, 17, 22, 30, 51, 54,
    59, 162, 228, 238, 248, 270
Holton (Halesworth) 224,
    225, 277
Homburg....30, 231
Honington....217
Hopfensitz, Fw. Wilhelm....80,
    81
Horham....115, 117, 119, 121,
    129, 153, 275
Horsham St. Faiths...173, 198,
    276
Holmes, Lt. Thomas....160
Huck, Sgt. Donald R. 72, 73
Hudson, S/Sgt Lowell....58
Hughey, S/Sgt Henry....64, 67
Hurtgenwald (Hurtgen
    Forest)...23, 172
Idar-Oberstein....176
Isbel, Jack....153
Isley, S/Sgt Eugene S. 63
Italy....96, 133, 171, 228
Jeffers, T/Sgt Quentin 58
Jena 245

Jodl, Generaloberst Alfred 8,
    13, 17, 93, 94, 240, 247, 251
Johnson, William E. 92
Jubach 213
Juhlin, Lt. Arthur 116
Junkerauth 30
Kaiseresch 180
Kaiserslautern 29, 30, 39,
    114, 117, 119, 120, 231, 279
Kaiser Wilhelm Tunnel 175
Kampfgruppe Peiper 179
Kapteina, Uffz Karl 81, 82
Kasselburg castle 190
Kausrud, S/Sgt Donald C. 70,
    72
Keitel, Wilhelm 8, 13, 93, 94,
    240, 247
Kelly, Lt. John....217
Keller, Hans-Peter...213
Kenworthy, Lt. Jay....130
Keur, Lt. John....217
Kiel....162
Klank, Lt. Walter C. 212
Kharkov....241
Kleinman, S/Sgt Stanley....76
Kilburg, Edward 181
Kilburg Sr., Lt. Donald F. 4,
    87, 100, 101, 102, 104, 105, 250
Killen, John....90, 287
King Jr., Lt. Robert....101
Kings Cliffe....162, 221

Kirch-Gons....154, 155, 160, 217, 218

Knettishall....35, 121, 122, 276

Koblenz....7, 29, 30, 40, 121, 129, 139, 174, 175, 180, 183, 184, 185, 186, 187, 202, 216, 218, 220, 221, 223, 225, 227, 239, 279

Kommando Olga 137, 138

Klose, Lt. Walter G. 183

Krajcik, Sgt. John L. 149

Kraker, Lt. Robert 77, 78

Kransberg Castle 12

Krebs, Hans....247

Kulp, Lt. Charles....73, 87, 102, 250

Kurfurst....17

Kursk....241

Kyll River....169, 171, 180

Kyllburg....30, 171

La Gleize....67

Labonte, S/Sgt Leo....149, 150, 217, 222

La Croix Andre....59

Landsberg War Crimes Prison....213

Lang, Lt. Kenneth....69, 72, 73, 249

Lang, 2Lt George....70

La Rochelle France....40

Lashenden....214

Lathrum, Lt. Donald K. 153

Latz, Lt. William F. 136

Lavenham....3, 5, 44, 45, 56, 64, 68, 74, 75, 77, 100, 101, 104, 105, 140, 186, 250, 276

Lay, Lt. Col Beirne....101

Lejeune, Jules....58

LeMay, Brig. Gen. Curtis E. 206

Lettau, Dr. Heinz H. 248

Leber, Col. Harry P. 142, 143

Lee, Colonel Robert M. 229

Leiston 51, 210

Lentz, Lt. Tony....119

Liege, Belgium 5, 40, 48, 51, 54, 55, 58, 59, 63, 65, 71, 77, 79, 80, 81, 85, 86, 100, 109, 127, 141, 149, 209, 210, 221, 226, 229, 230, 248, 249, 254, 269

Liesser River 203

Linge, Heinz 95, 96, 287

Little Walden 227

Linz am Rhein 146

Lohausen 233

Lommersun 180

London 41, 143, 145, 146

Lott, Lt. Harrison Dawes 86, 100, 102, 104, 250, 251

Lucas, Chris 44

Ludendorff Bridge 166, 243, 244

Luftwaffe Units...79, 80, 81, 103, 122, 137, 171,290

I/JG27...79

II/JG2...144,171

II/ JG11....112

III/JG2....79,142

JG3....59, 79, 80, 81, 99

JG4....103

III./JG 4....103

JG6....79

JG27....79, 80

IV/JG3...104

IV/JG4....134

IV/KG200....137

III/JG2....142

2/NJG 11....122

16/JG3...99

43/le.FlakAbt715. 122

Sturm Gruppe IV/(Sturm) JG3...81, 99

Lunt, James....223

Luxembourg, Duchy of....III, 49, 55, 95, 39, 168, 170, 173, 194, 201, 202, 203, 214, 228, 229, 230, 235, 238, 242, 248, 271, 288

Luxembourg City....23, 31, 49

Maastricht....51

MacArthur, General Douglas....21

MacDonald, Lt. Col. Robert D. 43

Machauer, Sgt David....76

Madison, Wisconsin....56, 248

Main, Lt. Delbert....106

Mainz....29, 91, 131, 139, 183, 240

Malmedy....25, 26, 27, 29, 79, 116, 172, 179, 194, 199, 221, 231, 232

Manchester....44

Mannheim....117, 139

Marburg....220, 250

Marche, Belgium....136

Marshall, General George A. 21

Matz, Sgt. Neil....76

Martlesham Heath....220

Mayen....177, 180, 182, 186, 187, 191, 279

McCauley, Charles "Mac" 29

McClendon, T/Sgt William....78

McConnell, 1/Lt. Joseph B. 149, 150, 217, 221, 222

McCubbin, Lt. James L. 218, 219

McDuff, S/Sgt Grover 87, 100, 102, 251

McGregor, Major J. A. 196

McKeogh, Sgt. Mickey 21

McNeely, Lt. Donald 200

McQuinn, Lt. William H. 48

Merseburg....146

Merzhausen 39, 154, 157,

158, 160, 221, 235, 279

McEwen, Lt. William 118

Melton, Lt. Ramon 126

Mendlesham 134, 139

Memphis Belle 250

Merck 121

Merritt, Lt. James....75

Metfield....201

Metz....202

Meuse River....8, 33, 79, 82, 84, 209, 217, 254

MEW control....50, 54, 85, 210, 212, 213, 214, 224, 225, 227, 255

Miller, Glenn....23, 69

Miller, Lt. Howard....72, 73

Mission 759....40

Mission 760....I, II, 1, 38, 40, 50, 77, 79, 89, 83, 84, 91, 100, 127, 130, 152, 160, 165, 174, 199, 227, 234, 267, 268

Mix, Lt. Kenneth....87, 88, 89, 90, 212

Mohne Dam....81

Molek, S/Sgt. Stephen....200

Molesworth....35

Mollerke, Uffz. Kurt....80

Monshau....17

Manteuffel, Hasso von....12, 13, 238

Montgomery, Field Marshal Bernard....22, 24, 191

Montgomery, Sgt. Henry....101

Mooney Jr., Cpt. William H. 212, 213

Moore, Lt. H. W. 125

Morell, Dr. Theodor....96, 97

Moscow....241

Mosel River....128, 175, 176, 177, 184, 192, 195, 196, 197, 200, 201, 202, 203, 233, 240, 271

Mossberg....219

Mulheim an der Ruhr...233

Munich....28, 139

Nahe River....182, 240

Nahe Valley Railway....183

Namur....51, 55, 84, 210, 217, 221, 223, 254

Nandrin...59

Narva....241

Nash, Anita....66

NASA....248

Nash, Major Lloyd W. 4, 60, 65, 66, 67

Nash, S/Sgt Robert A. 78

National Archives....III, 282

Naughton, S/Sgt James P. 3

Neckar River....119, 128, 129

Nesbit, 1/Lt. Charles H. 48

Nette River....186

Nettersheim....188, 189, 195

Neu, Lt. Russell C. 62, 63

Neumunster....247

Newcomb, Sgt Eathen....222

Nidda....39, 143, 144, 146, 154, 219, 235, 279

Ninth Air Force....28, 29, 78, 166, 228, 230

391st Bomb Group (M) 166

397th Bomb Group (M) 233

IXth TAC....229

XIX Tactical Air Command....28, 159, 227, 289

Norden bombsight....53, 145, 203, 252, 255

Normandy....7, 18, 228, 283

Nuremberg....107, 200, 248

Nuthampstead....48, 154, 276

"NUTHOUSE" 51, 54, 85, 87, 210, 211, 221

Nyrink family....59

Oakland Summary....86, 210

Oberettingen ("Ober") 190

Oberwesel....220

Oberlauch....198, 199

O'Brien, Lt. Douglas....131

Offenbach....134

Ohey Belgium....149

Old, General Archie....132

Old Brackenham....176

Olivieri, Sgt. Oliver....102

O'Neill, General James H. 34

Operation Bagration....231

Operation Bodenplatte....79, 99, 238, 246, 270

Operation Greif....9, 17, 82

Operation Stoesser....27

Operation Varsity....245

Ostend Belgium....40, 47, 53, 54, 55, 78, 113, 141, 155, 220

Ott....81

Our River....49, 168

Pagac, S/Sgt Samuel....75

Panzer Armies....8, 12, 29

1st Panzer Division (Peiper)....230, 232

5th Panzer Army....12, 178, 198, 238

6th Panzer Army....12, 178, 179, 194

150th Panzer Brigade (Skorzeny)....8, 232

Paris, France....26, 36, 71, 182, 203, 229, 249

Parke, SSgt Harold H. 150

Parker, Major Arthur C. 68

Parks, Sgt. Harland B. 149

Parshall, Lt. Raymond....173

Paske, S/Sgt Harold....222

Patton, General George S. 25, 31, 32, 34, 149, 159

Patton's 3rd Army....173

Peacock, S/Sgt Donald R. 128

Peiper, SS Lt-Col Jochen 27, 29, 179, 230

Pelm....182, 190, 191

Perkins, Colonel Nick....42, 43

Peters, Lt. Kenneth....116

Peterson, Major Richard....51, 55, 212

Pfalzel....40, 169, 175, 187, 191, 192, 195, 279

Pforzheim....39, 108, 110, 111, 120, 269, 279

Piekarz, Lt. Anthony....150, 222

Pinetree....40

Pippin, Lt. Jack....100, 101

Player, Major G. A. 196

Poddington....35, 48, 275

Polebrook....162, 164, 275

Potsdam....10

Powell, Lt. Roy N. 149

Preddy, Maj. George E. 225, 226, 227

Presswood, Lt. Martin 114

Procopio, 1/Lt. Bruno 57, 58

Prum....91, 141, 168, 173, 180, 182, 193, 194, 198, 199, 201, 227

Purdy, Lt. Glenn....118, 119, 203

Lt. Frank J. Purtzer....150

Putzhohe....170

Quakenbrück....80

Quesada, General "Pete" 229, 230

Quiring, S/Sgt Michael....4

RAF Bomber Command....28

Raisin, Lt. 156

Rasmussen, Lt. Lawrence....126

Raydon...220

Reed, Lt. Lloyd....4, 64, 65, 66, 67

Regan, Kevin....44

Reichs Chancellery....247

Remagen....145, 166, 244

Renner, T/Sgt. William....87, 100, 102, 250, 251

Racek, S/Sgt Edward....199, 200

Rescheid....194, 199

Rheine....39, 79, 135

Rhine River....128, 129, 130, 174, 192, 216, 223, 242, 269, 271

Rheinbach....40, 189, 195, 227, 279

Rhodes, Sgt Calvin....92

Richey, T/Sgt Earl....200

Ridgewell....128, 141, 143, 154, 156, 164

Ringheim....108

Roberts, 1/Lt. Scott....78

Rock, Lt. Philip J. 149

Rock Island National Cemetery....77

Rogister, Mr. 59

Rohm & Haas....121

Romania....228

Roosevelt, President Franklin D. 37, 247, 250

Roper, Major Leonard B. 162

Rougham....106, 107, 153

Royal Air Force....121, 233

Roudnice nad Labem....246

Rouvreux, Sprimont
    Belgium....63

Rowe, Lt. Claude....57

Rudd, Richard P. 92

Ruhl, Lt. Franz....80

Ruhr Valley....23, 233

Rundstedt, Gerd von....6, 11, 12,
    14, 17, 18, 32, 34, 80, 82, 92,
    157, 159, 161, 221, 237, 247

Russians....6, 7, 99, 244

Russian High....34

Ruwer....184, 192, 195, 197, 278

Saarbrucken....117, 182, 200, 202

Saarlautern....28

Sauer River....173

St. Dizier....227

St. Vith....142, 180, 187, 193,
    199, 222

St. Wendel....176, 200, 212

Stanteen, Wiltran....153

Saporito, S/Sgt Salvatore....74,
    75

Savage, S/Sgt. James J....149

Savannah....52

Sakyo, Sgt. Terry....150

Saxony....80

Scammenden....44

Schneider, Sgt Edward....118

Schmulewitz, Lt. Morris....78

Schnee Eifel....24, 193

Schoenecken....40, 168, 173, 191,
    198, 201, 227

Schroeder, Christa....93, 94, 95,
    289

Schwerdtfeger, Werner....10,
    17, 248

Seeber, 2/Lt. Robert A. 48, 147

Seesenguth, Lt. Donald L.
   138

Seething....222, 276

Sevick, Harry E. 92

Sheddy, S/Sgt. Donald L. 149

Shelton, Major O.W. 151

Shilling, Col. David C. 224,
    225

Shilling, Capt. Mayfield R.
    ....4, 18, 45, 56, 69, 86, 87,
    100, 101, 211, 251

Shoemate, Lt. Foy 203

Shuster, F/O Joseph 62, 63

Siegfried Line....14, 23, 40, 188,
    243

Siegen....152

Siletz OR....77

Skorzeny, SS Colonel Otto 8,
    12, 17, 25, 82, 232, 244

Smith, Bedell 22

Snetterton Heath....35, 123, 275

Souders, Lt. Braden 78

Spa Belgium....229

Spaatz, General Carl "Tooey"
    ....III, 22, 26, 36, 229, 285

Speer, Albert....17, 95, 97, 158, 241

Spencer, Lt. Joe B. 148, 149, 221

Sperber, Lt. Harold....65

Stalingrad....241

Stalag Luft I at Barth....207

Stalag Luft III at Sagan....216

Stafford, S/Sgt Kent....160

Stanton, T/Sgt Warren....77

Stauffenberg, Claus von....97

Stavelot....230

Steeple Morden...214

Stene, Lt. Peter E. 113

Stinson, Lt. Charles T. 218

Strong, Major General Kenneth....22, 23

Sundbaum, Lt. Carl P. 138

Struthers, Lt. James A. 203

Stuttgart 6, 7, 24, 107, 117, 125, 139

St. Vith....142, 180, 187, 193, 222

St. Wendel....176, 200, 212, 296

Sudbury....108, 111, 276

Sulkowski, Lt. Casimer....131

Sullivan, T/Sgt Vincent....130

Supreme Headquarters of Allied Expeditionary Forces (SHAEF) 20, 21, 22, 24, 26, 29, 37, 256

Swain, T/Sgt Lawrence....57, 58

Swaffham....123

Swiss Alps....106

Tattleston....186

Tedder, Air Marshal Sir Arthur....21, 22

Terwagne....58

Thetford....163

Thomson, Lt. Bryce....216

Thompson, Lt. Dick W. 220

Thompson, Lt. John....199, 200

Thoroman, T/Sgt Gordon....78

Thorpe Abbots.... 115, 275

Thurleigh....144, 145, 150, 153, 275

Tibenham....171, 187, 276

Tomeo, Lt. Gordon R. 64

Tomney, S/Sgt. Paul....67

Thompson, G.K. 131

Trans Eifel Railroad....176

Treble 4....56, 68

Trois Ponts....67

Turnquist, Lt. Howard A. 76

Ulm....38

ULTRA....9, 19, 24, 60, 99, 159, 257

Usingen....157, 163

US Army....I, 119

7th Armored division....27, 68

125th AA Battalion....59

333rd Field Artillery Battalion....27

518th Military Police Battalion....59

US War Department....37
Utz, Sgt. Charles R. 149
Valkyrie....18
Vandenberg, General
    Hoyt....228, 229
V1 rockets....43
VIII Bomber Command....39,
    40, 41, 159, 207
Versailles....20
Verstraete, Lt. S. A. 200
Verviers, Belgium....24
Vianden....49
Vick, Lt. Herbert....136
Vielsalm....67
Virgin, Lt. John R. 303
Vogt, Lt. Lawrence....92
Vulkaneifel....176
Wacht am Rhein....9
Wattisham....212, 220
Watton Station....163
Waldron, Lt. William J. 62, 63
Wales....30
Washington, DC....61, 72, 88,
    206, 207, 247
Wattisham....213, 220
Weber, S/Sgt James A. 71, 72
Wehrmacht....16, 17, 24, 29, 38,
    82, 104, 171, 172, 173, 174,
    175, 177, 178, 182, 183, 187,
    191,192, 194, 196, 228, 235,
    237, 242, 271

36th Field Artillery
    Regiment....104
62nd Volks Grenadier Division
    of the Fifth Panzer
    Army...198
Sixth Panzer Army...198
7th Army's LXXX Infantry
    Corps....171
7th Army...173, 184
15th Army...174
Fifth and Sixth Panzer
    Armies...178
1st, 2nd, and 12th SS Panzer
    division...194
Weiner, Barbara...56
Weltman, Lt....92
Wendling....191, 192, 196, 197,
    276
Wereth...27
West Point...52, 53
West Wall...23, 188, 194, 228,
    239, 242
Westcott...153
Wetteldorf...226
Weyland, General Otto...159
White, Lt. Jim....49
Wiesbaden...69, 134, 136, 220
Wilhelmsdorf...161
Wilhelmshaven...162
Wilkenson, Lt. A.C...250
Williamson, Lt. Col. W.H....198
Winter, August...8

Wisconsin, University of...56, 248

Wittge, Fw Max...138

Wittlich...40, 169, 173, 201, 202, 204, 280

Wolak, S/Sgt Alphonse...200

Wolsfelderberg...170, 171

Wolfsschanze...8-17

Wormingford...51, 215, 220

Worms...114, 270, 280

Wright, General W.H. Sterling...52

Wright, Walter...52

Xhos...59

Yowan, Sgt. Robert C....3, 70, 71, 249

Yugoslavia...228

Zeiss Optics...245

Zemke, Col. Hubert "Hub"...31, 206, 207, 209

Ziegenberg...12, 13, 14, 93, 97, 157, 160, 162

Zellhausen...213

Zuckerman, Solly...229

ZWG...10, 11

CPSIA information can be obtained
at www.ICGtesting.com
Printed in the USA
LVHW040134020423
743248LV00006B/47